CONFRONTING
THE
TRUTH

Confronting the Truth:
Conscience in the Catholic Tradition

Linda Hogan

PAULIST PRESS
New York/Mahwah, N.J.

Cover design by Cynthia Dunne

Library of Congress Cataloging-in-Publication Data

Hogan, Linda, 1964-
    Confronting the truth : conscience in the Catholic tradition / Linda Hogan.
        p.   cm.
    Includes bibliographical references and index.
    ISBN 0-8091-3981-2 (alk. paper)
    1. Conscience—Religious aspects—Catholic Church. 2. Conscience—Religious aspects—Catholic Church—History of doctrines. 3. Catholic Church—Doctrines. 4. Catholic Church—Doctrines—History I. Title.

BJ1278.C66 H64 2000
241'.1—dc21
                                                            00-062376

Published by Paulist Press
997 Macarthur Boulevard
Mahwah, New Jersey 07430

www.paulistpress.com

Printed and bound in the
United States of America

Table of Contents

Introduction   The Problem of Conscience   1

Chapter 1   Mapping the Moral Landscape:
            The Role of Conscience in the
            Contemporary Church   9

Chapter 2   "The Law Written on Our Hearts":
            Conscience in Greek, Jewish and
            Early Christian Thought   36

Chapter 3   "Discerning Moral Principles":
            Conscience from the Medievalists
            to the Manualists   64

Chapter 4   Conflicting Paradigms:
            Conscience and the Renewal
            of Vatican II   100

Chapter 5   Toward a Personalist Theology
            of Conscience   127

Chapter 6   Living with Contradictions:
            Disagreement and Dialogue
            in the Church   165

Notes   191

Bibliography   207

Index   217

ACKNOWLEDGMENTS

In the process of researching and writing this book I have received help and encouragement from many people. In particular I would like to thank the members of the Association of Teachers of Moral Theology in Britain, many of whom have read and commented on drafts of different chapters and from whom I have learned a great deal. I am also grateful for the help of colleagues at the Department of Theology and Religious Studies, University of Leeds. As a student I was privileged to be taught by four very different but equally inspirational teachers; Professors Patrick Hannon, Enda McDonagh, Thomas Marsh (now deceased) and Gerard Watson (also deceased). I am deeply grateful to each of them for the enthusiasm and expertise with which they taught their subjects and for the support that they gave me over the years.

Finally and most importantly I wish to express my gratitude to my parents and family. They continue to be a source of generous encouragement and love.

Introduction:
The Problem
of Conscience

Catholic moral theology today is characterized by deep divisions on a number of serious issues. There are two main schools of thought within the field. One is clustered around John Finnis and Germain Grisez, the other around Richard McCormick, Charles Curran and Josef Fuchs. While they share some approaches, the schools disagree on many fundamental issues, including the precise nature of morality, the significance of circumstances and intentions, the importance of scripture, the role of the magisterium and the status of conscience. A common thread that unites these instances of conflict is the question of where ultimate moral responsibility and authority resides. Contemporary theologians have approached this issue from many directions. However, although conscience is frequently mentioned in these debates, there has been little sustained analysis of the category. Yet it figures prominently in popular perceptions and discussions of these academic debates. This book places conscience center stage and through this filter attempts to deal with some of the current conflicts in ethics.

1

The aim of this book is to reconstruct a theology of conscience in light of the problems of contemporary Catholic moral theology. In so doing I hope to contribute to the current discussions of these issues and to offer insight into the history of the church's understanding of conscience. Thus I intend this text to have both historical interest and contemporary relevance. That the theology of conscience needs to be reconstructed requires some explanation. This is offered in the opening chapter. The Catholic approach to conscience is deeply ambiguous. On the one hand conscience is regarded as the most fundamental and directly personal way that the individual apprehends moral goodness and truth. The church's constant but little publicized teaching is that conscience must always be obeyed. However, there is also an expectation that the judgments of conscience will be in agreement with church teaching. As a result there is an immediate and inevitable tension between conscience and the other moral authorities in Catholicism. This situation will be explored in chapter 1 and will provide the context for our examination of conscience in the Catholic tradition.

This tension between the individual conscience and the institutional church has been evident in Catholic moral teaching from its very beginnings. It has led to conflict at various times in the church's history and has erupted under different guises. At one time the debate is about freedom and law, at another about subjectivity and objectivity in morality. Yet the core issue continues to be the relationship between individual moral discernment and the church as moral teacher. It is a central contention of this book that the current disagreements about the authority of conscience vis-à-vis church teachings are an inevitable consequence of the church's failure to confront the ambiguities in its own understanding of conscience. Assessments that blame the modern trends of individualism or relativism fail to appreciate the confusions that are part of the history of conscience. In order to sustain this thesis we will need to examine the development of Catholic thought on conscience. This will be the focus of chapters 2 and 3, in which we will analyze the evolution of the concept of conscience, with particular attention to the issue of its role and authority in the moral life. Chapter 2 will discuss both the pre-Christian sources of conscience and early Christian texts. Chapter 3 will focus on medieval and early modern thought. What will become clear is that although the essential message was of the primacy of conscience, this was frequently obscured and occasionally sacrificed. Throughout these chapters I will suggest that any reading that glosses over the inherent contradictions in the theology and politics of conscience is inadequate.

Within the contemporary debates the history of moral theology tends to be controversial. It may be an oversimplification to suggest that each school has its own version of history that supports its particular theology. What can be said, however, is that the schools tell the history of moral theology differently. They prioritize certain themes, theologians and events, and downplay others. This lack of consensus about the history of moral theology is in part responsible for the endurance of the theological disagreements. Within this fraught field the history of conscience is particularly contested. Selected highlights from history tend to be used to bolster theological positions. In addition there is an implicit suggestion from each of the schools that there is one simple and unambiguous understanding of conscience throughout history. It must be admitted that the history of conscience is rarely argued about explicitly. Rather, it is implied in the different versions of moral theology. These versions of moral theology are sustained by omitting certain elements of the history that do not conform to the account of conscience being proposed. Of course there are elements of truth on both sides. Each school prioritizes selective portions of the theology and history of conscience to establish the legitimacy of its own theology of conscience and all that flows from it. However, in so doing it must disregard the other, often contrary, strands of the tradition. My argument is that neither really acknowledges nor accepts the confused nature of the history and that each operates with a false sense of simplicity and unity in this regard. One of the reasons for revisiting the history is to complicate these received versions and to suggest that the true picture of conscience is one that involves many strands. As a result a constant theme running through the history chapters is that it is inaccurate to regard the story of conscience as one singular, uninterrupted narrative. As we shall see when we examine the development of conscience, a complex and often contradictory picture emerges.

Although the primary focus of the history section is on theological texts, the politics of conscience through the centuries will also be mentioned. Not only were there tensions between the different theological approaches, but the theology and politics of conscience were often also in conflict. One example will suffice at this stage. Although many of the great theologians and popes taught that it was a grave sin to act against one's conscience, down through the ages the church waged a savage war against heretics. The treatment of the Albigensians is a case in point. This "heresy" was a constant target of church censure. The Albigensians were not allowed to believe according to that which their consciences taught. As a result they were tortured and put to death in an effort to get them to conform to Rome. Even St. Bernard of Clairvaux insisted "if they prefer to die rather than to believe, let them die."[1] This position was sustained even though St. Thomas Aquinas wrote that "every conscience, true or false, is binding, in the sense that to act against conscience is always wrong."[2] This example suggests that the confusion at the level of theological reflection was made all the more extreme by the failure of the church in practice. Although a thorough investigation of the politics of conscience is beyond the scope of this work, key events will be used to highlight further the ambiguous nature of the church's approach to conscience. One can conclude that institutional politics adds yet another layer of complication to the understanding of conscience in the Catholic tradition.

There is a certain extent to which I could be accused of overstating the case. However, this tendency to ignore the contradictions in the history of conscience is certainly evident. A central purpose of this study is to problematize the history of conscience and to suggest that a hermeneutics of suspicion is necessary when looking at the story of conscience as implied in current theological debates. Therefore, in examining the history of conscience in the Catholic tradition I intend to confront rather than to neglect the many confusions and contradictions.

I then set about reconstructing a theology of conscience for Catholics today. I use the texts of Vatican II as my starting point. These are discussed in detail in chapter 4. Here again the double message is in evidence. Some of the conciliar texts prioritize conscience as the primary interpreter of the divine moral law. Still others seem to suggest that it is the teaching church through the magisterium that has this task. These contradictions must be confronted and resolved if one is to articulate a contemporary theology of conscience. The truth is that many of the key theological texts on conscience, including very recent ones, can be used either to promote or to curtail personal autonomy. The texts pull in both directions. Therefore some "external" theological vision or framework is needed to determine the way in which the texts should be interpreted. My argument is that the personalist theology of Vatican II ought to provide the impetus for and the focus of interpretation. This suggests that instead of valuing automatic conformity to church teaching, individual responsibility and autonomy should be promoted. Chapter 5 develops this personalist theology of conscience further and discusses both the accomplishments and the failures of conscience.

A fairly comprehensive account of the nature, role and authority of conscience emerges from these chapters. It builds on many diverse elements of the tradition. While it certainly prioritizes some elements of the tradition above others, I defend this by arguing that these emphases are suggested by the theological vision of Vatican II. Furthermore, I acknowledge that there are parts of the tradition that would lead one to construct a rather different understanding of conscience. The picture of conscience that I propose here is built on the beliefs that conscience discerns good and evil in the context of relationship with a loving God, that it is formed in the faith community, past and present, and that it is rooted in the narratives and traditions of the church. In addition it recognizes that intentions and circumstances are morally relevant, it attends to the particularities of each situation and rejects views of morality that evaluate acts in isolation from the context in which they are performed. This understanding of conscience also accepts that individuals may disagree with one another and with the church on the resolution of moral problems. It is also aware of the limitations and failures that are inevitably part of the human condition.

In the final chapter I deal head-on with the church's current difficulties with the theology of conscience, and I propose ways of living with the contradictions. I discuss briefly the current climate, which appears to value external conformity over honest disagreement on moral matters. I argue that this ethos, which is growing steadily in the church (both in the developing and developed worlds), is wholly at odds with the theology and ecclesiology of Vatican II. This chapter suggests that the discussion of the role of conscience needs to be recast. Instead of asking, What is the status of church teaching? What kind of authority does it have? What kind of obedience is it due? I propose that we ask firstly, How is the person to act on his/her conscientious decisions and what should her approach be when church teaching does not coincide with it? This seeks to avoid constructing two distinct authorities vying with each other.

I believe that the way forward for the institutional church is to adopt the theology of conscience outlined above and to apply it to its own institutions. This understanding of conscience is rooted in tradition but is interpreted in the light of the personalist theology of Vatican II. Many theological and ecclesiological changes would necessarily flow from this renewed appreciation of the primacy of conscience. This leads me to conclude that there is an urgent need to refocus the manner in which the institutional church engages with the people of God. Of course the church does have a very important role to play in the education and nurturing of conscience. However, it must do so in a way that is respectful of the seriousness with which most people engage in ethical reflection and that is supportive of their conscientiously held beliefs and values. We must come to appreciate that difference and diversity in the moral realm is not only inevitable, it is also valuable. Ultimately we will need to learn to live with contradictions within the church, not only in relation to our past history, but also in our present practice.

Chapter 1
Mapping the Moral Landscape: The Role of Conscience in the Contemporary Church

Conscience is a treasured commodity in contemporary culture. Although often vague and indefinable, it is rightly regarded with reverence. Indeed the language of conscience unites people of all faiths and none. This is because in modern Western society at any rate, conscience refers to the deeply held moral convictions of the person. It puts us in touch with that dimension of ourselves which seeks to do the good. Conscience refers to an inner sense of what is right or wrong in the person's intentions and activity. It directs the person to right action. It cannot be reduced to the routine feelings of guilt, remorse or fear that may cause a person to act in a particular way. Neither is it equivalent to deep-seated memories of childhood rules. Nor can it be equated with a blind obedience to the conventions of a particular social or religious group. Guilt, remorse, fear, the memory of childhood rules—each has some relevance when speaking about conscience. However, they are essentially underdeveloped or miscast elements of its activity.

They do not capture the moral maturity that conscience implies. The concept of conscience points to a degree of self-awareness in moral matters, which can never be equated with such things as mere obedience to rules.

Conscience is a difficult concept to come to grips with, since it refers to the inward workings of the mind and heart. As such it is beyond easy scrutiny. It is the term we use to indicate moral self-governance.[1] The conscience is an intensely personal category that identifies the self as a moral agent. It highlights a crucial feature of moral decision making and action, that is, it must be freely chosen. For decisions to be freely made and actions to be chosen, the person must be conscious of and honest about her/his motivations and desires. One must also be able to evaluate the likely consequences that flow from one's actions. The successful operation of conscience depends on this kind of self-consciousness.

Conscience is not merely instinctive, although an element of instinct is involved. It is also thoughtful, willed and rational and requires a high degree of sensitivity to oneself and one's context. But it would also be wrong to think of conscience as primarily an intellectual endeavor. Although it certainly includes an intellectual or rational dimension, the activity of conscience is much more than this. Conscience also draws on the emotional and intuitive aspects of the personality in coming to a sense of what is right and good in a given situation. Sidney Callahan describes this holistic activity of conscience as "a unified integration of thinking, feeling and willingness to act; it refers to those acts of a whole person who is simultaneously thinking, feeling and willing."[2] This integration of thinking and feeling is central to the proper working of conscience. If we are stunted either intellectually or emotionally, then the conscience will be limited or impaired in some important respect.

In addition to thinking and feeling, Callahan also mentions "willing" as a significant aspect of the conscience. Here she implies that the role of conscience is not simply an evaluative one. The work of conscience doesn't finish when the person has identified the right and good course of action. Conscience also involves the desire to do the good and right thing. It impels us to act on the basis of our own judgment. The judgment of conscience is not a disinterested, purely intellectual one. It also involves a desire, a commitment and an obligation to act on that judgment. This determination to pursue the good that one has identified is a core activity of conscience. It is not an optional extra. Conscience itself is comprised of both the decision-making aspect (involving reason and emotion) and the obligation to carry through such decisions. This explains why decisions of conscience are experienced as uncompromising.

It is obvious that people often disagree with one another about what is right and good in a given situation. This is not surprising given the complexities of making moral decisions. People can differ about the nature of the problem, about who is rightly involved, about which circumstances are relevant and which are not. We can also disagree about which solution is the correct one, how adequate it is and how it will affect other related concerns. We may not share the same priorities and goals, either in the long or short term. We may have different people in mind when we think about the wider implications of our decisions. At every stage in the process of rationally appraising a situation there may be conflict. But since the activity of conscience is not merely intellectual, other dimensions of personal experience are also relevant. The person's cultural and religious background, her/his education, emotions, past history and future plans each have a bearing on how she/he will evaluate a particular problem and what solution will be favored. Judgments of conscience are multifaceted, involving both rational and emotional elements. They reflect the many commitments a person may have. They also can be complicated and limited by the life experience of the person. It is quite likely therefore that people will disagree with one another on decisions of conscience.

When faced with the same moral dilemma, two people may differ completely about the right and good solution. Take, for example, the all-too-common problem of how to deal with a loved one who is in a coma and who is diagnosed as being in a persistent vegetative state. This means that the coma is normally nonreversible. The family frequently has to decide whether the patient should be given nutrition and hydration artificially. Although family members may be in possession of the same medical facts and the same advice, they may disagree as to whether artificial nutrition and hydration should be continued. One family member may be profoundly affected by the discomfort of the patient, the distress of other family members and the extreme unlikelihood that the patient will ever regain consciousness. As a result she may believe that the morally right and good course of action would be to stop all treatment, including nutrition and hydration. Another family member may be equally aware of all these factors but may abhor any such suggestion. He may believe that the good and right thing to do is to continue with treatment, even if there is no reasonable expectation that the patient's condition will change. In each case the decision that has been reached has been carefully considered. All the relevant factors have been taken into account. The alternatives, too, have been examined and rejected. Although sympathetic to the concerns that the other person has, once an individual has made a decision of conscience it is irrevocable. The person knows that she/he must act on it. It has a quality that cannot be compromised. But although the actual judgments of the individuals may differ greatly, they have some important elements in common. Judgments and decisions of conscience are those that are personal, and self-conscious. They comprise the person's best and truthful estimation of goodness in a given situation. They are held with integrity and involve an obligation to carry them through.

This powerful and demanding duty to act on decisions of conscience is evoked in Robert Bolt's play *A Man for All Seasons*. In the play Sir Thomas More is faced with the choice between acting against his conscience and thereby saving his life or sacrificing his life for his conscientious beliefs. In a famous scene the Duke of Norfolk pleads with More to act against his conscience and so save his life. However, More replies "And when we stand before God, and you are sent to Paradise for doing according to your conscience and I am damned for not doing according to mine, will you come with me, for fellowship?"[3] It is this irrevocable dimension of the conscience that accounts for its nobility. People are willing to endure hardship and even death for its sake. One can cite many examples, historical and contemporary, of individuals who have made great sacrifices in following the judgments of their consciences. The Burmese pro-democracy leader Aung San Suu Kyi, the late Ken Saro Wiwa of Nigeria and the Egyptian feminist Taslima Nasreen are just a few of the numerous martyrs, exiles and prisoners of conscience. Amnesty International continues to record and bring to public attention the countless individuals worldwide who suffer for their conscientiously held beliefs. Although few people may ever have to defend decisions of conscience to this extent, these instances highlight the fact that this personal, self-conscious ethical activity that we call conscience is part of the very dignity and uniqueness of being human.

Each judgment of conscience is based on the moral truth that the person has come to know. Because we must be guided by the moral truth as we understand it, we are obligated to follow our decisions of conscience. However, the moral truth as we understand it may be incomplete or even incorrect. History is replete with examples of people who followed their consciences and yet committed acts of atrocity, acts that most reasonable people find objectionable. But given all that has been said about conscience thus far, how are we to deal with such a contradiction? It can partly be explained by the fact that we are all the time speaking of fallible and morally frail human beings. Our intellectual shortcomings, together with our psychological and emotional limitations, do impair our judgments. Mental illness, trauma, misdirected socialization and many other difficulties can result in the malformation or malfunctioning of a person's moral sense.

Many war crimes can be understood in this way. War crimes occur when acts of war are regarded by society to be unjustified. Soldiers are trained to kill the enemy. However, they may be so socialized by the rhetoric and logic of war that they are no longer able to discriminate between acts that are legitimate and those that are not. Obviously, one would have to examine the extent to which each soldier is responsible for his actions, whether he could have resisted the logic of war and whether he had a duty to disobey orders. It is possible that a soldier might believe that the massacre of an entire village or ethnic group is right in particular circumstances. The soldier may indeed be acting on the moral truth that he knows. However, to most people this is a deformation of the moral truth. This is just one example from the many occasions when a person's apprehension of moral truth can be seriously wrong. The problems of accounting for and understanding this are immense. They raise questions about the formation of conscience and also about the authority of conscience. Is it always to be obeyed? How can I be sure that my judgment is right? Can I guard against situations in which my conscience might lead me in a wrong direction? Can I know if my decisions are compromised in some important respect?

The Catholic Context

There is nothing distinctively Christian about the view of conscience thus far. It is one that is shared by many in the Western world, regardless of whether they have a religious or a secular worldview. However, for Christians there is another level of understanding that must be taken into account. The Christian tradition gives a very particular orientation to discussions of the nature, role and authority of conscience. Presuppositions about the nature of morality, the role of individuals within the church and the authority of sacred texts and traditions shape the understanding of conscience in the Christian context. It is therefore impossible to consider the conscience in isolation from the other authoritative sources of Christian morality. Since conscience is the source of free and responsible decision making, it is rightly regarded as the supreme authority in ethics. However, Christianity operates with a community-based model of ethics not with an individualistic one. Therefore the understanding of conscience must reflect this. In addition Christianity regards the words and actions of Jesus, as revealed in scripture, as inspirational. This means that the Bible is an important source book for Christian moral thinking. There are different opinions on the role that biblical texts should play in Christian ethics. They range from the view that the Bible gives us definite guidance in the form of specific moral laws, to the view that it provides Christians with a distinctive but general vision of the virtuous life. However one conceptualizes this, there is no doubt that the sacred texts of Christianity have a central place in the moral formation of the person. The collective wisdom of Christians past and present, preserved through traditions and principles, also commands our attention. As does the guidance of those entrusted with preaching the Christian message today. The formation of the Christian's conscience must be mindful of these factors.

Within this general context our focus is on the Catholic tradition. It has a highly differentiated sense of the ways in which we learn moral discernment. Center stage is the church, which is believed to have an important teaching function. Its task is to enable individuals to recognize the moral truth in each situation. It does this in many ways: through moral formation, through the witness of exemplary figures and through preaching and formal teaching. Each of these forms of moral education is important, although the formal teaching through magisterial pronouncements and doctrine tends to be given most attention. To be a Catholic means one is always in dialogue with this multifaceted teaching tradition. One has the security of being part of this community of believers in which one's conscience is formed. As such, conscience takes its place as one of a number of sources of moral discernment. It is and ought to be shaped by the collective endeavor of the community. So too is it formed in dialogue with the central beliefs of Christianity. It is not therefore an utterly autonomous ethical sense. Rather, it is the individual's personal and self-conscious integration of collective moral wisdom with her/his own learned insight.

The church's attempt to balance these different aspects of ethical discernment has not been entirely successful. There is now and there has long since been a genuine confusion regarding the relationship between conscience and this collective wisdom, usually called tradition. It has been particularly difficult in relation to one particular vehicle of that tradition, that is, the magisterium. I use the term here to refer to the teaching role and authority of the hierarchy. Problems arise when the individual, in good conscience, comes to a decision that is not in accord with what the church teaches. In an ideal world the decisions of conscience and the teaching of the magisterium would be in harmony. Yet, history and personal experience indicate that there is often disagreement between serious-minded Catholics and the magisterium. The story of Catholicism reveals a church that is deeply ambivalent about the moral authority of the individual and has difficulty balancing the interconnected but often competing claims of the various sources of moral understanding, of which conscience is one.

The Church's View of the Current Moral Climate

When one examines recent magisterial pronouncements, it seems that the church's estimation of people's morality is predominantly negative. There is little value given to the fact that people are relying on their own moral judgments. Indeed, this tendency is regarded by the church to be a symptom of moral decline. For example, the encyclical *Veritatis Splendor* argues that certain trends in human society, namely individualism and subjectivism, have given rise to an ethical crisis of major proportions. The Anglican bishop of Oxford also echoed the central claim of the encyclical when he insisted that "many people today are inclined to think that moral values are simply up to each individual to work out for themselves, that they are subjective and relative." He goes on to affirm the message of the encyclical, which is that "moral values such as respect for the dignity of each individual, honesty and human rights belong to the objective order. We have the freedom to decide and act, but we do not invent the moral claims to which we seek to respond."[4] However, what the statement from Bishop,

Harries fails to acknowledge is that it is extremely difficult to identify whether individuals are acting on their legitimate "freedom to decide and act" or whether they are falling prey to the evils of subjectivism criticized by the encyclical.[5]

What then are these evils? The encyclical identifies a number of trends in contemporary society that it says are indicative of a severe decline in ethical values. The three main components of this corrupt form of morality are identified as (1) the belief that individuals create rather than discern values, (2) the view that morality is an exclusively private concern and (3) the conviction that there is no objective dimension to morality. However, I want to suggest that the extent to which these views are in fact held is unclear. Many individuals do react negatively to intrusions from either churches or governments on ethical matters. People are generally more vocal and determined regarding their right to make their own judgments. However, the encyclical has not considered whether these reactions are the result of a legitimate and necessary ethic of responsibility or whether they are the result of the corrupt tendencies it has already rejected.

Do People Really Believe That They Invent Rather Than Discern Moral Values?

The encyclical claims that they do. The crucial difference here is that the task of discerning moral values implies that these values exist independently. They do not depend on the individual's acknowledgement of them. These values therefore have a claim on us. We come to recognize what the good and correct solution to a problem is; we do not create it. However, *Veritatis Splendor* suggests that people "grant to the individual conscience the prerogative of independently determining the criteria of good and evil and then acting accordingly."[6] It also claims that the conscience is mistakenly viewed as having "the status of supreme tribunal of moral judgment which hands down categorical and infallible decisions about good and evil."[7] However, I am not convinced that people view conscience as a supreme tribunal acting in a radically independent manner. Statements like "I did nothing wrong. I followed my conscience," may give the impression that the individual is the inventor of value. In fact I think that this is simply a clumsy attempt to explain a difficult concept. Statements such as these express the belief that the person can only act on what she/he believes to be the correct course of action. They do not imply that the individual is the sole arbiter and judge of her/his own behavior. Nor do they suggest that morality is merely a matter of personal whim or fancy. However, they do illustrate the paradox that although the individual is the primary interpreter of her/his own moral life she/he is not exclusively so.

Veritatis Splendor is right to condemn the view that freedom is absolute, that each conscience determines the criteria of good and evil and that the individual creates moral values by acting with complete autonomy. However, I remain skeptical about the extent to which people hold these opinions. In my view *Veritatis Splendor* has misinterpreted as relativist the genuine efforts of individuals to act in an autonomous manner. I agree with Iris Murdoch, who suggested that "the ordinary person does not, unless corrupted by philosophy, believe that he creates values by his choices. He thinks that some things really are better than others and that he is capable of getting things wrong."[8] It may be legitimate to criticize the language of following one's conscience because it may create the impression that individuals determine the criteria of good and evil. However, for most Catholics, the purpose of employing this kind of language is to reinforce the thoroughly Christian view that regardless of all the other resources which she/he may have at her/his disposal, ultimately the individual has to act on the moral truth that she/he knows.

Do Individuals Really Believe That Morality Is an Exclusively Private Concern?

The second ingredient of this ethical crisis, according to *Veritatis Splendor*, is the privatization of morality. Here the encyclical is pointing to what it sees as the tendency to view morality as a purely personal affair. It implies that people put their ethical decisions on a par with decisions about their diet, how they spend their leisure time or where they choose to live. Each is exclusively a matter for the individual and of no concern to society at large. It is true that one does find examples of this kind of thinking in public discourse. Some of the most extreme "freedom of choice" arguments in relation to abortion, for example, insist that decisions about abortion are exclusively the domain of the individual women involved. Such views deny that these decisions also have a wider ethical significance. Popular discussions of a number of other complex ethical issues, notably new reproductive technologies and euthanasia, also use the idiom of the right to choose. Such language does seem to confirm that there is a tendency to view a substantial number of ethical issues as belonging properly and exclusively to the private domain.

As with the previous discussion, however, I wish to introduce a note of skepticism into this analysis. While it is certainly true that people are increasingly insisting that many ethical issues are matters of private choice, it is possible to identify at least two other reasons why this may be the case. One can explain this first by recognizing that the moral questions formerly regarded to be of legitimate public concern are changing. The cliché that the church should be more concerned with the boardroom and less with the bedroom reflects this changing climate. Traditionally morality was preoccupied with sexual and reproductive issues. Very little concern was focused on social or political problems. Although this is certainly changing, a disproportionate amount of attention is still given to bedroom issues. The general reluctance of people to listen to the magisterium on these matters may be a subtle way of saying that they themselves have more experience and greater moral wisdom in these areas and that the concerns of the church ought to be directed differently. Unfortunately the church seems to have difficulty in hearing this message. Thus far instead of taking this opportunity to rethink its own role, its main response has been to issue a denunciation of what it regards as the laity's moral corruption.

The language of private choice may also be explained by the fact that people are refusing to hand over their moral decision making to any external authority. Individuals are increasingly wary of the authoritarian exercise of power in every field. They are unlikely to follow blindly any point of view. Instead, each teaching, law and viewpoint is evaluated on its own merits, on its power to convince. This is the result of the gradual democratization of society. It is evident in all social and political institutions and seems to have been extended to the way in which people view the church's exercise of power. As with any other institution people have to be convinced that the views expressed by the church are right. They will not accept something simply because it is church teaching. A healthy skepticism of all authorities, including religious ones, is characteristic of this age.

The laity's hostility to church interference on issues of sexual morality is frequently cited by church authorities as an example of the general moral decline. It is said to illustrate the fact that morality is retreating into the realm of private choice. Yet this tendency could also be interpreted in a different manner. One could view the reluctance to obey church teaching on many sexual issues as either the result of the magisterium having lost touch with the conscientious moral judgments of the faithful or because people are coming to moral maturity and trusting their own moral instincts. The gap between what is taught, especially in the area of sexual ethics, and what is practiced can be explained in a number of ways. It cannot be dismissed with claims that people are retreating to their own private universes where they are doing what they please without any regard for morality. In failing to recognize that there may be many reasons for this state of affairs the church has ignored the obvious challenge to its own institutions. There is a discernible shift in attitudes to a number of ethical issues. Individuals are becoming more confident about acting on the decisions they have made in conscience. Yet *Veritatis Splendor* only explains the gap between church teaching and current practice by denouncing the tendency of individuals to rely on their own ethical decisions. But to undermine this tendency by branding it relativist is to do a great disservice to the vast majority of Catholics who are genuinely trying to live morally responsible lives.

Are Individuals Completely Subjectivist?

Perhaps the most serious charge that *Veritatis Splendor* levels against the moral sense of people today is that it is subjectivist. Individuals are said to believe that the rightness or wrongness of a decision is determined solely by their own evaluation of it. According to this view there is no external reference point for moral judgment, no objectivity. This means that two people can come to very different resolutions of the same problem and both can be right. The person does what she/he regards to be right, and that is the beginning and end of ethics. The individual's subjective assessment is believed to be absolute.

It is quite clear that this completely subjectivist account of morality is incompatible with Christianity. At the heart of the Christian moral vision is the belief that the difference between right and wrong is not an arbitrary matter. Morality is not simply about doing whatever I please. In short the Christian understanding of morality involves an objective dimension. The term *objective* here refers to the conviction that moral truth does not depend on one's personal belief. It exists and makes claims on us regardless of whether we recognize it or not. It stresses that there is always a right solution to any moral problem and that our task is to discover that solution through reflection on our own experience. This central belief of Christian ethics was traditionally expressed in the doctrine of natural law. For the Christian that which is right or wrong in a particular context is not random. It can be discerned from the nature of the person and her/his acts.

Although *Veritatis Splendor* identifies an absolute subjectivism as characteristic of this age, again I wish to enter a note of caution. It is true that Catholics seem to be rejecting moral systems that promote absolute and universal principles. They seem to be skeptical of ethical pronouncements that stress the objective dimension of morality and leave no room for subjective or personal assessment. For example, views such as "contraception is absolutely wrong" or "abortion is intrinsically evil" or "in vitro fertilization is wrong in all circumstances" are being rejected by many Catholics because they are too absolutist. People are reacting against these and other statements that fail to take any account of particular circumstances and that see morality in terms of black and white. But again *Veritatis Splendor* misinterprets this tendency. It regards such statements as endorsing the belief that morality involves no standards or objective criteria at all. Yet this is quite clearly not the case. The vast majority of individuals do believe that morality involves distinguishing between right and wrong and that the difference between the two is not exclusively a matter for their own judgment. People are introducing an element of provisionality into their own ethics. They are doing so because they recognize that moral dilemmas are complex, that they involve arbitrating between different values and that they rarely invite the luxury of certainty.

There is a lack of consensus on many ethical issues in the Catholic Church today. *Veritatis Splendor* interprets this as a symptom of a growing relativist mentality. The encyclical argues that individuals believe that they invent rather than discern moral principles, that they see morality as an exclusively private affair and that they reject the idea of any external, objective criteria in ethics. If such views are growing, as many commentators suggest, then church leaders are obligated to challenge them. However, there are good reasons to be cautious about such interpretations. It is wrong to regard the rejection of traditional moral authorities as exclusively the result of subjectivism. There are many reasons why individuals are relying on their own moral judgments. One of the reasons is that people are beginning to internalize the aspirations of Vatican II, which advocated the articulation of an ethic of responsibility. People are also redefining the boundaries between the private domain and public interest. In addition people are giving voice to the complexities of ethical decisions and are rejecting views that leave no room for exceptions or for compromise. The fact that there is an ever increasing gap between the teaching church and the faithful is also giving people the courage and determination to be more autonomous in their ethical decisions.

The shape and character of Catholic morality are certainly changing. The dominant trend seems to be toward personal autonomy and responsibility and away from adherence to externally imposed norms and principles. We are currently in a period of transition. *Veritatis Splendor* is but one example of the many texts and statements that express an understandable anxiety about the demise of one particular model of ethics. What the encyclical views as a radical growth of relativism and subjectivism can also be seen as an attempt to redefine Christian morality with the emphasis on the duties and responsibilities of individuals to shape their own moral lives. To label it subjectivist and then to condemn it represents a serious misunderstanding of what is in fact the emergence of a renewed ethic of responsibility.

Is Conscience Subjectivism under Another Name?

In Christianity the conscience refers to the individual's capacity to make autonomous and free moral decisions. Some fear that the language of the primacy of conscience promotes the kind of subjectivism criticized in the encyclical. Indeed, conscience can sometimes appear to be indistinguishable from the individual's subjective assessment of morality. Personal choice and belief seem to be given absolute status. The issue of moral rightness or wrongness seems to be reduced to the individual's arbitrary judgment. Similarities in language can create the mistaken impression that conscience is merely a synonym for subjectivism. However, the Christian understanding of moral autonomy expressed in the category of conscience is radically different from the subjectivist position. The differences relate mostly to the context within which conscience operates. There are subtle but important nuances within the Christian tradition that allow one to continue to use the language of conscience while resisting the subjectivist impulses of contemporary culture.

The most obvious difference is that in the Christian tradition conscience is believed to be the place where human beings come to discern the objective good in each situation. This involves an intricate relationship between subjective, personal elements and objective ones. Christian theology frequently expressed this idea by speaking of conscience as the site of the encounter between the individual and God, or of conscience as the voice of God. When conscience is situated in a theocentric frame of reference, it is obviously transformed. Conscience thus reflects the nature of the person who is oriented toward God and whose life is lived in relationship with that God. Conscience then becomes the person's consciousness of the obligations due to the other and to God. To use traditional terminology for a moment, Christians believe that it is through conscience, "God's abode in us," that we discover ethical values and thus direct our actions. This means that conscience is not only an expression of personal will and desire, but that it also aspires to be an incarnation of God's will. As the culmination of personal reasoning, reflection and discernment it is indeed the individual's subjective assessment of the rightness or wrongness of a particular decision. Yet by describing conscience exclusively in such terms we are emphasizing only one aspect of its meaning. For Christians conscience has a double orientation. It is the human realization of value, under the guidance of the Spirit of God.

However, this guidance of the Spirit should not be thought of as a catalog of divine dictates that the conscience has to enforce. To think in such terms would reduce the person to an automaton who applies general principles to particular cases. It would remove any need for personal assessment. Instead, the conscience is regarded as the site of a special encounter between the person and God, where moral value is discerned. This emphasizes the relational character of Christian morality. The work of conscience is not about systematically applying preconceived divine laws to situations but about responding in love to the demands of the other. The integrity of human freedom and responsibility involves more than an unreflective adherence to divine will. However, human freedom and divine will do coincide when the person chooses the good. In traditional theological reflection conscience is regarded as the place where the person discovers God's will on ethical matters. Here the person "is alone with God whose voice re-echoes in his depths. In a wonderful manner conscience reveals that law which is fulfilled by love of God and love of neighbor."[9] It is the place where human freedom is realized, in the context of divine love and guidance. It is the site of personal, subjective apprehension of objective morality.

Conscience is therefore firmly situated within the context of the objective moral order and is under the guidance of a personal and loving God. As such the autonomy of the Christian conscience is quite different from the autonomy characteristic of subjectivism. Its judgment may be said to be absolute, but only in the sense that it is the place where the individual authentically apprehends value. Yet, it is always subject to the limitations of human understanding and discernment. Its operation is also shaped by the individual's life in community and by respect for the moral norms and principles of the tradition. Conscience expresses the irreducible quality of the person's moral discernment, but always in light of its formation within an objective moral order. By situating conscience in this framework and by recognizing the deep affinity between the individual conscience and the community, the Christian tradition runs counter to the excessive subjectivism criticized by the encyclical. While it may be true to say that in the Christian tradition the authority of the personal conscience is absolute, this is so only within a strictly delineated context. It is not subjectivism by another name.

Conscience and the "Moral Law"

Traditional theologies of conscience also spoke of its role in the context of God's law. Although this terminology is rare today it is important to mention it briefly. The language of "divine law" or "moral law" functions primarily to reinforce the idea that the individual conscience operates within a moral order. The same point is being made with the metaphors of "God's will" or "God's voice" or "God's abode in us." The language of moral law, too, is metaphorical. It conveys the belief that God's will operates in the moral as well as the physical or natural world, that morality is governed by some basic laws. The concept of moral law is ultimately a device to express the belief that there is an essential order in the moral sphere and that it is the task of human beings to discover and live it. The term *law* here should not conjure up ideas of predetermined orders to be implemented always and without exception. Instead, one should think of the moral law as pointing to the right and good resolution of each moral problem. This underwrites the Christian view that there should be no innate opposition between human freedom—which is understood as a life lived under the beneficence of divine grace—and the moral law.

Of course the idea of moral law involves many subtleties. One thing worth noting in this context is that moral theology does distinguish among different types of moral law. These range from rather vague and abstract formulations of the natural law to the much more specific laws of church teaching on slavery or torture or sex. The natural law refers to general moral principles, such as "good is to be done," or "human beings should be loving and truthful." In contrast the moral law of church teaching can be very narrowly focused indeed. The authority of the moral law is believed to vary depending on its form. The claims of natural law are said to be more fundamental and authoritative than human articulations of the moral law in church or civil society. The general principles of natural law are universal in their claims. So, for example, in every moral dilemma I encounter I am to seek to do the good and avoid the evil. However, since the term *moral law* also covers far more specific formulations, we must be more skeptical about the authority that these have.

The church's approach to the torture of heretics provides a good illustration of this point. Through the centuries the teaching on this issue changed considerably. In 1252 a papal bull allowed for heretics to be tortured so that they would be forced to confess their error. In addition Pope Leo X refuted Martin Luther's claim that it is against the will of the Holy Spirit to burn heretics at the stake. But in 1953 Pope Pius XII said that torture should be excluded from judicial investigations.[10] The church sometimes allowed the torture of heretics and at other stages ruled it out. At each stage the church believed that its position was a reflection of the moral law. But this could not possibly be the case. This reality suggests that there are occasions in the church's history when what was regarded to be the divine moral law was fundamentally flawed. It also cautions us to be aware of the limitations of all human articulations of the moral law, whatever their provenance.

The church tried to overcome some of these difficulties by speaking about the different kinds of moral law, some more authoritative and reliable than others. However, this obviously does not resolve all of the problems. In addition to this, in many contemporary discussions these important subtleties and distinctions are ignored. So too is the fact that there is no consensus on what the term *moral law* actually refers to, how it is to be found, how we know the content of this law, what role conscience has in discerning it and how it relates to church teaching. There is also a reluctance to accept that the requirements of the moral law may be unclear or imprecise. As a result a person may have to act independently of, or indeed contrary to, that which is conventionally taken to be the moral law. Traditional moral theology assumed that both conscience and church moral teaching each play a part in discerning the divine moral law. If the person proceeds in good faith, then she/he is drawing on the discernment of conscience as the interiorization of the divine law. As a reflection of the eternal law, the conscience is bound to seek the good in each situation, regardless of how difficult this may be. "And so there should be no question of confusing law and conscience or letting the conscience be destroyed by the law. The conscience in the face of the clearest and most determinative law, always has the role and the value of interiorizing the law, to implant it by making it personal."[11]

In Christian morality the conscience is not regarded as an alternative court to divine will. Rather, it is believed to be a reflection of it. *Gaudium et Spes* gives expression to this understanding of the relationship between conscience and divine will. It suggests that "conscience is the most secret core and sanctuary of the person. There he is alone with God whose voice re-echoes in his depths."[12] While in secular contexts there may be genuine and irreconcilable disagreements between the individual conscience and the law, in the theological realm no such conflict ought to occur. Should such a scenario present itself one must conclude either that the person's conscience is deeply flawed or that the church's understanding of divine will, expressed through laws, principles or traditions, is obscured or limited in some important respect. This is one way of reconciling the church's conflicting attitude to torture. Conscience in the Christian tradition is not an independent, self-referencing faculty that simply rubber-stamps the arbitrary moral opinions of the person. Rather, the conscience is the locus of the individual's discernment of divine will on moral matters. To view its functioning apart from this context is to violate a central dimension of the Christian understanding of conscience.

Conscience in Catholic Theology Today

For Christians conscience involves the interaction of human and divine elements. However, explaining the precise nature of the relationship between the two has long been problematic. Difficulties arise on two fronts. First, the role of personal judgment in discerning the moral law has been disputed by some theologians. In addition there are problems in reconciling the role of conscience (as the personal apprehension of the moral law) with the other vehicles of the moral law, most especially with church teaching. Within the church itself there are differing opinions on these issues. Without wishing to oversimplify the debates I would suggest that these divergent views have given rise to two substantially different and often conflicting models of morality in the Catholic Church. One, usually called the legalistic model, is characterized by an emphasis on church teaching as the central way by which the objective dimensions of morality are known. It regards the magisterium as the primary vehicle of moral truth. Furthermore, it argues for the existence of absolute and universal moral principles.

It is also deeply suspicious of any ethic that gives more than a superficial role to personal moral judgment. This seems to be the model that *Veritatis Splendor* endorses.

The second model, called the personalist model, emphasizes the other side of the coin. It prioritizes the personal autonomy and responsibility of individuals in moral matters. It also focuses on conscience as the mediator of the divine moral law. Furthermore, it rejects any account of ethics that relies on absolutist principles. Instead it believes that every moral theory should give due recognition to the role of circumstances and intentionality. Both models share a vision of ethics that involves the subjective discernment of the objective moral order. Their disagreements relate to how the objective or divine elements are known to the individual. The legalistic model insists that they are known through church teaching. The personalist model puts stress on the individual as the primary interpreter.

The existence of these two models helps to explain why there are conflicts within the church itself about the role and authority of conscience. Problems arise mainly when very abstract statements about conscience have to be given explicit focus. These difficulties are exemplified by the discussion of conscience in *Veritatis Splendor.* The encyclical makes a strong case for the dignity of conscience. It speaks of conscience as the witness of the person's faithfulness or unfaithfulness with regard to the law.[13] It insists that the judgment of conscience has an imperative character,[14] and that its dignity derives from truth.[15] In addition it claims that "the maturity and responsibility of these judgments...are not measured by the liberation of the conscience from objective truth, in favor of an alleged autonomy in personal decisions, but, on the contrary, by an insistent search for truth and by allowing oneself to be guided by that truth in one's actions."[16] While it is true that maturity is not measured by liberation from "objective truth," the encyclical wrongly suggests that there is a sharp opposition between autonomy and objective morality. There is no innate opposition between "correspondence to objective morality" and "autonomous personal decisions." By setting up an opposition the encyclical implies that if a person arrives at a different conclusion from the one held by the magisterium, then it is the person's decision that is not in accordance with the objective moral order. While this may indeed be the case, it is not inevitably so. As we have seen from the approach to torture, the church, too, can be mistaken in its understanding of the moral law. Yet the encyclical seems to regard church teaching as the only reliable interpreter of the moral law. It fails to highlight that the conscience too has a primary role. It appears that those of us who are Catholic are encouraged, at an abstract level, to educate and inform ourselves and to take responsibility for our moral decisions. Yet when experience, reflection and prayer lead us in a direction that is at odds with church teaching, the overriding impression we are left with is that we should immediately and always suppose that the error lies with ourselves.

Underlying this is a more basic disagreement about which factors the conscience should take into account when making moral decisions. Again, there are two conflicting views in evidence. The legalistic model is reluctant to take the person's intention or the particular circumstances into account. It insists that "even though intentions may sometimes be good, and circumstances frequently difficult,...individuals never have the authority to violate the fundamental and inalienable rights of the human person. In the end only a morality that acknowledges certain norms as valid always and for everyone, with no exception, can guarantee the ethical foundation of social coexistence."[17] This is the view of John Finnis, one of the most vocal proponents of the legalistic model. What Finnis suggests here is a version of morality that regards norms as universally binding (always and everywhere) and as absolute (allowing no exceptions). In an exposition of his thesis Finnis uses the example of the commandment not to kill. He concludes that unless this and other norms are believed to be exceptionless and universally binding, morality will be robbed of its objectivity and eventually everything will be permitted. This is the slippery-slope argument. It claims that if one exception is permitted then everything is allowed. He suggests that "the first socially approved exception to a norm, such as one may never choose to kill an innocent person, shows that there is no reason why we should limit satisfying our desires provided we are willing to accept the cost or risk."[18] Thus "thou shalt not kill" should be an absolutely binding command. The traditional exceptions of war or self-defense do not hold. In this version of morality the circumstances of a killing are irrelevant. Finnis argues that once we begin to include factors such as intentions and circumstances in the judgment of the rightness or wrongness of our decisions, the whole edifice of morality crumbles. It is wrong to take account of context in ethics according to Finnis. He claims that "the reaffirmation that there are intrinsically evil acts, exceptionless specific moral norms and inviolable human rights is philosophically defensible and manifestly necessary to preserve the moral substance of Christian ethics."[19]

With this view of morality the only task for the conscience is to apply these universal, absolute principles to every situation. The conscience has no evaluative role because the particular circumstances of the individual are deemed to be irrelevant. It is useful to look at how the problem of artificial contraception would be dealt with in this version of Christian morality. If one were to implement this thinking then the role of the conscience would be to apply the church's teaching that artificial contraception is morally wrong. The conscience should not concern itself with the reasons why the person might consider using artificial contraception. According to this view there is no moral significance in the fact that a couple may use artificial contraception because they can just about take proper care of their existing children. Neither is there any moral significance in the fact that the woman may be trying to protect herself from marital rape or trying to protect herself or her partner from HIV infection. The conscience is said to have no use for this information because, in Finnis's view, circumstances are morally irrelevant. He claims that once an exception to the absolute ban on artificial contraception is allowed, then morality itself is under threat, robbed of its objectivity. The role of conscience here is to apply church teaching to each situation. Everything else, according to this model, is superfluous. One might say that the activity of conscience is restricted to obeying orders.

However, within the church one also finds a different approach to circumstances and intentions. Lisa Sowle Cahill argues that when we think about the morality of particular acts we do "not mark off absolute boundaries around the moral event."[20] Instead we take account of "the nexus of practical, physical, causal and moral relationships"[21] that are relevant. In her opinion it is incorrect to isolate an act, say telling an untruth, from its context, the reason why the person told an untruth and in what circumstances. According to this version of morality the fact that a person may have told an untruth for personal financial gain or in order to protect an innocent child from harm is morally relevant. Telling an untruth may be morally reprehensible in one situation but commendable in another. To claim otherwise is to go against the human experience of making moral decisions. When thinking seriously about what to do in a particular situation we do not focus exclusively on the action itself, endowing it alone with moral significance. Rather, we try to assess, in an honest manner, the circumstances of our decision and try to establish what our intentions and motives are. As a result it is impossible to regard norms and principles as either universally binding or absolute, save in a very abstract and general manner. This is because very specific principles can never take account of all the morally relevant factors. Therefore, they should be regarded as general norms of guidance, not as laws to be obeyed. This view accepts that morality involves an objective dimension. However, the objective rightness or wrongness of an action can only be judged by taking account of the circumstances and the intention, not by ignoring them. The role given to conscience here is rather different from the one envisaged in the legalistic model. The task of conscience involves scrutinizing one's intention, evaluating all the relevant circumstances and informing oneself of church teaching and other sources of moral wisdom. It is only when all these factors are considered that one can come to a judgment of conscience.

All these differences inevitably lead to conflicts of an ecclesiological nature. Again, one can discern two competing models of church in these theological texts. The legalistic model thinks of the institutional church primarily in terms of hierarchy. In addition it draws a rigid distinction between the teaching church (that is the magisterium) and the learning church, comprised mainly of the laity. With this model the learning church owes a duty of obedience to the teaching church. The role of the individual conscience is to dutifully assent to and apply church teaching to the problems that the person encounters. However, in the church today another model is also evident. It speaks of the church as people of God. It draws its inspiration from the vision of Vatican II, especially in *Lumen gentium.* It regards the church as "a community of disciples, united by baptism and all having a fundamental dignity and equality as children of God."[22] Although both laity and magisterium are believed to have distinctive roles to play, no hierarchy of authority is implied. Laity and magisterium are each always learning from the other. While it is the duty of each person to be informed of church teaching, this is only the beginning, not the end of the decision-making process. The role of conscience involves a complex process of evaluation and as a result of this may find itself in conflict with magisterial teaching. Disagreement on moral matters is seen as an inevitable feature of the business of ethics and faithful dissent from particular church teaching is accepted.

Conclusion

The role and authority of conscience in the Christian moral life is a complex one. It involves dealing with a number of difficult questions, such as how we come to know God's will, how it is revealed, how it relates to personal judgment and to church teaching. The best of Catholic theology attempts to do justice to both the personal and institutional discernment of moral truth. It is careful not to sacrifice either. However, this is not an easy task. Quite understandably people tend to emphasize one aspect or the other, which in turn gives rise to rival versions of morality. Such tendencies are not new. Indeed, the entire history of Catholic moral theology can be seen as an ongoing attempt to explain the subtleties of the relationship between the individual and the church on ethical matters. For the most part conscience was the theological territory on which these difficult questions were debated. Raphael Gallagher highlights this when he suggests that historically the conscience has been the place where the duel between freedom and law has been fought.[23]

In the following chapters we will map the evolution of the concept of conscience in the Catholic tradition. We will consider how we can explain its existence; what kinds of qualities it has; how it is formed; how it operates in real life; how it makes moral decisions; how it relates to the intellectual and emotional life of the individual; how we know when its judgments are right and how and why they can be wrong. Alongside questions of its nature we will discuss its role in the Catholic context. This involves asking where conscience gets its authority; how it relates to the other moral resources in the Catholic Church; whether conscience ever loses its dignity; and if each person is obligated always to follow it. The often contentious answers to these questions also unfold in the history of conscience in the Catholic tradition.

As this chapter has shown, contemporary moral theology is engaged in a number of debates, each of which impinges on the understanding of the authority of conscience. This text should be seen as one contribution to this ongoing discussion. The Catholic tradition has always respected the centrality of the individual's conscience. The historical analysis of the forthcoming chapters confirms this. Although there are many inconsistencies and conceptual difficulties with the category of conscience, theologians through the centuries have continued to affirm its primacy. Yet the conscience is formed and operates always in dialogue with the tradition's other sources of moral wisdom. As a result balancing these relationships requires a delicate hand. In response this text attempts to articulate a thoroughly traditional account of conscience in the

Catholic Church, one that neither compromises the authority of the individual conscience nor the importance of the other moral resources. I will suggest that the existing tradition can indeed provide the basis for a renewed theology of conscience, one rooted in personal responsibility but formed by the church community.

Chapter 2
"The Law Written on Our Hearts": Conscience in Greek, Jewish and Early Christian Thought

The purpose of this chapter is to examine the early history of conscience. As with many theological concepts, the origins of the Christian notion of conscience can be found in Jewish religion and in the philosophical traditions of Greece and Rome. These biblical and classical antecedents will be the focus of our attention in the first half of this chapter. The second half of the chapter discusses the early Christian appropriation of these ethical ideas. Our examination of conscience in the New Testament will be limited to the theology of Paul, whose letters to the Romans and to the Corinthians are particularly important. Paul's theology of conscience is highly significant, not only because of the manner in which he developed particular ideas, but also because of the place given to it by patristic and medieval writers. The chapter will conclude with a brief survey of the concept of conscience both in the rich and varied patristic tradition as well as in the era of the penitentials. Before beginning, however, it is necessary to make some general methodological points.

We are now accustomed to using the term *conscience* in an exclusively moral sense. However, it is important to note that it has not always been reserved for the realm of morality. In many early Greek and Latin texts the word *conscience* refers not only to moral but also to nonmoral fields. Indeed, this is still the case in many languages, including Greek, Latin and French. Conscience in these languages can mean "awareness" or "consciousness" in any sense, including an ethical one. The meaning of *syneidesis* (the Greek word for both "conscience" and "consciousness") or *conscientia* (the Latin equivalent) may or may not refer to ethics. It is the context in which the term is used that enables the reader to discover whether its orientation is ethical or not. This means that there are many texts in which the words *syneidesis* or *conscientia* appear that are not relevant to our concern. Any survey of the frequency of the use of *syneidesis* or *conscientia* in the texts of the tradition must therefore take this into account. Otherwise, we will have a false impression of the prevalence of the term.

A second, and in some ways contradictory, problem also arises. In the literature of the pre-Christian and early Christian eras there are relatively few instances of *synderesis* or *conscientia* being used in a strictly ethical sense. However, the same reality is often spoken about using different terminology. Analogous concepts such as *heart* or *wisdom* are frequently used instead. These also convey the meaning of conscience. Therefore, the rarity of the term *conscience* in its explicitly moral form does not actually represent the full extent of the historical sources we have at our disposal. This can be explained by the fact that Indo-European languages only developed philosophical terms gradually. In place of abstract terminology a host of more concrete images were used to express philosophical, psychological and moral meanings. This is true not only in relation to the understanding of conscience, but also in relation to many other philosophical and theological ideas. Our discussion of the evolution of conscience will deal with this by also examining analogous concepts. In biblical, classical and early Christian writings the analogous ideas that are most prominent are *heart, wisdom* and *prudence.* These carry many of the meanings of *conscience* without the explicit terminology and are particularly important in the early history of the concept. In focusing on the word *conscience* in early Jewish, Greek and Latin texts we are thus working with two opposing constraints. First, we accept that the word *conscience* can have nonethical connotations and, second, we recognize that the idea of conscience may be conveyed with different, non-philosophical terminology.

Since this is not intended to be an exhaustive treatment of the history of ethics, our discussion of these highly sophisticated ethical traditions will be limited. I will focus specifically on the features developed in subsequent Christian texts. This will involve a discussion of the term *conscience* and of the analogous notions of *heart, wisdom* and *prudence.* Theological and philo-sophical texts will be our main resources. However, we will also mention the texts of casuistry from each of the traditions, since these also play a significant role in the development of the con-cept of conscience. Any historical survey of this kind is some-what arbitrary. Inevitably there will be omissions. The purpose of this chapter is to gain an overview of the origin and evolution of the concept from the early centuries. We will identify the cen-tral preoccupations, the main themes and the important inno-vations in each historical period. We will also discuss the consolidation of certain traditions as well as the emergence of contradictory ones. As Christianity developed one of its main concerns was to explore the nature of the moral demand. The story of conscience forms a major strand of the search for clar-ity and certainty in this regard. As we shall see in the following analysis, the concept of conscience gradually acquired precision and sophistication. As such it represents an important compo-nent of Christian reflection on morality.

The Greek Tradition

Democritus of Abdera, a philosopher of the fifth century B.C.E., is said to be the first to use the term *syneidesis,* the Greek word for "conscience." In one of the surviving fragments of his work he uses the term *syneidesis* in a moral sense, saying, "There are men who are quite ignorant of what is to follow the dissolution of their mortal nature; yet because their conscience is burdened with the memory of their evil conduct, they torment themselves, all their lives long, by inventing myths and fables about a life after death."[1] Conscience here refers to a faculty of self-reflection. It plays a judicial role, pronouncing judgment on past actions and invoking feelings of guilt and remorse. The term *conscience* stems from the verb *sunoida*, which means "I know in common with." It is used in a number of different grammatical configurations and can imply "knowledge about another person, which can be used in witness for or against him." It can also mean "I bear witness," or "to share knowledge with oneself," or "to know with oneself," or "to be a witness for or against oneself."[2]

From the fifth century B.C.E. on, the term *syneidesis* appears sporadically in Greek literature but with no consistent meaning. Many of the instances speak of conscience in an explicitly moral sense, and of these most refer only to a bad conscience. Euripides' play *Orestes* is one such text. In the play Orestes has just killed his mother. He kills her because she and her lover have already murdered Orestes' father, Agamemnon. Even though he was avenging the death of his father the play tells us that he was tormented by his actions. He is in a terrible state and is asked by Menelaus which sickness has overcome him. He replies "Conscience—to know I have wrought a fearful deed."[3]

Here Orestes is speaking explicitly of a bad conscience. When Plutarch, writing much later, refers to this play, he gives a vivid description of Orestes' remorseful conscience. He says:

> My conscience, since I have done a dreadful deed, like an ulcer in the flesh, leaves behind it in the soul regret which ever continues to wound and prick it. For the other pangs reason does away with, but regret is caused by reason itself, since the soul together with its feelings of shame, is stung and chastised by itself. For as those who shiver with ague or burn with fevers are more distressed and pained than those who suffer the same discomforts through heat

> or cold from a source outside the body, so the pangs
> which Fortune brings, coming as it were, from a source
> without, are lighter to bear; but that Lament, None is to
> blame for this but me myself, which is chanted over one's
> errors, coming as it does from within, makes the pain
> even heavier by reason of the disgrace one feels.[4]

This description of the terror, shame and regret that the person feels when he/she has done a bad deed is as terrifying as any one can find.

The term *syneidesis* used in a moral sense is curiously absent from the philosophical works of both Plato and Aristotle. However, both do have ways of speaking of moral self-reflection. Delhaye mentions only one place in Plato's *Republic* where *syneidesis* is used in a moral sense. Again, it refers to a bad conscience. Plato says "When a man feels that death is approaching...he runs over and examines the injustices which he might have committed. If he finds many iniquities in his conduct he finally awakens from his slumber...he is afraid and lives a dreadful expectation."[5] The relative absence of the term, however, should not suggest a lack of ways of speaking of this moral self-awareness. In place of the term *conscience* Plato and Aristotle use a number of different terms and concepts. Of these the most important are *wisdom* and *prudence (phronesis),* which carry with them the sense of ethical self-consciousness.

Although not strictly analogous to conscience the terms *wisdom* and *prudence* do highlight many of the features of the person's moral life, which were later expressed by the term *conscience.* The most obvious similarity is the way in which both Plato and Aristotle associate wisdom and prudence with knowledge. For Plato wisdom is the knowledge that enables the person to conduct her/his affairs with good judgment. It is knowledge, not in a specialized or technical sense, but knowledge that helps one to recognize and live by the virtues. In Aristotle wisdom or prudence has an even more practical orientation. *Prudence* or *phronesis* for Aristotle is the virtue of practical wisdom. It is the disposition that enables the person to discern the art of living well in each context. *Phronesis* is the person's ability to "decide correctly what is good and useful for their happiness."[6] This focus on the practical resolution of ethical questions was to become an important feature of the Christian conscience in later centuries. It was especially the case once the distinction between the habitual and the actual conscience was established.

There is one aspect of Plato's work, however, that has been the source of much scholarly disagreement. It relates to whether Socrates' *daimon* is an early form of the conscience or not. Socrates frequently refers to his *daimon,* which he says "began in my early childhood—a sort of voice which comes to me."[7] For Socrates the *daimon* is a sort of intermediary being that guides his actions. D'Arcy and Maurer disagree as to whether this *daimon* is an early version of what the Christian calls conscience. D'Arcy suggests that this internal monitor or *daimon* of Socrates is the conscience in all but name.[8] However, Maurer insists that the Socratic *daimon* cannot be equated with conscience, because "as a divine voice, which cannot be explained rationally, it delivers impartial judgments on Socrates' acts. But its admonitions relate only to approaching decisions, not to those that belong to the past."[9] Although there may be similarities between the two, I am inclined to agree with Maurer's assessment that since the *daimon* does not judge past decisions it cannot be regarded as identical with the conscience.

Two other strands in Greek thought are also relevant in tracing the emergence of conscience in the moral sense. The first is the Stoic idea that each person has a divinely appointed overseer. For the Stoic philosophers this is what makes moral and intellectual decisions possible and is referred to occasionally as *syneidos.*[10] For example Epictetus tells us that "when we were children our parent handed us over to a nursery slave who should watch over us everywhere lest harm befall us. But when we were grown up, God hands us over to the conscience [*suneidesei*] implanted in us, to protect us. Let us not in anyway despise its protection for should we do so we should be both ill pleasing to God and have our own conscience [*suneidoti*] as an enemy."[11] In this text we can see hints of the positive, guiding role that the concept of conscience developed later. However, this did not happen in any coherent way until the Christian era.

The second relevant strand is the tradition of meditation, which one finds in some Greek philosophy. This practice of nightly self-examination originated with the Pythagoreans and is very similar to the Christian practice of the examination of conscience. The practice begins with the recommendation that "thou shalt not take sleep to thy gentle eyes until thou hast considered each of the day's acts: Where did I fail? What was a right act? What was left undone? Begin with the first, go through them, and finally when thou hast done wrong rebuke thyself and when thou hast done good rejoice."[12] This certainly prefigures much of the moral self-examination associated with conscience. Although it would be wrong to interpret every reference to ethical self-reflection as conscience, in these texts we can clearly see the origins of the concept.

The Latin Tradition

In Latin literature the term *conscientia* is a direct translation of the Greek word *syneidesis*. As in Greek literature its meaning is not confined to the ethical sphere, although it appears far more frequently than the Greek term does. The term does achieve a significant moral elaboration, especially in the works of Seneca and Cicero. Etymologically, the word *conscientia* mirrors the Greek term, being a combination of *con* and *scientia*. It means "knowing with," that is, either knowledge shared with other people or knowledge within oneself, self-consciousness. Cicero (106–43 B.C.E.) is credited with being the first author to use the term *conscience* in its exclusively moral sense with great regularity. Davies mentions that he uses the term seventy-five times.[13] His positive recognition of the role of conscience in the moral life in his *De Senectute* is often quoted. Of conscience he says, "The consciousness of a life well spent and the remembrance of numerous deeds well done—this is a blessed thing."[14] The more usual association of conscience with negative judgment of misdeeds is also present in Cicero's works. In his *De Finibus* he advises us to cultivate the virtues that will guard against "the pangs of anxiety night and day gnawing at [our] hearts." He asks, "What can wickedness contribute towards lessening the annoyances of life, commensurate with its effect in increasing them, owing to the burden of a guilty conscience...?"[15] The conscience is so powerful an accuser that, according to Cicero, it is the judgment of conscience and not fear of the gods that determines and regulates our conduct. Thus, even if the city removed all images of the gods and if the gods were to be ignored, sin would not prevail. This is because, according to Cicero, an innocent or a guilty conscience is a sufficiently powerful force in its own right.[16]

The Roman Stoic Seneca had a similarly well-developed notion of conscience. He speaks of conscience as the moral faculty, inherent in the person, that passes judgment on past actions as either worthy or unworthy. In his *Epistle* (41,1) he refers to a spirit dwelling in the person that is "an observer and guardian of good and evil in us." In this text Seneca is advising a friend. He encourages him to do good deeds because of this "sacred and august spirit which resides within us."[17] The conscience in Seneca plays two different roles. It accuses the person because of bad deeds and encourages the person to engage in virtuous action. This helps to cultivate a good conscience. The conscience is given a place of significance in the moral life by Seneca because the person lives always under its shadow. Indeed, he suggests that "a good conscience enlists a multitude of friends; a bad conscience is distressed and anxious, even when alone."[18] Yet although we can find many similarities between Seneca's use of the term *conscience* and the later Christian concept, there is at least one important difference. In Seneca the "reference is still to the conscience which follows after or is at the most concurrent."[19] There is no anticipatory role for conscience in Seneca's texts. This guiding or future oriented dimension of conscience was not properly present in the literature until Paul's letters.

Roman Casuistry

Within the Latin philosophical tradition the practice of casuistry is also significant. Although the term *casuistry* is often now used in a pejorative sense, the tradition of casuistry plays a vital role in enabling individuals and institutions to come to decisions involving complex dilemmas of conscience. The *Oxford English Dictionary* defines casuistry as "that part of ethics which resolves cases of conscience, applying the general rules of religion and morality to particular instances in which circumstances alter cases or in which there appears to be a conflict of duties." Although this tradition has fallen somewhat into disrepute (the attack on the casuistry of French Jesuits by Pascal in his *Provincial Letters* is well known), it had a crucially positive role in the articulation of Catholic understandings of conscience. The practice of casuistry is important because it attempts to bridge the gap between "the abstract grasp of idealized theories and the concrete mastery of practical situations."[20] Although the Catholic tradition did not develop a formal casuistry of its own for many centuries, it was deeply influenced by Roman and rabbinic systems of casuistry.

There are elements of casuistry in Greek philosophy, especially in the philosophies of the Stoics and of Aristotle. However, it is in Cicero that we find the earliest and most systematic texts of casuistry. *On Duties (De Officiis)* deals with a number of cases, both real and hypothetical, in which the individual's conscience is genuinely perplexed. Cicero recognizes that such dilemmas occur because, in attempting to cultivate virtue, we encounter moral duties that conflict with one another. We also encounter dilemmas of conscience, because what initially appears to be the right course of action may in the end turn out to be wrong. For example, "There are occasions when even promise keeping or returning something left in your charge would not be right when, for example, it would be harmful to the one to whom the promise was made, or would do more harm to you than good to him."[21] In *De Officiis* Cicero acknowledges that "the cultivation of virtue" or any other phrase that might describe the art of ethical living will only bring one so far. In itself it is not a sufficient guide to decision making. We must also learn the art of moral deliberation so that we can identify and pursue the good in complex cases. It is not appropriate here to discuss the criteria and axioms that Cicero thought ought to guide the resolution of cases. However, it is worth noting that Cicero recognized that actual circumstances make the simple application of ethical principles and duties well nigh impossible. As a result "in the performance of all these duties, we shall have to consider what is most needful in each individual case. In this way we shall find that the fundamental moral claim of social relationships is not identical in every circumstance....These different circumstances should be carefully scrutinized in every instance of duty, so that we may become skilled evaluators of duty and by calculation perceive where the weight of duty lies."[22]

Cicero discussed many cases of conscience. He drew on different sources for his discussions. Some were real cases of conflict. Some were drawn from history and literature. Still others he invented. In each instance he set out the problem case, identified the conflicts of duties or principles and then went on to propose different ways of resolving each case. He used the cases of "the shipwrecked companions who cling to a plank that is buoyant enough to support only one; the merchant who brings grain to a drought-ridden city, knowing that a plethora of grain will arrive in a following fleet (The merchant has to decide whether or not to charge the inflated prices which pertain because of the drought.); the real-estate agent who advertises houses that are termite-ridden;...the story of the noble Regulus, who had to decide whether he would keep a promise to return to his captors, knowing that this return would mean his death."[23]

The practice of casuistry illustrates very clearly that reflection on the nature of morality was pursued, not with theoretical arguments alone, but also by engaging with specific moral cases. These discussions in Cicero's *De Officiis* contribute a great deal to our understanding of the process of decision making. Furthermore, they highlight the fact that, in addition to the sophisticated theoretical discussions, there was also an appreciation of the complexity and indeterminacy of morality as lived. In surveying the history of conscience these practically oriented treatises must therefore be taken into consideration. Together with the more abstract philosophical texts already mentioned, they were important resources for the development of a comprehensive account of conscience in Christian moral thinking.

The Jewish Tradition

Hebrew Bible

There is a virtual absence of the term *conscience* from the Hebrew Bible. There are two or perhaps three specific mentions of the word. One occurs in the Book of Wisdom, a book greatly influenced by Greek thought. It reads, "wickedness is confessedly very cowardly, and it condemns itself; under pressure from conscience it always assumes the worst."[24] This text and the other less certain references mirror the meaning that *syneidesis* had in the prevailing Greek culture. The absence of the term can be partly explained by noting the lack of introspection and self-examination in early Jewish thought. Instead, the focus tended to be on morality as obedience to the law and the covenant. Maurer draws our attention to the fact that Judaism was oriented to the God of revelation, whose presence determines all human efforts and responses. As a result the self-knowledge to which the term *conscience* refers occurs in a different way. Knowledge of the self arises, not through probing the depths of one's being, but in remembering and keeping God's law revealed in God's word. It is God's word that makes self-understanding and hence a good moral life possible.

Psalm 139, which is often described as a hymn in praise of God's omniscience, embodies this fundamental orientation of Judaism very well. Here the author says, "Yahweh, you examine me and know me,...you read my thoughts from far away...you know every detail of my conduct...God examine me and know my heart, probe me and know my thoughts; make sure I do not follow pernicious ways, and guide me in the way

that is everlasting."[25] The rational autonomy that is characteristic of later understandings of conscience is nowhere present
in this thinking. As Maurer suggests, in the Hebrew Bible "the
reflection of the I about itself is thus obedient listening to
God....Conscience is hearing in the sense of willing adherence. The voice of God and one's own voice agree...in the harmony of the I with God's will. It is because of this radically
distinct conception of the situation of the moral person in
relation to God that that which we have come to term conscience is absent in Hebrew thought at this time."[26]

It would be wrong to think about biblical morality as being
primarily concerned with external conformity to God's law.
There was also a very strong emphasis on the need to interior-
ize the divine law, to cultivate virtuous behavior and to value
good acts. The metaphor of the heart *(lêb)* is the most frequently used motif in this regard and is described by many
commentators as a notion analogous to the Christian conscience. The heart bears witness to the moral worth of our
deeds, condemning or exonerating us. For example, in the
Book of Job we read of Job insisting at one stage, "my heart
reproaches none of my days."[27] In the Greek translation of the
Hebrew text this word *heart* is replaced by a phrase that
includes the word *synoida,* which in English becomes *conscience.*
Here we already have the Hebrew word for *heart* replaced by
the word *conscience.* In some English translations the verse
becomes, "my conscience gives me no cause to blush." This
connection between the two concepts is also illustrated very
clearly in the Vulgate translation of a text from the Book of
Ecclesiastes. The text reads, "you may hear that your servant
has reviled you; your own heart knows how often you have
reviled others."[28] In the Vulgate the word *heart* (*cardia* in Greek)
is translated by the Latin word *conscientia.* This indicates that
the moral meaning expressed by the Jewish idea of the heart
was most appropriately translated by the term *conscience.*

There are a number of other ways in which the use of the
heart metaphor highlights this affinity. "Hardness of heart"
indicates a distortion of the moral faculty. A "contrite heart"
expresses remorse at wrongdoing, as does a "change of

heart." These and other such phrases appear with regularity in the biblical texts. The authors of Exodus tell us that the Pharaoh's heart was stubborn.[29] Zechariah describes the doers of evil deeds as having "made their hearts adamant rather than listen to the teaching and the words [of] Yahweh."[30] The exhortations of the prophets that the people of Israel have a change of heart also supports this view. The guilt and remorse that accompany the realization of evil deeds done are expressed in the prophet's description of "contrition of the heart." Jeremiah, for example, says, "my heart is broken within me."[31] It is a change of heart that is needed and prayed for in Psalm 51. Here the supplicant asks Yahweh to "create in me a clean heart, O God, and renew a right spirit within me."[32] Over the centuries the heart became an important metaphor for describing certain features of the person's moral faculty. The attribution of new qualities and functions to the heart was part of this development and indicates its growth in importance. Maurer plots this gradual development and concludes that it prepares the ground for the emergence of "a concept hitherto unknown, in the Greek world, that of the good conscience...."[33] This was another feature that grew in prominence as the concept of conscience developed.

It is not possible to survey the vast corpus of Jewish moral thought. However, two Jewish philosophers are also worth mentioning. One is the first-century Jewish philosopher Josephus. He used the term *syneidesis* fairly frequently but did not introduce any significant developments. In his writings it is present in a moral sense, but its precise meaning is often disputed. In the works of another early Jewish philosopher, Philo, one finds consistent use of the term *conscience* as *the* moral faculty. While an examination of the precise parameters of the discussion in Philo is well beyond the scope of this text, it is worth making a few points about Philo's account of conscience. In Philo's texts conscience has both a judicial, condemnatory role and also (though rarely) a positive function of guiding action. This, as we have already seen, is not unique, though it is unusual. The second feature worth noting is that although Philo was deeply indebted to Greek philosophical thinking, his account of conscience is closely related to the ethic of the Hebrew Bible, wherein the conscience echoes the voice of God. The conscience is essentially "an instrument in God's hand to bring men to conversion," behind whose person stands "God as Accuser and Judge."[34] In the history of the origins of conscience it is clear that Philo stands at a significant intersection of Jewish and Greek thought. This was something that early Christian theologians continued to do with significant consequences for the development of particular concepts. Indeed, the concept of conscience was one that benefited greatly with the fusion of these two traditions.

Jewish Casuistry

In addition to the scriptural and theological texts of Judaism, there were also many texts of casuistry. An interest in elaborating on and interpreting the law for particular contexts has long been a central feature of Judaism. It forms the basis of many aspects of Jewish theology, including the laws and doctrines of the Talmud. Our interest in Jewish casuistry must be limited to the early centuries of the common era. Of particular importance is how this tradition deals with the individual's resolution of ethical conflict, a role ascribed to the conscience in Christian theology. There are significant differences between Jewish and Latin casuistry. However, both traditions remind us that although the term *conscience* is rare, the activities subsequently identified with the conscience were very much of concern to philosophers and religious teachers of that time.

In this casuistic tradition the main focus was on the impact that different cultures might have on the practices and observances of Judaism. The Pentateuch contains "613 commandments governing the daily religious and secular life of the people" and "the Mishnah comprises 63 treatises...covering different aspects of life: prayer, holy days, marriage, civil and criminal law, temple ritual, and ceremonial purity."[35] Inevitably, given the extent and complexity of Jewish law, some rules might conflict with one another, some might be impossible to adhere to and some might contravene civil law. Others might need to be adapted as a result of encountering new and unanticipated situations. These issues were discussed in the Halakhah, which comprises the source book of casuistry for rabbinic Judaism. These texts discussed actual and potential moral dilemmas associated with Jewish law. They also provided distinctive principles and methods for resolving dilemmas of conscience, which the Christian tradition developed much later.

In conclusion, then, when we examine early Jewish theology we discover that the term *conscience* is not significantly present. However, similar ideas were developed in other ways. The interiorization of the law expressed through the metaphor of the heart was an important comparable notion. The tradition of casuistry was also significant. These suggest that a number of features of the moral life subsequently expressed through the term *conscience* were of great concern in Jewish theology.

The New Testament Tradition

The term *conscience* is rarely used in the gospel texts. There is only one certain use of the word. It appears in John 8:9. However, many scholars regard this as a later interpolation. The text occurs in the story of the woman caught in adultery who is about to be stoned for her misdeed. The narrator tells us that after Jesus had defended the woman, the audience "convicted by their conscience,"[36] went away one by one. Other texts like Mark 3:5; 6:52 and Matthew 15:10 don't use the word *conscience* but use the metaphor of heart in a comparable way. These rather scanty references indicate that in the gospels other mechanisms for speaking of the moral life and its demand were used. However, one cannot identify anything that could reasonably be described as analogous to the conscience.

In the writings of Paul the category of conscience figures more prominently. There is disagreement among biblical commentators as to the number of times the term *conscience* occurs in the Pauline letters. This depends on whether particular letters are attributed to Paul or not. One point on which scholars do agree, however, is that in the letters to the Corinthians and

Romans Paul introduced and developed a concept of conscience. In these texts Paul speaks both about the nature of conscience and about resolving problems of conscience. He deals with the nature of conscience particularly in his Letter to the Romans. Here he claims that the "spark of conscience" is not the exclusive preserve of Christians. Instead, he regards it as a moral faculty that nonbelievers, that is, Gentiles, also possess. In Romans 2:14 he writes, "When the Gentiles who have not the law, do by nature what the law requires, they are a law to themselves, even though they do not have the law. They show that what the law requires is written in their hearts, while their conscience also bears witness and their conflicting thoughts accuse or perhaps excuse them...."[37] In drawing this distinction between the moral resources that Jews and Gentiles possess, Paul ascribes an important role to the conscience. Jews have the law to guide their behavior; Gentiles have their consciences. It is significant that Paul speaks of the conscience as belonging to the person by nature. Here, both Jews and Gentiles are credited with having the capacity to discern the moral quality of their behavior. In the case of the Gentiles, who have not the law, the conscience performs this function.

In Paul the conscience is a faculty present in Gentile and Jew alike. It forms the basis of our capacity to judge our own and others' actions. Paul gives conscience a prominent role in the evaluation of his own behavior. "I am speaking the truth in Christ, I am not lying; my conscience bears me witness in the Holy Spirit."[38] What is clear from this and other texts is that the judgment of conscience is not a purely personal evaluation. It has both subjective and objective dimensions. The objective dimension is the "divine character of conscience [which] is even more marked in the Christian, since the conscience is inhabited by the Holy Spirit who guides and enlightens it."[39] This way of speaking about the objective dimension of conscience was continued in the Christian tradition. Since the whole outlook of the Christian is shaped by faith, it is reasonable to expect Paul to speak of conscience in this way. It is repeated in Romans 14, where conscience is again closely identified with faith in Christ. The voice of conscience, even though it is our own personal response to our circumstances, is also shaped by the demands of the gospel. It is the requirements of faith that give it its objective reference.

The subjective dimensions of the person's conscience are also discussed by Paul. He makes many references to the good conscience. This is by no means a fait accompli; rather it is a state to be worked toward and aspired to. It is achievable by a constant determination to seek the good in each situation. For example in his Letter to Timothy he discusses how he keeps his own conscience clear. He says, "Night and day I thank God, keeping my conscience clear and remembering my duty to him...."[40] It is significant that Paul can be confident about the state of his own conscience. In another text, speaking for both himself and Timothy, he writes, "There is one thing we are proud of, and our conscience tells us it is true: that we have always treated everybody, and especially you, with the reverence and sincerity which comes from God...."[41] Paul can make these astoundingly positive statements because of his sense that he is doing God's will, obeying God's commands. His judgments are not purely personal and autonomous; rather they are based on and reflect the word of God.

The interplay between the subjective and objective dimensions of the conscience are very much to the fore in Paul's discussion. The confidence with which he accepts the judgment of his own conscience sets his writings apart from those of his contemporaries and his predecessors. Not only does the conscience have a role in making negative judgments, but Paul also speaks of conscience affirming and applauding one's behavior as well. Although these texts still focus on judgments after the event, the role given to the positive pronouncements of conscience is significant.

Paul developed thinking on conscience significantly in his discussion of an erroneous conscience. Although mentioned in a number of different texts, the main discussion occurs in his First Letter to the Corinthians.[42] Here Paul is responding to a specific moral problem that the community was not able to resolve. In giving his advice on how to approach this question he ascribes a central role to the conscience. A dispute had arisen among Christians as to whether it was permissible to eat meat that had already been offered to idols. Most of the available meat would have been in this state. Some argued that since the gods to which the food was offered did not exist, then the dedication of the food had no significance. It could therefore be eaten. Others were more scrupulous and insisted that it was wrong to eat such food. Paul set about resolving this dispute, not by talking about the acceptability of eating such food in itself, but by discussing the effect that such actions would be likely to have on the wider community. In doing this he invokes the ideas of a good conscience, a bad conscience and a weak conscience.

Paul's answer is that there are members of the community who do not comprehend that the meat offered to idols has no significance because the idols do not exist. Because they do not have this knowledge, "they eat this food as though it really had been sacrificed to the idol, and their conscience, being weak, is defiled by it."[43] As a result those who are strong and whose consciences allow them to eat this food (on the correct premise that since idols do not exist, sacrifice to idols is meaningless) are encouraged, out of respect for the weak, to refrain from eating such foods. This is because "by sinning in this way against your brothers, and injuring their weak consciences, it would be Christ against whom you sinned."[44] The conscience of the weak person dissuades that person from eating the meat and must be obeyed. It must be obeyed even though it is mistaken. Two aspects of this discussion became very important in later Christian theology. The first is the idea that a judgment of conscience can be wrong. This was not present in earlier texts. The second is the insistence that even if it is in error the force of conscience is such that one is obliged to follow it. The conscience may be weak or erroneous for a number of reasons. Its judgments may be wrong because of lack of knowledge, out of habit, or because it is not able to withstand the example of others. Whatever the cause of the weakness, according to Paul, its force is binding.

Paul is also credited with giving conscience a guiding or legislative role. In a continuation of the discussion on eating meat Paul implies that the conscience plays a role before an action is performed.[45] The text can be translated in two ways. It can mean that because of conscience one should avoid asking questions about whether the food has been sacrificed to idols or not. It can also mean one can eat any food sold in the market without letting scruples of conscience induce one to ask questions about it. Whichever way the text is translated, most commentators agree that Paul uses the term *conscience* to indicate deliberation prior to performing an action. Romans 13:5 also speaks of conscience as having a guiding role. Here Paul is advising Christians on how to relate to civic government. He encourages submission not only because of fear of punishment, but also "for conscience' sake."[46] Although it is possible to read this as meaning submit to civic government in order to avoid a bad conscience, it could also mean submit "out of duty, conviction, or other moral considerations suggested by conscience."[47] Eric D'Arcy insists that in Paul the conscience plays a directive role, that is, before action takes place.[48] I am not convinced, however, that the textual evidence would allow for such an unambiguous claim. These are difficult and much disputed texts. All one can confidently say is that Paul prepared the ground for and occasionally hinted at a guiding role for conscience.

Paul certainly developed both the understanding of the nature of conscience and the range of ways in which it could be used in explaining moral decision making. He was unambiguous in his statements about the presence of "the spark" of conscience in Jews and Gentiles alike. He was similarly sure about the primacy that must be given to judgments of conscience, even when, as in the case of eating food offered to idols, its evaluation is in error. He not only stressed this subjective element of conscience, but also discussed the relationship between the conscience and "the will or judgment of God." This was an important aspect of his theology because of his conviction that the correct verdict of conscience is that which is in accord with God's word. He also prepared the way for the directive role attributed to conscience in later centuries. Although he gives neither a coherent definition nor an analysis of the role that conscience plays, he extended the discussion in many important respects. As a result some essential characteristics of Christian morality were given fuller expression. In Paul's texts "it is no longer a question of a reference to God the lawmaker and judge; the law is itself interiorized, it guides the action, it judges it after the fact."[49] This is the Christian conscience in embryo.

The Patristic Tradition

Any attempt to discuss the range of patristic thinking on conscience is bound to be limited. The variety of perspectives of many significant theologians means that it is difficult to form a coherent picture of the category. For this reason I will focus on a few texts and authors who in some sense can be regarded as representative of patristic thinking on conscience. These texts are chosen because they also consolidate the achievements of Paul.

Patristic theologians wrote in both Latin and Greek. As a result from the second century on there were theological texts in which both the terms *syneidesis* and *conscientia* appear. Although one word is a direct translation of the other, the terms do not always overlap in these texts. This is because neither word had yet been so refined as to be the specialized moral term it was later to become. Some patristic texts also continue the Jewish tradition of using the metaphor of the heart to express the ideas later associated with the conscience. This is evident in a great number of patristic writers, including Origen, Cassian and Augustine. Indeed, Mahoney highlights this, suggesting that "patristic development of the theme of conscience relied heavily on Paul, stressing the idea he adopted from the Old Testament prophetic literature of a moral law written by God on men's hearts."[50] A further point which is important in relation to patristic uses of the term conscience is that there is a genuine polyvalence in the meanings of the word. A number of meanings suggested by the concept are developed and given priority in different texts. As a result, although one can identify a range of ideas that the concept of conscience includes, it is impossible to give a precise account of its meaning and use.

The consequent conscience that pronounced judgment on past actions was the most well-developed aspect in ancient thought. It is unsurprising therefore that in patristic writings it is also important. Themes of the anguish and remorse that result from wrongdoing frequently occur in these texts. In many cases the statements are uncompromisingly harsh, leaving the faithful in no doubt as to the torment visited by the conscience as a result of bad behavior. John Chrysostom's *De Lazaro* is often quoted as an example of such texts. He warns his readers,

> Even in this life...the sinner finds punishment for his fault....Look at his conscience, there you will see the tumultuous agitation of his sins, in fear, tempest, discord. As a sort of tribunal, the mind sits as it were as a judge on the royal throne of conscience, using the memory of what one has done as so many executioners, suspending the course of thought, cruelly causing the sins committed to be exploited. It is impossible to silence its accusing voice even when it is a question of things known only to God.[51]

The ferocity of the feelings of remorse are usually related to the heinousness of the crime. The perpetual torment of the person judged sinful by conscience is a recurrent and central theme. Ambrose and Augustine[52] also speak of the judgment of the consequent conscience bringing feelings of guilt to the sinful person. Indeed, as one reads these patristic texts one is struck by the formidable power of these negative judgments of conscience.

Whereas up to this point the dominant theme was of accusation, in many patristic texts there is a lesser tradition of the good or harmonous conscience. Many texts also speak of the inner peace and joy that pronouncements of conscience can foster in the individual. Although less frequent (and also less dramatic) many texts witness to the experience of moral well-being that positive judgments of conscience can create. Ambrose, for instance, speaks of the pleasures that a contented and reconciled conscience brings. He insists, "As for me, it is not the bodily well-being that represents happiness, but the depth of wisdom, the pleasure of a good conscience, the generosity of virtue."[53] And according to Chrysostom "the greatest festival is a good conscience....For the man who lives and acts in a good way, even ordinary days are festivals, because in this case a very pure joy is the fruit of the conscience...."[54] This positive role, which was much underrated in earlier texts on conscience, was given greater attention in the writings of patristic theologians.

The legislative conscience also appears in patristic writings, although it is not as prominent as the judicial conscience. The most frequently cited is a text from Origen that speaks of conscience as having both a directive and a judicial role. In the text in question Origin is discussing Paul's Letter to the Romans 2:14. This is the text where Paul speaks of Gentiles having a conscience to guide them. Of this conscience Origen says, "I would say that conscience is that spirit which, the Apostle says, is found in the soul as tutor, companion and guide. Its function is to advise one about the best course of action, and to rebuke and chastise one for sin."[55] Here we have a very early unambiguous statement of the dual role of conscience as both judge and guide. This is the form that subsequent discussions of conscience take.

Many patristic theologians speak of the judgment of conscience as binding. Both in terms of accusation and affirmation, the voice of conscience is authoritative. Delhaye mentions Justin, Clement of Alexandria, Origen, Gregory of Nyssa and many more to support the view that patristic writers like Paul attributed great importance to the pronouncements of conscience. "Let us fear the judgment of our conscience,"[56] advises Jerome, with his characteristic tone of admonition. Its authority comes directly from the belief that the conscience is the individual's discernment of divine judgment. However, this claim that the judgment of conscience is binding was not unanimously accepted. Augustine in particular insists that the conscience must defer to the will of God. His argument is a complex one and will be examined in the context of medieval discussions of the authority of conscience.[57]

Patristic writers developed the link between the inner voice of conscience and divine guidance. The inborn power of conscience, which enables the human being to discern good and evil, is a gift from God. Since this discernment is a rule of behavior within the self, one can never escape its judgment. As Justin says in his *Apology,* everyone has been given "the faculty to act rightly and do good."[58] Therefore there can be no excuses for transgressing the divine law. Many patristic writers make the point that through the faculty of conscience every person has the ability to discern good and evil. This ability resides in the conscience, which is the voice of God in the depths of the person.

The idea of natural law has been traditionally used in theology to express the idea that there is an objective dimension to morality. Natural law theory claims that there is an "unwritten moral law," one that is prior to and independent of human law, that we must discern. The conscience is the faculty by which we discern this natural law in our daily lives. It is also our interiorization of the divine law. As such it is always to be obeyed. As Delhaye explains, in many patristic texts one finds the idea that "even before the law existed, or outside its confines, man [*sic*] knows his moral duty, solely from the governing force of the natural law speaking in his conscience."[59] It is a theme present in the commentaries of Ambrose, Cyril of Alexandria, Chrysostom and Jerome.[60] More and more, conscience was being spoken of as a personal moral faculty reflecting divine guidance and judgment. As such it had an undisputed priority. This interplay between the objective and subjective dimensions of conscience, evident in embryonic form in Paul's account of conscience, is very much to the fore in patristic texts. It accounts for the growing importance of the category and for the dignity that it gradually acquired.

In addition to theological discussions, some patristic writers also produced texts of casuistry. Cyprian's *On the Treatment of Lapsed Christians* and Clement of Alexandria's *Can a Rich Man Be Saved?* are examples of texts that deal with cases of conscience. These patristic-era texts suggest that there already was a recognition that the accepted principles of Christian living are often insufficient to resolve dilemmas of conscience. They highlighted the fact that principles can often conflict with one another, can be inapplicable or can be too vague to allow a person to determine the right course of action. These many discussions of actual cases of conscience prefigure a significant theme in later theological reflection, that of the perplexed conscience.

A Turning Point

Patristic discussions developed the ideas of conscience as judge and guide. They emphasized the link between conscience and divine law and also spoke of the binding nature of judgments of conscience. As D'Arcy says, "...had this been the entirety of patristic thinking on conscience, the evolution might have been straightforward."[61] However, this was not to be the case. As a result of an error on the part of the theologian Jerome the entire discussion of conscience was recast. But the impact of Jerome's mistake did not become clear until this text was commented upon by the great medievalists many centuries later.

Jerome's error was simply one of transcription. It resulted in the introduction of a new term, *synderesis,* into the theology of conscience. The mistake occurs in Jerome's *Commentary on Ezekiel,* in which he deals with various interpretations of Ezekiel's visions. He regards the animals in the text as metaphors for the Platonic divisions in the soul. He identifies the eagle with the spark of conscience, which the Greeks call *synderesis.* It is worth quoting the passage here in full. Jerome writes,

> These writers interpret the vision in terms of Plato's theory of the three elements of the soul. There are Reason, Spirit, and Desire; to these correspond respectively the man, the lion, and the ox. Now, above these three was the eagle; so in the soul, they say, above the other three elements and beyond them is a fourth, which the Greeks call *synderesis.* This is that spark of conscience which was not

quenched even in the heart of Cain, when he was driven out of paradise. This it is that makes us, too, feel our sinfulness when we are overcome by evil Desire or unbridled Spirit, or deceived by sham Reason. It is natural to identify *synderesis* with the eagle, since it is distinct from the other three elements and corrects them when they err. This is that spirit which, as we read in Scripture, "intercedes for us with groans beyond all utterance." "Who else can know a man's thoughts, except the man's own spirit that is within him?" This is that spirit which Paul prayed might be kept unimpaired with soul and body. And yet in some men we see this conscience overthrown and displaced; they have no sense of guilt or shame for their sins; as it is written, "Little the godless man recks of it, when he falls into sin's mire." They deserve the rebuke, "Still never a blush on thy harlot's brow."[62]

Of course the Greeks do not call this spark of conscience *synderesis*. They call it *syneidesis*. *Syneidesis* is the term used to refer to all those ideas that our word *conscience* includes. It is the word which, when translated into Latin, gives us *conscientia*. So Jerome's word *synderesis,* although similar, is not the same. Nor did it exist as a word before Jerome invented it.

The introduction of this new word, although in error, determined all subsequent discussions of conscience. We will consider the precise impact of this error in the next chapter. For the moment it is sufficient to note that medieval theologians retained both terms and used them to highlight the different aspects of conscience. *Syneidesis* was used to refer to particular judgments of conscience, whereas the new term *synderesis* denoted the "spark of conscience," which inclines human beings to discern and do good. All subsequent moral theology made this formal distinction between the innate disposition toward good, which it called the habitual conscience and the specific judgments of conscience, called the actual conscience. While these distinctions were occasionally hinted at in earlier authors, the actual source of the distinction can be traced to an error in a text of Jerome that was copied and continued by subsequent commentators.

The Penitential Tradition

The penitentials originated in the Celtic monastic traditions of Ireland and Wales and eventually spread over most of western Europe. They were texts, written from the sixth century on, used by clergy for guidance in the practice of confession. The penitentials introduced a primitive form of casuistry into the administration of the sacrament of penance. They cataloged various sins, put them into categories, produced lists of questions that the priest should ask the penitent and suggested degrees and forms of penance appropriate to the different sins. Although they did not develop the theology of conscience in any significant way, nonetheless they are relevant. Their relevance for this study lies in the sophistication with which they deal with the process of decision making.

These texts rarely use the language of conscience. However, they recognized that moral responsibility and culpability is a complex matter. As a result they introduced systems for dealing with the distinctiveness of each situation. For example the *Penitential of Bede* advises that

> not all persons are to be weighed in one and the same balance, although they be associated in one fault, but there shall be discrimination for each of these, rich or poor; freeman or slave; small child, boy, youth, young man or old man; stupid or intelligent; layman, cleric or monk....The priest shall make a distinction for the character of the sins or of the men; for acts performed wilfully or by accident; in public or in secret; with what compunction a penitent makes amends; under compulsion or voluntarily....[63]

This excerpt is fairly typical of many of the penitentials. The texts were concerned primarily with establishing the nature and extent of a person's culpability and with prescribing the appropriate penance. In doing so these texts also contributed indirectly to the development of conscience. This is because they promoted an understanding of morality in which the person's motivations and intentions together with the particular circumstances of acting were considered to be relevant.

Conclusion

From the early decades Christians were concerned with moral questions. They reflected on the inevitable difficulties that they would encounter in trying to live out the ethical imperatives of their religion. This gave rise to the distinctive tradition of moral theology. Moral matters were not considered in isolation from other questions of faith. Instead, issues of morality were regarded as all of a piece with those of faith. One can see this very clearly in the way conscience was reflected upon in the texts of the first five centuries. Conscience was understood both as the individual's discernment of God's law in ethical matters and as a faculty by which the person makes moral decisions. For the Christian these are but different sides of the same coin. Determining the right course of action is just another way of describing the process of discerning the divine law in each concrete situation.

The concept of conscience is not distinctively Christian. Both the idea and the terminology were present in earlier literatures. However, in Christianity it acquired special meaning, since it was the mechanism by which theologians explained the dual strands of Christian morality, the human and the divine. Yet its career was not to be a smooth one because it attempted to hold these two different orientations together. It is unsurprising then that conscience became a site of tension in Christian morality. The subsequent centuries were to see many debates about the relationship between the human and the divine, the subjective and objective aspects of Christian morality. In most cases the category of conscience was central to these debates. Although one could perhaps predict such tensions, they were not obvious in the early centuries of theological exposition. For the most part, in the texts we have examined, theologians were concerned with finding an adequate language with which to express the uniqueness of the Christian moral demand. In this regard conscience emerged as one of the primary categories of the Christian moral life.

Chapter 3
"Discerning Moral Principles": Conscience from the Medievalists to the Manualists

---

In the medieval era theological scholarship flourished. There are many reasons for this. The emergence and growth of the universities throughout this period is important. So, too, is the prominence that theology gained within these establishments. In Europe for the first time in many centuries there was access to Arabian philosophy and theology. This in turn led to the recovery of the philosophy of Aristotle in the West. As a result there was a dramatic growth in the corpus of logic, metaphysics and science. There was also a growing commitment to apply rational inquiry to faith. A distinct medieval theological tradition grew from these and other factors.[1] Within this context there was also a significant evolution in the theology of conscience.

In this chapter we shall consider first the impact that Jerome's now infamous error had on subsequent thinking on the concept of conscience, changing it completely and forever. We will do this by looking at the reception of Jerome in the works of a number of theologians, such as Peter Lombard, Philip the

Chancellor and Bonaventure. This gave rise to a minor debate between two schools of thought on the nature of *synderesis* that is worth mentioning. Of greater significance during these early centuries was the work of Peter Abelard who, without discussing the category of conscience directly, introduced some ideas on subjectivity and on the importance of the person's intention. These ideas in particular were to have a major impact on subsequent ethical thinking, especially in relation to conscience.

The moral theology of Aquinas represents a high point in the Middle Ages. His various treatises on conscience are also significant and will be the focus of our third section. We will follow Aquinas's own distinctions, examining first the nature of conscience and then exploring questions of its power and authority. Although Scholastic thinking (especially Thomism) can be said to have endured in Catholic moral theology down to the 1940s and '50s, the course of the history of conscience was far from smooth. In addition to the significant impact that the reformations of the sixteenth century had on thinking about conscience, the seventeenth and eighteenth centuries, too, were times of great ethical debate, with the category of conscience as the primary site of contest. Although it will not be possible to look in detail at these fractious centuries, we will focus, in our final sections, on specific debates that shaped thinking on conscience.

During these centuries the understanding of conscience went through many permutations. At times its importance was stressed; at others it was downplayed. Yet, despite the various emphases, one can say that the centuries in question gradually evolved what one might call the classical doctrine or theory of conscience. As such it demands our attention. It is important too, since it is against this backdrop that the personalist theology of Vatican II, with all its implications for conscience, was articulated.

The Early Middle Ages

Early medieval discussions of conscience were dominated by decades of "muddled, uncritical exegesis"[2] reminiscent of

Jerome's *Commentary on Ezekiel*. This is the text in which Jerome invented the term *synderesis*. Medieval theologians either failed to notice this error or were reluctant to point it out. Either way they accepted the presence of both *syneidesis* and *synderesis* and set about explaining and defending their existence. As a result the early medieval treatises on conscience tended to be divided into two parts, one headed *Synderesis* and the other *Conscientia*. But as we have already noted in the previous chapter, *synderesis* is "just a corrupted transliteration of *syneidesis*,"[3] which is the Greek word for *conscientia*. The fact that this spurious distinction was made inevitably caused problems. Indeed, one of the greatest difficulties for the modern reader is that the confusions and inconsistencies in the terminology are rarely acknowledged explicitly in the medieval texts. They are simply passed over. The reader is expected to accept the author's analysis and ignore the difficulties presented by Jerome's text.

The early medievalists were broadly concerned with four issues. They discussed (a) whether *synderesis* is a faculty, (b) whether it belongs to the intellect or to the will, (c) whether it is something that can be lost and (d) what the relationship is between *synderesis* and *conscientia*. These questions were approached from various perspectives and were resolved differently by individual theologians. Nonetheless, they emerge as the defining questions in the medieval debates on conscience. So much so that by the time Aquinas was writing his *Summa Theologiae* in the 1260s and early '70s there was already a significant body of material on conscience.

Stephen Langdon was the first medieval theologian to undertake a systematic study of the topic, although one does find occasional references to *synderesis* in the works of earlier theologians like Peter of Poitiers, William of Auxerre and Master Udo. Stephen Langdon dealt with the question of conscience in the context of his treatise on free will. In the process he contributed at least one enduring insight to the theology of conscience. Langdon proposed that *synderesis* "is concerned with moral judgments at the level of very general principle."[4] His overall theory of *synderesis* as a faculty that inclines the reason toward good is very confused and without any lasting significance. However, his suggestion that *synderesis* operates at the level of the general, whereas *conscientia* works at the level of the particular was an important distinction. Langdon did not discuss the nature of *synderesis* very comprehensively, and there are many inconsistencies in the conclusions that he drew. Yet this clarification of the "realm of operation" of both *synderesis* and *conscientia* was to prove an important insight for later theologians. This discussion of the respective natures of *synderesis* and *conscientia* will dominate this chapter, much as it dominated medieval debates.

It is easy for moderns to dismiss these discussions of now obsolete categories as insignificant; however, to do so would undermine their enduring, if hidden importance. The medievalists' distinction between the general orientation toward the good, which everyone possesses *(synderesis),* and the concretization of this orientation in particular decisions *(conscientia)* continues to be significant. It allows us to make a distinction between the basic goodness of a person and the occasional lapses into bad judgment, of which we are all capable. In an important sense it prefigures a very modern recognition that although individuals may make wrong decisions or act against what they know to be right, this does not mean that their basic or fundamental orientation is flawed. People who are essentially committed to the good can sometimes, either knowingly or unknowingly, act against their values and principles. This point is central to Häring's concept of fundamental option, which could not have been developed without the medieval distinction between *synderesis* and *conscientia.* However, as we shall see in later chapters, it is an insight that continues to be controversial in the contemporary church.

In the early thirteenth century Philip the Chancellor wrote the first medieval treatise explicitly on conscience. It later became the model for all subsequent discussions. Philip was also concerned with the four issues we already identified and dealt with each of them either explicitly or by implication. He began by asking "about *synderesis,* which is called the spark of conscience, is it a potentiality of the soul or some connatural disposition which is in the soul from the beginning?, if it is a potentiality, is it the higher or the lower part of reason...?, if there exists the power of sinning in respect of it, as in respect of free choice, whence has this arisen?, in what sense is it extinguished and in what sense not, and in respect of what?"[5] These questions are undoubtedly confusing for the contemporary reader. They relate to the issue of whether conscience belongs to the rational or the emotional/affective aspects of the personality. However, modern psychology has effectively rendered this language meaningless. We no longer think about human beings as constituted in this way. Nonetheless, these deliberations were important, because the way in which they were resolved determined the direction in which the theology of conscience developed.

In the first two questions Philip is dealing with the issue of whether *synderesis* is a faculty or not and whether it belongs to the intellect or will. He does this by asking how *synderesis* fits into the structure of the soul and how it relates to reason. His conclusion is "that *synderesis* is innate and not acquired...and that it is not a potentiality distinct from reason."[6] The meaning of this statement is far from clear. Potts suggests that Philip's main contention is that "*synderesis* is akin to a potentiality in being innate, but akin to a disposition in embodying a tendency, namely, to what is good."[7] Here we can see shades of a later debate concerning whether *synderesis* belongs to the will or the intellect. Although Philip does locate it in the will, he also links it with the intellect by saying that it is on the level of the "rational, not sense, appetite."[8] However, his discussion is not particularly illuminating.

One can sense that Philip is dissatisfied with the categories with which he is working. However, he continues to work within them. Nonetheless, his attempt to locate *synderesis* within the established anthropology indicates that the concept had become part of the theological landscape. Although Philip is quite clear in his treatise that *synderesis* is a habitlike faculty belonging to the will, he fudges the issue slightly by saying that it belongs to the "rational, not sense, appetite" of will. The purpose of this qualification is to associate *synderesis* with the "spiritual, rational side of human nature, and not with the desires or drives which spring from the animal side."[9] Although we now regard this radical distinction between reason and will to be problematic, it was an important one for medieval theologians. Contemporary theologians have continued to consider this issue but do not use the same language. In a sense Philip's questions are precursors to the modern realization that the operations of conscience necessarily involve both the emotional and intellectual aspects of the person. Yet, Philip's hesitation suggests that he was not entirely comfortable with his own conclusion about the nature of conscience and how it relates to the other aspects of the person.

Philip then goes on to ask whether *synderesis* can be mistaken and whether it can be lost. While discussing the question of whether it can be mistaken, he employs the distinction, made by Stephen Langdon, between *synderesis* and *conscientia.* Philip maintains that *conscientia,* which involves the application of principles, can be mistaken, but that *synderesis* cannot. This is because *synderesis* refers to the apprehension of general principles and cannot be in error. However, *conscientia,* which is the conjunction of *synderesis* with free choice, can err. The final question raises the issue of whether or not *synderesis* can be lost. Again, his answer to this depends on the distinction between *synderesis* as the apprehension of general principles and *conscientia* as the act of application. Philip insists that *synderesis* cannot be lost. This is illustrated by the example of the heretics whose *conscientia* urged them to die for their (mistaken) faith. He explains that

> ...the effect of *synderesis* considered as such, is paralyzed in them because of the lack of faith, which is the basis of everything good. But the exercise of *conscientia* thrives in them, the evidence of which is that the man is ready to undergo martyrdom, because he supposes that what he believes is the faith. It is not, however, *synderesis* which does this, but what belongs to free choice or reason. Moreover, *synderesis* is not extinguished in such a person because, although he may be mistaken about the particular matter, evil in general still displeases him.[10]

Although he still lacked clarity regarding the precise relationship between *synderesis* and *conscientia,* Philip drew a clear distinction between the two. Jerome had introduced the term *synderesis* and then blurred its meaning. Subsequent exegetes occasionally saw *synderesis* and *conscientia* as identical, and at other times dealt with them as distinct. Some understood *synderesis* as belonging to the will; others thought it belonged to the intellect. Confusions abounded in the early Middle Ages, and were, to some extent, set to continue. However, Philip the Chancellor represents one important stage in the evolution of a comprehensive account of conscience as including both *synderesis* and *conscientia.* His contribution was to ensure the survival of the distinction between the two categories, which he did by defining their spheres of operation in relation to each other.

The limitations of Philip's treatise soon became obvious with the gradual emergence of two opposed schools of thought. One supported Philip's view that *synderesis* is a habit that inclines the will toward good. This position is known as voluntarism, coming from *voluntas* the Latin word for "will." St. Bonaventure is the theologian most associated with the voluntarist position, although he departs quite substantially from Philip's way of coming to the same conclusion. D'Arcy summarizes Bonaventure's conclusion rather simplistically yet accurately: "...both reason and will have a part to play in our moral life, and each of them needs to be given some direction or inclination towards moral goodness. [*Conscientia*] does this for the reason; *synderesis* does it for the will, where it resides as a 'natural bias' inclining the will towards moral goodness...."[11]

The alternative is the intellectualist school, which represented the view that *synderesis* is a habit belonging to the intellect and in particular to the practical reason. It was associated with the Dominicans and especially with the work of Albert the Great. In opposition to both Philip and Bonaventure, Albert understood *synderesis* as belonging to the practical reason. Instead of thinking of *synderesis* as a separate faculty inclining the will to desire the good, Albert speaks of it as knowledge of the universal principles of morality. In the same way as speculative reason guides the intellect to the self-evident principles of the speculative order, so, too, the practical reason grasps the first principles of morality. *Synderesis* is the aspect of practical reason that enables the person to grasp the first principles of the moral order. For Albert and the intellectualists *synderesis* was still associated with general principles rather than applications. However, it was associated with reason (and thereby knowledge) and not with the will.

The debate between the voluntarists and the intellectualists is important because it highlighted a number of substantive issues for the theology of conscience. Many of the arguments had implications for the way in which the role of conscience was subsequently understood. It is also significant because it moved theological speculation on the nature of conscience onto a new plane. Within a century discussions had shifted from being rather confused commentaries on two badly understood and somewhat random terms to a sophisticated attempt to discern the place of each of the terms, both in relation to existing anthropological categories and in relation to each other. The distinction between *synderesis* and *conscientia* was established. So too was the belief that *synderesis* could neither err nor be extinguished. Still in dispute was whether *synderesis* was most appropriately understood as belonging to the will or the reason. The precise relationship between *synderesis* and *conscientia* also remained rather vague.

By this time, then, some major points had been agreed upon, points that were to shape the developments of the following centuries. The point of agreement that was to be most enduring and most significant was the distinction between *synderesis* and *conscientia.* Although there was little clarity as yet regarding the way they related to each other, the clear designation of different spheres of operation was truly innovative. It enabled theologians to deal more precisely with the complex matter of the interior dimensions of moral judgment. It allowed them to draw a distinction between the person's moral sense and his/her actions. However, this distinction was not in any sense an absolute one, because at the same time they retained a strong link between *synderesis* and *conscientia*. This subtle interlinking of moral orientation and action, which enables one to assert the intimate connection yet make some necessary distinction, was in many respects acomplished in the early Middle Ages. This model, although significantly refined in subsequent centuries, remains a cornerstone of contemporary moral theology.

A second point, which was being debated by this time and which continues to be important, is the issue of whether conscience belongs to the intellect or the will. As we have already mentioned, although this language does not resonate with contemporary Catholics, the question continues to be relevant. The indecision of Philip together with the emergence of two contrary schools of thought indicates that there was deep dissatisfaction with the radical separation of conscience from either the intellectual or the emotional aspects of the person. In fact Aquinas reinforced the intellectual dimensions of conscience, and it was this which became enshrined in moral theology for many centuries. However, through the centuries there was also a sense that an important aspect of the operations of conscience (that is, the emotional) was being ignored. In the twentieth century especially there has been a resurgence of interest in the role of the emotions in the moral life of the individual. The neglect of the emotions has seriously impoverished our understanding of the workings of conscience, yet the early medievalists had recognized their significance. Contemporary theologians have come to realize that there is much to be learned from the struggle between the intellectualist and voluntarist schools. Indeed, our reconstruction of a theology of conscience later in this text is greatly indebted to the insights of these early medievalists. It attempts to give a prominent role to the emotions while also recognizing the intellectual aspects of conscience. The irony is, however, that this very struggle was played out many centuries ago.

The Rise of Subjectivism

Although he did not explicitly address the question of conscience, Peter Abelard had an important impact on its development. His contribution arose from his concern with the issue of intentionality. His moral theology was controversial because he emphasized subjective values rather than objective criteria. He was interested in determining how to "distinguish between conduct worthy of praise or blame by God."[12] In this context he drew much from a contemporaneous discussion on the nature of universals. Abelard took the controversial step of suggesting that the goodness or badness of actions derives exclusively from the intention of the person who performs the action. In his *Ethics,* which he called *Scito te ipsum (Know Thyself),* he discusses his theory of intention and how it relates to moral goodness or evil. He argued that "God thinks not of what is done but in what mind it is done; merit and praise accrue to a human agent not for his actions but for his intentions. Deeds, being common to the damned and to the elect, are all in themselves indifferent and are called good or evil only on account of the intention of their agent."[13] However, it would be wrong to categorize Abelard as a complete subjectivist. He very definitely believed in the existence of objective criteria. He considered that the objective criteria of morality could be discerned and ought to inform the person's intentions. He also insisted that it was the duty of the Christian to align his or her intentions with the objective criteria of divine law. So although the intention determines the morality of actions, for Abelard intentions ought to be in accord with divine law.

Abelard's view—that the moral quality of a person's actions reside not in the act itself but in the intention with which actions are performed—was novel. However, it did build on Augustine's view that the will is the principle by which we act. According to Augustine virtuous action is characterized by love of God. Yet while he did stress the interior disposition of the person, Augustine restricted this view of intention to good actions. He insisted that the performance of good acts is the result of the presence of love of God. Abelard extended this focus on interior disposition to evil acts as well, concluding that "consent to evil [is] the univocal definition of sin."[14] He insisted that works or acts in themselves do nothing to merit praise or damnation. Rather, it is the intention of the person acting that determines whether they are good or evil. Here we can see the significance of the phrase "know thyself " in Abelard's ethics, since it is only in reflecting on one's intentions that one can have a sense of the moral quality of one's actions. This way of viewing morality also has very modern resonances. People frequently evaluate actions on the basis of whether the intentions of the person are worthy or not. For many people today good decisions are equated solely with the intention to do good. This is often seen in dilemmas about truthfulness. For example, in deciding whether or not to tell the truth about a particular situation my main concern may be to avoid causing pain or offense to another. I may regard this to be of paramount importance, and so my intention, which may indeed be good and laudable, may lead me to disregard all other aspects. In this scenario the value of truthfulness is subordinated to my "good intention" to avoid another's pain or offense.

Abelard's focus on intention is important for our discussion of conscience, because it threw into sharp relief the subjective dimension of morality. Although few followed Abelard unambiguously, by focusing on intention he highlighted an aspect of morality that had been neglected. For Abelard actions themselves are morally indifferent, and personal merit resides in cultivating and sustaining good intentions. With this attribution of moral significance to the intention alone came the importance of self-knowledge. His *Ethics* is an argument for self-reflection and personal responsibility in the ethical domain. The propositions forwarded in Abelard's *Ethics* generated much debate. Very few were prepared to accept his position that nothing matters other than the person's intention. However, in the process of refuting his ideas theologians began to give considerable attention to intentionality and to other subjective dimensions of morality.

These and other debates all fed into the ideas about conscience that were being discussed at the time. Indeed, the category of conscience itself later became the receptacle of many of the ideas about the subjective and interior dimensions of morality. Furthermore, many of the discussions about the relationship between the subjective and objective aspects of morality were pursued in the context of the theology of conscience. The explicit treatises on conscience in which theologians were trying to unravel the confusions of contradictory definitions and imprecise terminology were significant. In addition, alongside these particular texts, other medieval discussions of ethics were also important. This is particularly true of Abelard's stress on intentionality in the moral domain. These and other developments made a significant contribution to the growing importance of the category of conscience in medieval theology.

Aquinas on Conscience

As with most medieval theology the figure of Thomas Aquinas looms large in discussions of conscience. Aquinas systematized and developed earlier thinking, and as a result his contribution to the topic is significant. Aquinas discussed conscience in three texts. His first consideration was in his *Commentary on the Sentences.* Theological commentaries were like dissertations by which aspiring teachers established their theological credentials. His was a commentary on Peter Lombard's *Sentences,* a standard text of the time. He also addressed the issue of conscience in more detail in his *Questiones Disputatae de Veritate,* said to date from the end of his stay at the University of Paris, between 1257 and 1259. In his great work, the *Summa Theologiae,* Aquinas also examined the question of conscience. In the *Pars Prima* he tried to unravel the confusions and discussed the nature of conscience. In the *Prima Secundae* he dealt with its authority. In attempting to do justice to the nuanced discussion of Aquinas I will focus on the *Summa Theologiae,* which is his most mature work. However, I will also draw on the other texts, especially the *De Veritate.* In looking at the texts of Aquinas it is worth remembering that the treatises on conscience come from many different phases in his lengthy career. As such they represent his changing concerns. Any inconsistencies that exist can mostly be explained by the fact that his thought was constantly developing. We will approach the topic as Aquinas did, first by examining the nature of conscience and then by considering the problem of its authority.

The Nature of Conscience

Aquinas discusses conscience in question 79 of the *Pars Prima* of the *Summa Theologiae*. He had considered the topic earlier in his *De Veritate,* questions 16 and 17. His primary concerns in the *Summa* were to establish whether *synderesis* is a separate faculty, whether it belongs to the will or to the reason and to explain the relationship between *synderesis* and *conscientia*. These are the same questions that had concerned theologians like Stephen Langdon and Philip the Chancellor in the previous century. Aquinas claims that it is "a habit, not a power,"[15] that is not a separate faculty. Furthermore, it is a habit of the reason, specifically of the practical reason. By speaking of *synderesis* as a habit of the practical reason he aligned himself with the intellectualist school of thought. He makes *synderesis* into a habitual, intuitive grasp of the primary principles of action. As Delhaye explains, "the practical reason asks of itself what it must do, and judges the actions of the past. For that, it must begin with first principles."[16] It is through *synderesis* that we apprehend these primary principles of action. As Aquinas describes it, "*synderesis* is said to incite us to good and to deter us from evil in that through first principles we both begin investigation and judge what we find."[17] Although this terminology seems rather strange to us today, the purpose of his inquiry is very relevant. Here he is engaged in a close scrutiny of how human beings come to know that we should do good. Aquinas tries to explain the workings of *synderesis* by comparing it with speculative reason. Just as humans have a natural disposition by which we apprehend the principles of theoretical disciplines, so, too, we have a natural disposition by which we apprehend the primary principles of behavior.[18] Mahoney describes the work of *synderesis* thus: "...just as we have a grasp of the rules of grammar, so we have a habitual grasp of the basic rules of morality."[19] This metaphor was in fact used by Aquinas himself, in another context, when he discussed the issue of natural law.[20] *Synderesis,* then, belongs to our very nature as human beings. Aquinas has a very positive view of human beings. He insists that this capacity and desire for good, although it may become blurred or weakened through constantly choosing against it, is never actually extinguished. Once he had established that *synderesis* is a habit of the practical reason, he moved on to discuss the nature of *conscientia.*[21] Aquinas suggested that *conscientia* applies the principles known by *synderesis* to each particular situation. This distinction was already evident in earlier discussions. We saw that Stephen Langdon and Philip the Chancellor both spoke of *synderesis* as pertaining to general principles and of *conscientia* to the particular. However, neither theologian had any clear mechanism for explaining the way they related to each other. Aquinas envisaged a very direct relationship—that *conscientia* is nothing other than the application of these first principles to particular situations. "Strictly speaking *conscientia* is an act, not a power."[22] Aquinas drew on the etymology of the word *conscientia* to defend this position. *Conscientia,* he claimed, "denotes knowledge ordered towards something, since it means knowledge-along-with-another *[cum alio scientia].*"[23] Commentators dismiss this argument since it has no serious etymological foundation.

However, the relationship he envisaged between *synderesis* and *conscientia* does not depend on etymology. It is based on his claim that *synderesis* is the apprehension of the first moral principles. In addition it builds on the distinctions made by earlier theologians. He also supports his case by examining the ways in which conscience occurs in common usage. He gives examples of situations where it is clear that the work of conscience is an act. He quotes Ecclesiastes, saying that "knowledge is applied in a second way when through our conscience we judge that something ought to be done or ought not to be done."[24] He also considers the case when, "by conscience we judge something already done to have been done well or ill. In this case we speak of conscience excusing or accusing or tormenting. It is obvious that all these things follow actual application of knowledge to what we do. Hence strictly speaking conscience is the name of an act."[25]

Aquinas describes *conscientia* as being nothing more than the application of first moral principles to particular situations. This language may give the impression that *conscientia* is merely a mechanical act of applying general rules to particular situations. However, this is certainly not the case. Aquinas recognized that what he called the first moral principles are rather vague. When he speaks of the first moral principles he has in mind something like good is to be done and evil avoided. Principles such as murder is wrong or theft is wrong are not what Aquinas means when he speaks of first moral principles. They are far too specific to belong to the realm of *synderesis*. When Aquinas says that the activity of *conscientia* is to apply the first moral principles to particular situations, he recognizes the abstract nature of these principles. As a result the task of applying them is complex.

Conscientia must identify which of the first moral principles are to be applied. Even after doing so the task is difficult. For example, the process of applying the principle that good is to be done and evil avoided in a particular context involves a range of complicated judgments. The work of *conscientia* involves coming to an accurate understanding of the problem and recognizing all the morally relevant features. This involves a range of skills and good moral judgment. Thus, it would be wrong to see the task of *conscientia* as one of routinely applying specific preordained rules to self-contained, predefined situations. This completely misunderstands both the nature of the first moral principles and the process of moral judgment. When one reads Aquinas's articles on conscience in the context of the rest of his moral theology, one can see that he recognizes that moral decision making involves great complexities and ambiguities. However, as with the case of *conscientia,* these can often be masked by his very precise and scientific language.

The complexity of the application of general moral principles to specific contexts is evident in every moral dilemma.

Take, for example, the case of an administrator in a large phar-maecutical company who believes that a new product is being released onto the market without the proper testing having taken place. She knows that many among the scientific staff are worried, but they are under orders to behave as though all is well. She has seen the paperwork and knows that certain tests that would ordinarily have been carried out have not been done. She is determined to make the right choice in this situation, but she is unclear as to what this is. She knows that if she raises her worries with more senior people she will just be told that it is none of her business. She does know some journalists to whom she could give this information secretly, but she is afraid that she would lose her job were the whistle blowing traced back to her.[26] Within the Thomistic framework one could say that her *synderesis* is appropriately oriented and that she is determined to make the good and right decision. However, in attempting to determine which of the many values should be given priority, her *conscientia* is troubled. There are many values at stake; there are also many principles that could be relevant and applicable. In addition there may be many conflicting opinions as to the best and most effective way to ensure the right outcome. All of these issues come into play after the person has decided that she is committed to the good in this situation. However, the work of conscience is only just beginning at this stage and, as we have seen clearly in this scenario, involves a great deal more than the simple application of preordained principles to particular situations.

In question 79 of the *Summa* Aquinas set out his account of conscience. He formalized the distinctions arising from Jerome's error, which resulted in there being two different words for conscience. In an effort to make sense of the two terms for conscience theologians after Jerome focused on different aspects of its operations. By the time Aquinas had completed his account of *synderesis* and *conscientia*, their respective and distinctive roles were well and truly established. *Synderesis* became the habitual grasp of the first moral principles, and *conscientia* their application.

The Authority of Conscience

Although this general discussion of the nature of conscience was important, there were other issues to be examined. Once he had established an account of the nature of *synderesis* and of *conscientia* together with a clear sense of how each category related to the other, further questions had to be considered. These relate to the authority of conscience, specifically how and in what ways it binds the person. These questions became the source of much controversy in subsequent centuries, as indeed they had been in the centuries before. Here Aquinas's theology represents an important consolidation of a number of earlier insights, associated primarily with Albert the Great. In addition he established important new theological principles.

Within the theological tradition there was a broad spectrum of opinion as to whether the judgments of conscience were binding or not. Some, like Augustine, argued that conscience in itself never binds. Others suggested that conscience sometimes binds. Very few expressed the view that conscience always binds. It was this latter position that Aquinas, following his master, Albert the Great, set out to defend. He approached it by arguing for the obliging force of conscience in general and went on to extend this to the erroneous conscience as well.

The dominant view of the time was the Augustinian one. This proposed that "conscience has no authority except that which it receives as God's delegate."[27] Augustine likened the relationship between God and the person's conscience to that of the emperor and one of his officials, such as a proconsul. In a text that was much commented upon by medieval moralists Augustine insisted, "The command of a subordinate authority does not bind if it runs counter to the command of a superior in authority; as for instance if the proconsul were to enjoin what the Emperor forbade."[28] According to Augustine, the conscience operates as a proconsul does. It is only when it speaks as "God's delegate" that its judgment is binding, just as it is only when the proconsul speaks on behalf of the emperor that his command is binding. According to this view, if the conscience commands something in opposition to divine law, it is not binding. Similarly, if the proconsul commands something that opposes the emperor's law, neither is it binding. In this theology the authority of conscience is rather weak. It is binding only insofar as its judgments are in accordance with divine law. Since Augustine regarded the teaching church to be the preeminent interpreter of divine law, we can assume that it, rather than the conscience, should be followed in cases of conflict.

In contrast, even in his earliest text, the *Commentary on the Sentences,* Aquinas argued that "every conscience, true or false, is binding, in the sense that to act against conscience is always wrong."[29] Aquinas's argument revolves around the claim that the conscience seeks to identify the good in each situation. Even if its judgments are defective, they must be followed because these judgments are presented to the person as the good in each situation, and one is obliged to seek and do the good. But what if a particular judgment of conscience is in conflict with divine law? Aquinas's answer in question 17 of *De Veritate* is that "no one is bound by a law save by one means alone: knowledge of that law."[30] From this Aquinas drew two conclusions that were crucial for his discussion in the *Summa Theologiae.* He insisted that a person who is incapable of knowing a precept of the law is not bound by it. He also suggested that a person who does not know a particular precept is not bound by it either, except insofar as the person should have known it.[31]

The Erroneous Conscience

In question 19 of the *Prima Secundae* Aquinas deals with the thorny issue of the erroneous conscience. The ethical question is whether a person is bound to follow the judgment of a conscience that is mistaken. In formulating his argument Aquinas takes on the Augustinian position and refutes it. Augustine had insisted that the lower authority (the proconsul or the conscience) must give way to the superior authority (the emperor or divine law). Aquinas argues against this, suggesting that the conscience always presents its judgments as being in accordance with divine law. He insists that we can have no knowledge of divine law in particular circumstances other than through the conscience. Therefore, the conscience could not be aware of any conflict.

The prevailing theological view was that the erroneous conscience should only be followed on neutral matters and not on those that are good or bad in themselves.[32] Aquinas argued against this. He suggested that human beings should desire that which they perceive to be good. Aquinas's approach is that we should will (desire) that which is presented to the will by the reason as good. Furthermore, he writes, "...we should state quite simply that every act of will against reason, whether it is right or wrong, is always bad."[33] He illustrates his argument with two examples. The first is a case of fornication, which Aquinas says we know is bad in itself. However, if a person sincerely believes that fornication is good, then for that person to refrain from fornication is bad. The reason mistakenly presents fornication as good. If the will does not pursue the good as presented to it, it sins. The second example pertains to Christian belief. Aquinas says that to believe in Christ is good in itself and necessary for salvation. However, if a person mistakenly believes that Christian faith is evil, then it is a sin for that person to embrace Christianity. Although the reason may be mistaken and the judgment of conscience may be in error, one is still obliged to follow it. This position is ultimately based on the fact that if conscience believes a particular course of action to be God's will, then to choose to do the opposite is sinful.[34] The conscience must follow the good as it perceives it.

Aquinas investigates the issue further by asking whether or not a person is culpable for following an erroneous conscience.[35] His answer is that it depends on whether the error of conscience is blameworthy or not. This in turn depends on whether the ignorance of the person is voluntary or not. Errors of conscience can result from the kind of ignorance that is culpable. In such cases ignorance may be in some sense willed or chosen in order to excuse wrongdoing. I may choose to remain in the dark about a situation in order to absolve myself of wrongdoing. For example, the trials at Nuremberg after World War II heard many testimonies from people who deliberately chose not to know about the extermination of the Jews, though they knew that some terrible things were happening. This voluntary ignorance is not excusable according to Aquinas, because a person is merely using freely chosen ignorance to excuse wrongdoing. Ignorance can also occur through negligence or carelessness. Aquinas refers to the ignorance resulting from inattention as *"ignorantia malae electionis."* He calls negligence with regard to matters of fact *"ignorantia supina,"* and negligence pertaining to matters of law *"ignorantia universalium juris."* None of these forms of ignorance is excusable. For "if, then the reason or conscience is mistaken through voluntary error, whether directly or from negligence, then, because it is on a matter a person ought to know about, it does not excuse the will from evil in following the reason or conscience thus going astray."[36]

However, there may be situations in which the person is blameless. The crucial factor for Aquinas is whether the ignorance in question makes an action involuntary or not. He uses the term *involuntary* to highlight the fact that the person is not choosing that particular action. That is, the person does not intend or will it.[37] He gave the example of a homicide to explain this distinction. In question 6, article 8, Aquinas describes a situation in which a person kills another who is in his line of fire and whom he has not seen. This killing is clearly involuntary. The person was ignorant of the fact that the victim was in his line of fire. Aquinas calls this *"ignorantia antecedens,"* that is antecedent or prior to the act of will. The ignorance is unwilled and therefore causes the act of killing to be involuntary. This distinction between voluntary and involuntary actions is a crucial one for Aquinas. If the action is involuntary, then it is not blameworthy.

Aquinas accepts that there are other kinds of actions which may also be blameless. A person through no fault of his/her own may be ignorant of some morally relevant circumstances. Aquinas calls this invincible ignorance. In such cases the erroneous conscience is excused, and the individual is not guilty of evil. He gives the example of a man who believes that he is obliged to have intercourse with another man's wife. That man's conscience is obviously in error. If the error arises from the man's belief that it is good to commit adultery, then his error is culpable. It is culpable, says Aquinas, because the man's reason is ignorant of "a law of God he ought to recognize."[38] Ignorance of divine law is culpable. He should know that it is wrong to sleep with another man's wife. However, the man may sleep with another man's wife, believing her to be his own wife. In such a case "his willingness to have intercourse is exempt from evil, since his mistake arises from ignorance of a circumstance which excuses and renders his act involuntary."[39] This distinction between voluntary and involuntary ignorance alleviates the problem of an erroneous conscience significantly. If the error arises through involuntary ignorance, then the person is blameless. If on the other hand it arises through chosen ignorance, then "a man is not hopelessly involved, for he can go back on his error since his ignorance is voluntary and can be overcome."[40] The distinction between vincible and invincible ignorance was one of his most important innovations and featured prominently in all subsequent discussions of conscience.

One final point is worth noting. Although Aquinas talks about actions arising from invincible error as "not sinful," he resists describing them as good. He appeals to Dionysius's view that for an act to be called good it must be good in every respect. Thus, although an act may not be sinful, neither could it be called good. Even though one is bound to follow one's conscience when the judgment of conscience is wrong, this act of following one's conscience cannot be called good. It could only be called a good act if the judgment of conscience itself was right. Since the actual judgment of conscience is wrong, even though the determination to follow one's conscience is right, it cannot be called good. One can only say that it is not sinful. Let us return to Aquinas's example of the man who sleeps with a woman, believing her to be his wife. This does seem rather unlikely, I admit. However, it might happen that the woman was already lawfully married to another. In such a case the second marriage would be invalid. According to

Aquinas the man's act of sleeping with his wife was wrong because the woman was not his wife. However, the man's ignorance of this means that his erroneous judgment is not blameworthy. Yet Aquinas would not be prepared to say that his action was good. The intention must be good, as it clearly is in this case. The man intends to express his love for the woman whom he regards to be his wife. In addition the act itself must be objectively right. In this case the act is objectively wrong. The concession that Aquinas is prepared to make is to say that the act is not sinful; however, he would not describe it as good.

Aquinas was both a great synthesizer and an original thinker. One can see this in his work on conscience, which became a benchmark for all subsequent work on the topic. Prior to Aquinas, thinking on the subject was random and disconnected. Although some significant features of both the nature and tasks of conscience had been established, there was no coherent account of the role of conscience in the Christian life. Although there are some confusions and inconsistencies in Aquinas' work, he does have a coherent account of both the nature and authority of conscience. However, his conclusions did not go uncontested. His claim that the work of conscience involves complex deductive reasoning and is not simply a mechanical act of applying principles to cases was controversial. So too was his argument for the primacy of conscience, even the erroneous conscience. These and other issues were the subject of much debate in subsequent centuries, debate that continues up to the present day. As I suggested in chapter 1, in the contemporary context we can see that although the basic principles of Aquinas's position on the authority of conscience are accepted, they are frequently compromised and fudged in many important respects.

The Challenge of Nominalism

In his moral theology Aquinas promoted a balance of objective morality filtered through personal, subjective experience. He argued that each individual has the capacity to discern the nature of things and that in moral matters this was seen in the person's ability to discern the good in each situation. This view is based on the assumption that one can speak of "the nature of something." For example, one can speak of the nature of law or theft and refer to something intrinsic to or inherent in law or theft. In the early fourteenth century, however, this very Aristotelian view of reality came under attack precisely on the point that one could speak of the essence of a thing.

William of Occam was one of the theologians who led the attack against the idea that one could speak of the nature of something. He argued, against Aquinas, that one cannot apprehend what is good or bad by examining the nature of things. One cannot do so according to Occam, because one cannot speak of anything having a nature in any real sense. He suggested that since God is completely free, he could have made, and can make, everything utterly different. In the moral sphere he could have commanded, and can command, something entirely different as well. Because this is the case, morality should be concerned only with aligning one's will with God's will. Morality only involves obeying the commands of God. However, since God can "change his mind" about what is required of humans, morality is also provisional "concerning the moral commandments and laws which God has issued and not so far (or so far as we know) nullified or changed."[41] According to Occam, "...morality did not issue from within reality, but was painted on to it from the outside, and absolutely speaking it could change color overnight."[42]

The impact of Occamism and the nominalism that it spawned was far-reaching. Although it came under attack from papal and other sources, the ideas of nominalism flourished in the universities of Europe, especially in the fifteenth and sixteenth centuries. Occamism reduced morality to an encounter between "the individual and the will of God." It downplayed the role of reason completely and recast the work of conscience. Conscience was no longer the site of a complex relationship between reason and revelation. Instead it became the place where the individual appropriated the somewhat erratic commands of God. Again one can see vesitges of this thinking in some contemporary discussions about morality. Occasionally morality is expressed in terms of its being the will of God, with morally good behavior being equated with obedience to God's commands. The issue of how God's will is known is often addressed differently by the various exponents of such a position. Some Catholics speak of the utterances of the magisterium as unambiguously expressing the will of God. Others see a more direct link between individual discernment and God's commands, whereby the individual believer is understood to apprehend it directly. One can think of many debates in the public forum that proceed along these lines. Many of the religiously motivated interventions in debates about the morality of homosexuality and abortion use this kind of language and could be said to appeal to a type of modern modification of nominalism.

Aquinas spoke of conscience as being a collaboration between the objective and subjective elements of morality. In so doing he imagined the relationship between divine law and conscience in terms of a dialectic. With the advent of Occamism, however, this relationship was recast in terms of a confrontation between divine law and conscience. According to Occam the law comes from God alone and is founded on his authority. Conscience on the other hand represents the strivings of reason. It can either align itself unquestioningly with divine law (through absolute obedience) or it can disregard divine law and pursue its own path. Either way the dialectic between reason and divine law through conscience is lost.

The Impact of Luther

Although the focus of this study is on the somewhat erratic development of the concept of conscience in the Catholic tradition, it is necessary to discuss, however briefly, the important contribution of Luther. Of course Luther's theology of conscience is significant in its own right; however, in this context our interest lies in its relation to the development of Catholic thought. In the history of conscience Luther is discussed both in terms of his personal history and because of his writing. There is a long tradition, going back to the Enlightenment, of regarding Luther as someone whose personal stance at the Diet of Worms in 1521 inaugurated "a new era in the history of freedom, that of the religious freedom of the individual conscience."[43] His famous reply to the request that he retract his writings tends to be the basis for such a claim. At this crucial time he insisted:

> Unless I am convinced by the testimony of Scriptures or by clear reason (for I do not trust either in the pope or in councils alone, since it is well known that they have often erred and contradicted themselves), I am bound by the Scriptures I have quoted and my conscience is captive to the word of God. I cannot and I will not retract anything, since it is neither safe nor right to go against conscience. I cannot do otherwise, here I stand, may God help me. Amen.[44]

However, in order to avoid an anachronistic attribution of modern values to Luther it is important to consider his theological reflections on the nature and authority of conscience. It is only in this context that we can properly evaluate the meaning and significance of his stance at Worms.

In his *Action and Person* Baylor argues convincingly that Luther's contribution to the theology of conscience should be analyzed both in terms of its affinity with medieval (especially late scholastic) thought and also in terms of its own distinctiveness. Scholars who fail to see that Luther's stand is intelligible on the medieval principles that (a) it is a sin to act against conscience and (b) conscience ultimately derives its authority from God alone ignore a significant dimension of Luther's theology. However, it would also be incorrect to regard Luther's stance as unambiguously based on these principles of medieval thought since his theology does represent an unparalleled break with the past.[45] In the process of analyzing the many texts in which Luther discusses conscience one can see these two aspects, that is, both his dependence on late scholasticism, especially the *via moderna* of Occamism, and his innovative recasting of the concept within a new theological framework.

Within this necessarily truncated discussion of Luther's theology of conscience it is essential to consider just a few of its central features. Although he never articulated a detailed account of his understanding of the nature and authority of conscience, Luther discussed the issue constantly, if often indirectly. He frequently refers to conscience while explaining his theology, as well as when he defends his own personal position vis-à-vis the religious authorities of his day. However, although the frequency with which he employs the notion of conscience gives us many fruitful avenues for exploration, it also creates many difficulties, especially since Luther's understanding of both its nature and function went through many permutations and changes.

Most commentators agree that in Luther's earliest writings and lectures we see a concept of conscience that was strongly indebted to the later scholastics, especially Biels. Initially, at any rate, he accepted the distinction between *synderesis* and *conscientia* that, working together, produced a knowledge of good and evil actions. Like the scholastics he also thought of *synderesis* as belonging to the rational aspect of the person, although not in any exclusive sense. Furthermore, he thought of *synderesis* as having a definite content, as is evidenced in his lectures on the Epistle to the Romans. There is, however, much scholarly disagreement regarding the precise nature of this content, specifically in relation to the extent to which this involved spiritual as well as moral truths.[46]

On the issue of the authority of conscience the early Luther also followed the scholastics in many important respects. In his first lectures on the Psalms he repeated the central principle of scholasticism that "he who acts against his conscience sins."[47] In his comment on the problem of those in the community who are weak (Romans 14) he reaffirmed this position in relation to the erroneous conscience. However, in this discussion he introduced an important qualification that anticipated one of the places where he was to depart significantly from the scholastic position. This related to his overwhelming sense that it is by faith alone that Christians are justified. For Luther it is only the presence of faith that can generate morally good acts; anything that does not derive from this faith is sinful. This basic position that he gradually began to delineate more clearly and forcefully introduced a significant modification to the scholastic framework. Indeed, it was on this basis that even in his Romans lectures Luther dismissed the concept of invincible ignorance as a solution to the problem of the erroneous conscience. This is because he claimed that the weakness which produced the error was itself sinful.

In a sermon entitled *On the Proper Wisdom and Will* of 1514 Luther introduced a novel idea that he later abandoned, at least in its formal aspects. Here he preached about *synderesis* as being both cognitive and volitional, rational and emotional. Indeed, he even spoke of the *synderesis* in the will, which "remains forever, for it wishes to be saved and to live well and beautifully," and the *synderesis* of the reason, which "pleads inextinguishably for the best, the true, the right, and the just."[48] Although he had discarded the whole notion of *synderesis* by 1519, yet he retained his commitment to the affective and intellectual aspects of conscience throughout his work. Again, there is no consensus among scholars on the reasons why he abandoned this notion of *synderesis,* which was so crucial to the scholastics. Some argue that it is because Luther regarded it as a semi-Pelagian notion; others suggest it is because it is unbiblical or because it was too closely associated with the Aristotelianism of the scholastics, with which Luther was growing increasingly intolerant.[49] Although there are undoubtedly elements of truth in each of these analyses, I am inclined to agree with Baylor that *synderesis* was not so much rejected "but it was being eclipsed by a view of conscience that lay outside the framework of the *synderesis* and the practical reason."[50]

It was when Luther set aside the scholastic notion of *synderesis* that the truly innovative and distinctive aspects of his theology of conscience became obvious. One crucial distinctive dimension was the focus on the emotional aspect. This had already been prefigured in his concept of "*synderesis* in the will," but was extended and developed in his later work. Conscience was no longer a judgment of the practical reason but was associated with a deeper reality that involved a unity of reason and will. A second and indeed related innovation refers to the object of the judgment of conscience. In scholastic thought conscience judges the person's actions. However, Luther insisted that conscience judges not only the person's actions, but the person as a whole. Indeed he was only concerned with the person's actions insofar as they reflected the presence or absence of faith in the person. This does represent a significant break with the tradition since it reflected a very different understanding of the person before God.

For Luther the judgment of conscience paralleled the judgment of God over the individual. However, this judgment was not considered to be one that the individual generated autonomously. Luther regarded it as a divine judgment revealed to the person. Thus, both the good and bad conscience were viewed by Luther as replicating God's judgment of the individual. Since all persons are sinners, both the righteous and the self-righteous should fear God's condemnation. However, according to Luther all persons are simultaneously justified through faith in Christ. It is this ambiguous state of being both condemned and saved in Christ that is reproduced by the conscience. The good conscience, then, is dependent on faith in the gospel. Furthermore, it is faith and not external actions that generates the good conscience, which is attainable only in Christ. This central conviction is seen in Luther's lectures on Romans, especially in his comments on Romans 14. Here he noted that "in the New Law all things are free and nothing is necessary for those who believe in Christ, but (as the apostle says) charity is sufficient, from a pure heart and a good conscience and a faith that is not false."[51] He reinforced this point in his tract *On the Freedom of a Christian* when he insisted that "faith redeems, corrects and preserves our consciences so that we know that righteousness does not consist in works, although works neither can nor ought to be wanting."[52] Thus, for Luther, good or bad works and a good or bad conscience can only be judged according to the presence or absence of faith.

One can see from this brief comment on Luther's theology of conscience that he both depended on and departed from the well-developed scholastic tradition. He is often regarded as the theologian who augmented the authority of conscience far beyond anything that the tradition had seen up to then. In some ways this is true. He certainly shifted authority away from the institutional church toward the individual. However, it is essential to remember that Luther directed authority in religious affairs toward the individual, but it is the individual who is the hearer of the word of God. For Luther it is not that conscience is a supreme authority but rather that scripture and reason are the authorities. Luther did not regard conscience to be an authority like scripture—quite the opposite in fact. He believed conscience to be entirely governed by and reflective of the word of God. Thus, although some subsequent interpreters elevated conscience to the status of a supreme authority, this was a far cry from the position of Luther.

The Tradition of Casuistry

The fifteenth and sixteenth centuries were times of serious political and theological upheaval. In the centuries following the demise of Scholasticism and the rise of the reformed churches moral theology changed considerably. In place of the treatises on the nature of morality, a tradition of casuistry developed in Catholic moral theology. There were many reasons for this. After Occam confidence in ecclesiastical law as the mediator of divine law waned. Occam regarded divine law as nothing other than the arbitrary will of God and reduced morality to the absolute obedience to divine will. As a result the treatises on the nature of morality became redundant. Another factor that influenced this change was the renewed interest in Augustinian theology. This was one of the legacies of Luther. As a result of this the role of personal intentionality in the moral sphere came to the fore again. Thus, the focus was no longer primarily on the action itself (the *finis operis*). Instead, the intention of the person acting (the *finis operantis*) was also given prominence. Because of this personal responsibility and freedom received more emphasis. Ecclesiastical changes in the Catholic Church also played their part in the development of the new "form" of moral theology. The Council of Trent had called for a renewal of the discipline of moral theology, particularly as it influenced the norms operative in the sacrament of penance.

These and other factors resulted in a considerable change in the way in which moral theology was done. A new genre of manuals of moral theology was developed in which the problems of conscience played a major role. These *Institutiones Morales,* as they were called, were manuals for the study of cases of conscience. Although they included some discussion of the nature and foundations of morality, their primary concern was with the analysis of specific moral dilemmas.

The late sixteenth and early seventeenth centuries produced a number of celebrated manualists, people like Azor, Navarrus and Jean Caramuel-Lebkowitz. They refined the method and ensured that casuistry emerged as the main form of moral theology. The manuals discussed some general themes in their opening sections. They considered subjects like the nature of moral acts, conscience, sin and law. They then moved on to examine problematic cases of conscience. This structure did not vary and remained more or less constant until the middle of the twentieth century. They used standard methods of exposition and resolution that became precise and sophisticated. Their focus on the theoretical and practical dimensions of morality was important. It gave rise to an ethical framework that recognized the uniqueness of each particular case while at the same time identified certain categories of cases. This tradition also acknowledged the importance of circumstances as well as the relevance of intention. These texts emphasized the situation in its totality, that is, the act, the circumstances and the intention.

As a result of these theological developments the role of conscience was upgraded. Conscience became the instrument by which the complexity of circumstances, intentions and actions were analyzed and resolved. Conscience involved establishing the true intentionality, interpreting the significance of circumstances, marshaling a range of opinions as to the correct resolution of the dilemma and ultimately coming to an objectively correct decision. Although it is true that this was also part of the Thomistic understanding of conscience, it is certainly the case that the casuistry of the manuals developed it significantly.[53]

Probabilism

As casuistry developed the cases became more complicated and the methods of resolution became more inflexible. As a result by the middle of the seventeenth century moral theology was riven by debates and disputes. The disputes arose mainly because of the practice of listing, comparing and contrasting all the probable opinions regarding the resolution of each case. Frequently, manuals didn't give an answer to the dilemma or even advice as to how best to answer it. They merely identified the range of opinion on the matter. This became a central feature of casuistry and resulted in a vigorous debate. The debate was over the issue of probabilism. Probabilism refers to a particular way of choosing one of a range of possible resolutions of a case. When all the probable opinions regarding the right solution were listed, one had to decide how to choose one. From the 1550s to the 1650s the dominant doctrine was probabilism. This was the view "that, if an opinion is probable, it is licit to follow it, even though the opposite is more probable."[54] This thesis was proposed by the celebrated Dominican casuist Bartolomeo Medina. It allowed a person to follow a course of action if it was probable, even if an alternative course seemed to be more probable. A person could follow a course of action that didn't have great moral certitude and was only probable. If a person was in doubt as to the correct moral resolution of a problem, she/he was permitted to decide on the basis of something being probably right, despite the person's recognition of another opinion that was more probably right.

This thesis was devised so that the individual could choose confidently, even if there was intellectual doubt about the correct course of action to follow. One of the values of casuistry was that it recognized that there could be genuine doubt regarding how to resolve a dilemma even if a person approached the situation with serious moral purpose and prayerful reflection. The reality of moral doubt was not compromised or glossed over. The main aim of the casuists was to establish practical certainty in each case, even if there was a theoretical dispute about the correct resolution. This was necessary because the casuists taught "that it was sinful to act while in doubt: to do so was to hold the law in contempt."[55] In the first century of casuistry this practical certainty was accomplished by the doctrine of probabilism. During this time the role of conscience was greatly enhanced because its task of moral deliberation was recognized to be a complex one of weighing opinions and assessing the moral relevance of each factor.

The essence of the doctrine of probabilism is that a person can take advantage of any reasonable doubt regarding the obligation to be bound by any moral, civil or ecclesiastical law.[56] This presumption toward freedom, although not fully articulated in the doctrine of probabilism, led to laxist opinions among some casuists. This resulted in one of the most turbulent periods of moral debate in the Catholic Church. Laxists argued that one could follow an opinion in favor of freedom from a particular law even if these arguments were only tenuously probable or even if the opinion in favor of the law was far more probable. A person only had to find an alternative opinion, however unlikely or spurious, to be released from the obligation to obey the law. These laxist tendencies were the subject of a damning criticism by Blaise Pascal in his *Provincial Letters*. They also brought the entire tradition of casuistry into disrepute. In fact in 1679 a number of positions associated with laxism were condemned by Innocent XI in his *65 Propositions*.

The opposite extreme also caused great controversy. This was the tendency to tutiorism. Those who held this view argued that one always has to choose the opinion to follow the law, even if the opinion for freedom is more probable. Therefore it considerably restricted the person's ability to choose by imposing the obligation to follow the law. Although less popular, it did have its proponents among the casuists. Tutiorism became associated with Jansenism, and in 1690 absolute tutiorism or rigorism was condemned by Pope Alexander VIII.

These conflicting mechanisms for resolving doubt in cases of conscience were the focus of heated and acrimonious debate for the best part of a century. Focusing on the extent to which one had freedom from the law, different casuists argued for virtually complete freedom (laxism), no freedom (tutiorism/rigorism) or for freedom provided that the other opinion was solidly and truly probable (probabilism). The controversy was only abated when Alphonsus de Liguori, who dedicated his professional life to finding a solution, introduced the moderate position of equiprobabilism. Equiprobabilism proposed that an opinion for freedom could be followed if it were equally as probable as the opinion for obligation to the law. This was quite similar to the probabilism introduced by Medina in the 1650s in that it allows one to follow a probable opinion in opposition to the law. However, it stops short of permitting one to choose the less probable opinion in the face of a more probable one.

The designation of an opinion as probable was complex and involved a number of criteria. Cases could be argued on the basis of intrinsic or extrinsic probability. The authority and reliability of the authors of the various opinions were also considered to be significant. So too was the nature of the case involved. There were certain moral dilemmas, like those relating to the sacraments, that were regarded to be beyond the scope of probabilism. In these cases one was always obliged to follow the obligation in favor of the law. There were many limitations on the use of each of these methods. However, Liguori's equiprobabilism continued in the manual tradition until the 1950s.

The Modern Manual Tradition

The manuals of the nineteenth and twentieth centuries were very similar to the earlier texts. However, in the later manuals theologians returned to Thomism as *the* expression of Christian faith. Most of the manuals of this period exhibited identical philosophical and theological presuppositions. They also followed a common structure and discussed moral problems in a uniform manner. They each began with a section on "general moral theology," involving a consideration of human acts, the nature of morality, conscience, law and sin. The second section of each manual involved an exposition of particular sins, identifying the nature, species and seriousness of particular sins. They focused on the acts themselves rather than on any other features of the situation. There was a slight variation in the way they discussed the particular sins. They were organized in relation to their violation either of the virtues or of the Ten Commandments. The third and final section of the manuals presented the canon law of the sacraments, thus framing morality entirely in a penitential context.[57]

Although the manuals had some obvious limitations, they did have many good qualities. The inherent moral framework was one that had an optimistic view of human nature. However, this was masked by an excessively legalistic form. They acknowledged the importance of both reason and will in making moral decisions. Furthermore, they recognized the interplay of subjectivity and objectivity in the moral domain. In short they embodied many of the positive elements of Thomistic moral theology. Conscience was accorded a prominent role. However, the language and context of the operation of conscience are interesting to observe. According to Gallagher, "conscience was construed as the subjective norm of morality; it referred to the intellectual capacity of individuals to perceive what the moral law required of them."[58] Furthermore, as is evident from the manuals of McHugh/Callan or of Noldin/Schmitt, conscience was not interpreted as expressing an autonomy in the moral realm. Rather, "The standard of morality...is not each one's wish or opinion, but God as the Last End and the external natural and positive law as the means to the end."[59] Conscience is regarded as a form of reasoning within a legalistic framework. In the manual tradition the parameters of morally acceptable behavior were already delineated by church law.

Here one can see clearly the limitations of conceptualizing the role of conscience within the framework of law. Inevitably, one confronts a power struggle between the objective and subjective poles of morality, between divine law and conscience. Ultimate responsibility for ethical decisions is located with the person. Yet, the boundaries of ethical inquiry are drawn very tightly by the law. Law limits the scope of moral questioning. Conscience could be described simply as a faculty that gives the illusion of ethical autonomy within an already strictly limited ethical arena. Of course the teaching that "an erroneous conscience binds" still pertained. In this sense the manuals retained the Thomistic account of conscience. However, the dialectic between conscience and divine law that Aquinas had so carefully crafted had become reified by centuries of debate. As a result the conscience of the manuals had the rhetoric of autonomy, but without the freedom. In these late manuals the conscience is like a swimmer in a swimming pool, told that she/he is free to swim where she/he wishes, but limited always by the (unspoken) boundaries of the swimming pool. While any truly Christian account of conscience needs to retain both subjective and objective dimensions of the category, the manner in which the relationship between the two is envisaged is all important. By the end of this tradition it became clear that moral thinking had outgrown both the language and the methodology of the manuals.

Conclusion

It is commonplace now to critique casuistry and the methods it employed. Through the filter of the renewed moral theology of Vatican II casuistry appears to reduce moral discernment to an arithmetic calculation of the probability of opinions. Although there is a certain amount of truth in this caricature, as a method of achieving certainty when faced with complex ethical dilemmas, casuistry did have a great deal of value. The underlying philosophy recognized the difficulty of achieving certitude in the moral domain. It envisaged a prominent role for the informed conscience of the individual.

This role was not limited to the mechanical application of pre-determined principles to already defined situations. On the contrary it involved a range of activities, from finding an accurate analysis of the dilemma to evaluating the many possible resolutions. However, by the time this tradition became enshrined in the manuals, this intricate reasoning and discernment had been reduced to a mechanistic calculation of the merits of probable opinions. This was a far cry from casuistry in its early and uncorrupted form.

The manuals of moral theology lasted until the middle of the twentieth century. By then changes in philosophical, psychological and scientific thinking had taken hold, leaving the genre of the manuals unable to respond to these shifts in mindset. Eventually the emergence of new ideas, associated primarily with the desire for a more biblically based moral theology, resulted in the demise of casuistry and the manual tradition. This happened in an amazingly short time span and recast yet again the role of conscience in the Christian life.

In this chapter we have discovered that there have been many changes in the way conscience has been understood throughout the Christian tradition. It is not simply that the concept has grown in sophistication and complexity. It is also the case that it has been conceptualized differently with various grades of authority ascribed to it. Augustine suggested that the conscience should defer to divine law, whereas Aquinas would not accept that the relationship between conscience and divine law could necessitate such a choice. He understood the conscience to be the person's appropriation of divine law. Occam changed the nature of the relationship yet again, insisting that morality is nothing other than obedience. Later, the casuists attempted to restore the place of personal discernment, and the manuals continued this tradition, albeit with the difficulties mentioned above. Yet through all these changes conscience remained one of the central moral categories in the Christian tradition. It remained so even though there were many ambiguities and tensions that were not resolved.

Chapter 4
Conflicting Paradigms: Conscience and the Renewal of Vatican II

In the last forty years the language, concepts and concerns of moral theology have undergone significant change. This has been part of a more widespread "revolution" in Catholic theology that has affected all aspects of the discipline. The phrase "paradigm shift"[1] has often been used to describe these changes, which began cautiously in the 1940s and '50s and which were developed by the Second Vatican Council. A paradigm is described as "a framework of thought, a scheme for understanding and explaining certain aspects of reality."[2] It refers to how we envisage the place and purpose of human beings in the world. Of course our understanding of reality is always evolving and in that sense paradigms never remain static. Occasionally, however, there are such significant changes in our understanding that we need to abandon many of the presuppositions, categories and traditions that have sustained the old paradigms, and establish new ones. This is essentially what has been happening in Catholic theology since the 1940s.

Brian Johnstone makes the important point that "the transitions from paradigm to paradigm are not made by an irrational leap in the dark from one to another....A transition from paradigm to paradigm becomes necessary when traditions or certain elements within the tradition lapse into...crisis...when the tradition...by its own standards, becomes unable to make further progress...and is...not able to deal with new questions which have arisen."[3] This is precisely what had been happening to the manual tradition in the late nineteenth and in the twentieth centuries. It was in crisis, unable to close the gap between its understanding of reality and the lives of Catholics worldwide. The paradigm on which it was based could not incorporate the changes in philosophical, scientific and psychological thinking that the twentieth century had heralded, and so a paradigm shift became inevitable. However, the move to a new paradigm is never a simple process, nor can it be accomplished unproblematically. Indeed, since the close of the Second Vatican Council there has been a struggle between those who want to retain the old existing paradigm, and those who are developing the new one.

In this chapter we will examine the extent of the paradigm shift in moral theology. We will begin by looking at the early years of transition, when the old paradigm continued to be enforced and the new one was only beginning to be tentatively proposed. Catholic responses to the situation ethics debates of the 1950s provide us with a snapshot of these paradigms in transition. We will move on to discuss the main features of the new paradigm, often called the personalist paradigm. We will do so by examining the documents of Vatican II in which the renewal is advocated. We will focus primarily on how the new paradigm affected the manner in which the role of conscience was understood. Within these documents, however, one can see paradigms not only in transition, but also in conflict. We will consider these conflicts in relation to Vatican II's understanding of conscience. We will also look at the politics surrounding *Humanae Vitae* as an instance of these paradigms in conflict. In the final section I will argue for a fully developed moral theology based on the personalist paradigm. I will discuss the main features of such an ethic and will identify some of the reconceptualizations that are needed. This will prepare the way for an exploration of the nature of conscience in the context of this new theological paradigm.

I have argued from the beginning that in both theory and practice one can discern two conflicting accounts of morality in modern Catholicism. It is a duality that permeates moral theology from its foundational concepts to its practical conclusions. It can be seen in the reactions to *Humanae Vitae* and to *Veritatis Splendor,* as well as in the manner in which the tradition is interpreted. I suggested in chapters 2 and 3 that many of these tensions were present through the centuries. The history of moral theology and especially the history of conscience suggest that there were many contradictions and ambiguities that have never been resolved. With this current conflict of paradigms many of the old issues of institutional versus personal moral authority arise again. One paradigm looks to Vatican II for support for its renewed morality. The other is determined to return to an absolutist and authoritarian morality. The theology of conscience that I propose in this chapter is a personalist one. I do so because it is my firm conviction that this is what is warranted by the challenge of being human.

Paradigms in Transition

Much of the impetus for reform grew out of the modernist crisis and the church's response to it.[4] However, it was not until the 1930s that this movement for change was felt in the sphere of moral theology. We have already discussed the reasons for the growing dissatisfaction with the manualist tradition. This dissatisfaction combined with some innovative ideas on the part of individual moral theologians exacerbated the perceived gap between theology and "life." Since it is not possible to discuss these developments in detail, I will focus on those that influenced moral theology most. It is worth remembering, however, that in these decades the entire theological tradition was confronted with radical critiques of the discipline. In terms of the shifting concerns of moral theology three developments in particular are worth examining. These are (1) the introduction of historical consciousness into theological reflection; (2) the growing resistance to neo-Thomism on the part of particular moral theologians; and (3) the controversy surrounding the situation ethics debates of the 1950s.

1. The Introduction of Historical Consciousness to Theology

By the mid–twentieth century many philosophers and theologians argued that it was impossible to speak of human beings as though they were all essentially the same, regardless of their culture, history or language. This involved recognizing the importance of historical consciousness in all disciplines, including theology. The Catholic theologians who developed this *nouvelle theologie* were people like Danielou, Chenu, de Lubac and Congar. They rejected the idea of a timeless theology uncontaminated by the exigencies of history. Instead, they insisted that since theology is our attempt to understand the mystery of God in time, it is unambiguously historical. Our rootedness in history has a profound effect on the way we do theology, since each theological system is primarily a product of its context. This recognition had a major impact on the understanding of moral theology, since the natural law tradition tended to regard human nature as though it were abstract, disembodied and universal.

Once it was introduced, the perspective of historical consciousness became ever more important. Karl Rahner's theological anthropology, for example, relied on the premise that one could not speak of human beings in terms of immutable essences. His model was based on identifying the material, biological and spiritual dimensions of the person,[5] each of which highlights its uniqueness. As a result he argued that a transhistorical and universal concept of human nature is inappropriate. This development eventually led to what Richard McCormick has called "the age of experience"[6] in moral theology. There was a gradual realization that the neo-Thomism of the manuals depended on a concept of universal human nature against which the particularities of individual existence were insignificant. Rahner was only one of an increasing number of Catholic theologians who began to direct attention toward the human person in all his or her particularity. Real human beings rather than abstract human nature became the subject of theological reflection. This turn to the subject represented one of the most serious challenges to the manuals, which had relied on discussing individuals in terms of genus.

2. The Growing Resistance to Neo-Thomism

Although they did not challenge the dominant theological paradigm directly, individual moral theologians such as Häring, Lottin and Tillmann began to question particular aspects of the neo-Thomistic manuals. For example, in his *Law of Christ* Häring insisted that human beings ought to be thought of not in terms of their nature but of their personhood. In addition he argued that morality must arise from a personal relationship with God, one that enables the person to discern value. He spoke of morality in relational terms and viewed legalism as the great moral danger.[7] Lottin's concern was to reintegrate moral and dogmatic theology and to remove moral theology's excessive preoccupation with the confessional. Tillmann attempted to make moral theology more consistent with the themes of the New Testament and sought to reconnect the religious and moral dimensions of Christian life. Although at this stage there was no distinctive movement that challenged the manual tradition, these theologians were important because they introduced alternative ways of thinking about morality.

Herbert Doms is another theologian who challenged the hegemony of the old paradigm. In his *The Meaning of Marriage,*[8] published in 1939, he proposed that the categories which moral theology had inherited should be rethought. In fact Doms can be credited with introducing personalism into the field of moral theology. Specifically, in terms of Doms's work this meant an "explicit turn to marital experience as a resource"...construing "sexuality's meaning in terms of a range of values, especially intersubjective ones"...and precipitating "a basic shift in the way the priority of the traditional purposes of sexual acts (procreation and unity) is understood...."[9] The precise conclusions of

Doms's work on the nature of Christian marriage cannot detain us here. What is significant for our purposes is his methodology. Here he gave priority to the actual experience of married couples in constructing a theology of marriage. Doms's work was ordered to be withdrawn from publication in the early '40s by the Congregation of the Holy Office.

His work conflicted with existing papal teaching on marriage because it did not focus on the procreative potential of all sexual intercourse. In fact his true innovation was that he began to write a theology of marriage that put the experience of married persons ahead of church tradition. It must be said, however, that Doms did not highlight or develop these methodological implications of his work. With the benefit of hindsight one can see that giving priority to experience was bound to be controversial and groundbreaking, but Doms did not draw attention to this. Yet his work became a major resource for the theology of marriage of Vatican II, which in turn was to become the basis of the personalist moral theology of the renewal.

3. The Situation Ethics Debate

In the situation ethics debate of the 1950s one can see the different approaches to morality that existed within the Catholic tradition. Extreme forms of situation ethics that denied the existence of any moral objectivity were rightly denounced by the magisterium. However, many important insights were also dismissed in the process. Yet, many of these insights were subsequently accepted in the renewal of the '60s and '70s. Those who adopted a moderate situationist position argued that the moral law should not be regarded as immutable. Instead, moral theology should deal with persons in their concrete particularities. They insisted that morality involves discerning ethical obligation by examining the situation itself. They claimed that in the neo-Thomistic system conscience was reduced to a process of applying general principles to particular cases. Instead, the situationists emphasized that conscience "is a faculty which under the guidance of the Spirit of God is endowed with a certain power of intuition and discovery which allows it to find the original solution appropriate to each case."[10]

Pope Pius XII unreservedly condemned situation ethics in 1952 and in 1956. His most detailed criticisms were contained in the *Instruction of the Holy Office on "Situation Ethics."*[11] His condemnation focused on two distinct concerns. Firstly, he rejected the tendency of situationists to conceive of human nature as "an existing and partly changing concept" rather than a "static and absolute"[12] one. He criticized situationism for asserting that morality is fluid and changing. This he claimed was a consequence of their belief in an evolving human nature. He rejected the view that morality must be read from the situation. Instead, he insisted that it can be determined by the mechanical application of predetermined, universal laws to each particular situation. In this document Pius XII refused to recognize anything other than applying universal moral laws to particular situations as authentic Christian living. Furthermore, he regarded these moral laws as absolute and unchanging.

His second objection related to the way in which situationists think of the role of conscience in the moral life. He claimed that "Having accepted these principles [above] and put them into practice, they assert and teach that men are preserved or easily liberated from many otherwise insoluble ethical conflicts when each one judges in his own conscience, not primarily according to objective laws, but by means of that internal individual light based on personal intuition, what he must do in a concrete situation."[13] Indeed, in each reference to the role of conscience in situation ethics, Pius XII came back to the role given to the intuition and interior judgment of the person. He was instinctively reluctant to accept moral insight of this kind and focused instead on the rational dimensions of moral decision making. But as Mahoney rightly points out, Vatican II and much subsequent papal teaching on morality have stressed the importance of not limiting moral decision making to its rational components.[14] Of course simply appealing to one's intuition that something is wrong is not sufficient from a Christian point of view. One must also articulate the reasons why one thinks that something is wrong, and to give a coherent account of one's point of view. However, in his condemnation of moral insight, Pius XII failed to recognize a truth long accepted in the Catholic tradition, that reason is but one component of moral decision making.

Yet although he was concerned about the relationship between reason and moral insight, it is my view that Pius XII was more troubled about the pastoral implications of recognizing the importance of personal moral insight. Of course the tradition did recognize the legitimate functioning of the individual conscience in the moral life. However, its sphere of activity was carefully circumscribed by "the objective moral law." This resulted in an excessive focus on the external action, with little attention being given to the intention of the person performing that action or to the circumstances in which it was performed. Situation ethics sought to reestablish the importance of intentionality in the moral realm. As a result it challenged the neo-Thomistic tendency to give excessive weight to the act itself. The implications of this for the prevailing paradigm in moral theology were significant. Moral authority would move away from universal pronouncements about the objective morality of particular acts and toward the individual in his or her particular situation. The role of conscience would likewise be transformed.

The New Paradigm Articulated

The documents of Vatican II provided the building blocks for a new understanding of moral theology. In a range of documents traditional ethical categories (such as conscience) were reinterpreted in the context of a more biblically based, personalist ethic. One can see this particularly in *Gaudium et Spes,* where the focus is on the interior morality of the person. Fuchs explains that this concern for the interior morality of the person lies in the Council's conviction that "when speaking about humanity...the first subject is salvation as given by God."[15] *Gaudium et Spes* describes the Christian moral demand as a personal response to the divine initiative in salvation. The free response to this invitation is the basis of the new morality and requires a reorientation of heart and mind. The effect of this is that the Christian "lets himself be reshaped, and reshapes himself in inner freedom; thus he is not a sinner, but redeemed."[16] The significance of this in terms of a new paradigm is noted by Fuchs when he reminds us that "it is important in reflecting on the statements of the Council that salvation be viewed in direct relation, not to acting in the world, but to the person in his freedom."[17] It involves openness to other persons (G.S., 38), a readiness to work for the good of others (G.S., 39) and to care for the right shaping of the world (G.S., 39).[18]

The thrust of *Gaudium et Spes* is toward nurturing a disposition responsive to the mystery of salvation. Love of God and love of neighbor frame this interior life and ought to become the basis of our actions in the world. This cultivation of personal moral goodness, this personal ethic based on an inner freedom, ought to be our response to the gift of salvation. One can see clearly that both in terms of language and concepts this description of Christian morality departs substantially from existing ones. Of course the core elements of the tradition remained, but they were given a very different emphasis.

The consequence of framing morality, thus, was that the person moved center stage. In these texts the actions and choices of the individual are a reflection of the kind of person one is and one will become. Actions are not considered in isolation from the person performing them. Furthermore, the person at the center of morality is "part of the material world, interrelational with other persons, a social and historical being."[19] As a result the relationships and circumstances which go to make up the subject's experience do have real and enduring moral significance. *Gaudium et Spes* puts forward a model of morality in which the person is the source of ethical discernment and action. In so doing it initiates a move toward a new paradigm, one that emphasizes personal responsibility rather than obedience.

Gaudium et Spes's discussion of marriage and sexuality introduced a further innovation. It proposed that "the moral aspect of any procedure...must be determined by objective standards which are based on the nature of the person and the person's acts."[20] The person is thus regarded as the criterion of what is morally right and wrong.[21] This is quite an extraordinary statement. The official commentary made it clear that this principle was applicable, not only to marriage, the context in which it was first articulated, but as a general principle that applies to all actions. McCormick insists that the importance of this statement cannot be exaggerated. It involves a radical departure from the previous theology because it commits us to an entirely different way of assessing the morality of human actions. In practical terms it means that each action must be evaluated in the context of the person considered holistically, that is, in light of the person's circumstances and relationships. It follows from this principle that acts like contraception or abortion cannot be evaluated in isolation. The context in which the person makes a decision, the intention, the effects on relationships, together with the consequences each contribute to the moral significance of the act. This principle commits moral theology to an approach that places human experience and relationships at the heart of moral evaluation and assessment.

Conscience in the Documents of Vatican II

The popular perception is that the documents of Vatican II stress the dignity and autonomy of conscience. While this is true in a very general sense, there are a number of different, often conflicting, views about the nature and role of conscience present within them. The teaching of the Council on conscience can at best be described as ambiguous. James Gaffney goes further and argues that the term *conscience* is employed "in a combination of senses which not even the most benign exegetical subtlety can rescue from incoherence."[22] The incoherence can be seen in (1) the relationship between conscience and law, (2) the issues of discernment and obedience, (3) the problem of the erroneous conscience and (4) the role of the magisterium. Many of these ambiguities existed in the theology of conscience from the beginning. They go to the heart of the problem of the role of conscience in the Christian life. Is conscience about following church law or about determining for oneself what is right and good? Is conscience about obedience or discernment? How can conscience err if it is the voice of God? What is the relationship between individual and institutional moral authority? These are questions that Catholics need help in answering. Unfortunately, the documents of Vatican II did little to remedy the confusions. In fact they further complicated the issue. However, my view is that wherever ambiguities exist, they should be interpreted in light of the general moral framework proposed by Vatican II. This means explicitly situating conscience within the personalist paradigm.

1. Conscience and Law

There has long been a difficulty with articulating the precise role of conscience in relation to divine law. This difficulty is also evident in the documents of the Council. It is especially obvious in *Dignitatis humanae,* which deals with conscience in relation to religious freedom. Fuchs suggests that in *Dignitatis humanae* there are two different accounts of conscience and its relationship to the divine law. In the first instance *Dignitatis humanae* declares that "the highest norm of human life is the divine law."[23] However, since divine law is not directly accessible to human beings (nor to the magisterium) we have been given the capacity to "participate in this law"[24] through our conscience. "The human person sees and recognizes the demands of the divine law through conscience."[25] This phrase suggests that conscience is understood as the capacity for moral consciousness,[26] the traditional *synderesis.* However, when one examines the account of conscience in *Gaudium et Spes* a different understanding is evident. Married couples are told to "conform their conscience to the law of God." They "must be ruled by conscience—and conscience ought to be in accord with the law of God in the teaching authority of the church, which is the authentic interpreter of divine law."[27] Here the role of conscience is identified with (and reduced to?) implementing church teaching. Its activity in ethical discernment is limited to obeying the teaching authority of the church. Thus, the two strands of conscience that had been relatively successfully integrated by Aquinas are present in the documents, not together but as competing accounts.

2. Discernment or Obedience?

Further ambiguities flow from the manner in which the activity of conscience is described. The ambiguity is extremely obvious in the *Gaudium et Spes* text that has become the classic articulation of the activity of conscience. It is worth quoting it at length.

> Deep within their consciences men and women discover a law which they have not laid upon themselves and which they must obey. Its voice ever calling them to love and to do what is good and to avoid evil, tells them inwardly at the right moment: do this, shun that. For they have in their hearts a law inscribed by God. Their dignity rests on observing this law, and by it they will be judged. Their conscience is people's most secret core, and their sanctuary. There they are alone with God, whose voice echoes in their depths....Through loyalty to conscience, Christians are joined to others in the search for truth and for the right solution to so many moral problems....[28]

In the early part of the passage the work of conscience is described simply as obedience to the objective moral law. The task of conscience is to obey. Yet, in the later sentences the idiom changes substantially. The paradigm of law is abandoned. Instead, it is the voice of God echoing in one's depths that orients the person to seek the good in each situation. Furthermore, the passage affirms that this capacity to discern the law is present in all peoples, regardless of whether they are Christian or not.

However, what is not at all clear is how we understand the phrase "objectively right." We are given no guidance regarding whether the "objective moral order" is composed of very specific, concrete, universal norms or whether it consists of more general values. The latter would allow for a significant amount of moral pluralism. It would accept the likelihood of different cultures or, indeed, different individuals giving expression to core Christian values in a variety of forms. The former understanding would rule this out. Furthermore, the latter understanding "is not a ready-made and only passively accepted 'law' but rather a law that is discovered actively by us men and women and in human (and ecclesiastical) society and is found in this way."[29] The first account would lead to a very different model. It would view the objective moral order "as the (possible) knowledge of every norm of correct moral behavior in the world, that is without drawing a fundamental distinction between an objective law and the concrete solutions, for in this case (the solutions) too, would be objective moral law."[30] Such an understanding would severely circumscribe the activity of conscience. It would limit moral discernment to informing oneself of the teaching of the church on each and every moral matter and implementing it without question. The primary work of the conscience would simply be to obey. The difficulty for those of us who look to these texts on conscience for guidance is that they pull in two contrary directions.

3. The Erroneous Conscience

The documents speak of conscience as the voice of God echoing in the depths of the person. However, they also teach that conscience can be in error. This error can be because of ignorance, carelessness or bad habits. Cardinal Ratzinger points to a contradiction here when he wonders "how conscience can err if God's call is directly to be heard in it, is unexplained." He suggests that "the fathers of Vatican II were anxious not to allow an ethics of conscience to be transformed into the domination of subjectivism and they were not willing to canonize a limitless situation ethics under the guise of conscience."[31] These comments highlight the fact that the logic of one aspect of Vatican II's concept of conscience suggested giving more weight to the subjective assessment of the individual. However, the church authorities regarded this as dangerous and so tried to counteract it. They did so by reintroducing traditional formulae. In so doing they disregarded the consequences of this for the coherence of the understanding of conscience.

Yet, there are elements within the tradition itself that allow one to explain how people do err even when they aspire to make the right judgment. The explanation revolves around the distinction between goodness and rightness. James Keenan has argued that in the theology of Aquinas one can find a mandate for this important distinction. He suggests that Thomism would support the contemporary tendency to separate these two aspects of morality. He proposes that we should think of rightness as being a judgment of reason, whereas goodness pertains to the heart.[32] This distinction allows one to recognize that a decision may be in error but may arise from moral goodness. Erroneous judgments can come from the desire to do what is truly loving. Keenan suggests "the distinction between goodness and rightness could be stated in this form: goodness measures whether out of love one strives to attain a rightly ordered self....Rightness on the other hand, measures whether one actually attains a rightly ordered self."[33]

The Vatican II documents limited the discussion of the erroneous conscience to the issue of whether the error was caused by vincible or invincible ignorance. However, if the distinction between goodness and rightness is placed at the center of the problem of the erroneous conscience, one can explain how a person acting out of goodness (the heart), through an error of reason, can make a decision that is objectively wrong. While this aspiration to do good does not guarantee a right judgment, its presence is sufficient to speak of the goodness of the person. This distinction between rightness and goodness would allow one to endorse the Council's view that conscience is the voice of God calling the person to love and do the good. The essential aspect of conscience is this "summons to love and fidelity." The dignity of the erroneous conscience depends on the fact that it is oriented toward this goal, even if its judgment is mistaken. Indeed, the concept of the erroneous conscience "presupposes that, despite one's mistake, one is striving to obey its summons to fidelity."[34] However, although necessary to reconciling the conflicting ideas of the erroneous conscience, in the texts no such distinction was made. As a result, in Ratzinger's words, "the Council's position on the binding force of erroneous conscience is rather evasive."[35]

4. The Role of the Magisterium

The practical implications of such confusions can be seen in the Council's failure to deal with the authority of conscience and its relationship with the magisterium of the church. There are two different models of conscience at play in these texts. One model emphasizes that conscience is an active faculty that discovers and discerns the good within the complexity of each situation. It is the site of autonomous moral decision making and bears the responsibility for acting rightly. The second model emphasizes that conscience must be aligned with the objective moral order. This is true also of the first model. However, the difference is that the second model elaborates on this by insisting that "conscience ought to be in accord with the law of God in the teaching authority of the church, which is the authentic interpreter of divine law."[36] But is conscience itself not the authentic interpreter of divine law? Is this not precisely the role that the documents ascribe to conscience? If not, then what is its role? Passive implementation of the teachings of the church? Mechanistic application of predetermined principles?

Of course it is possible to hold that conscience and magisterium should not be seen in terms of conflicting authorities. Instead they should be regarded as mutually supportive sites of engagement with divine law. This is undoubtedly the model that is aspired to. Yet, in every century of the church's history we can see that this model ruptures when there is disagreement about some moral problem. When there are conflicting views about the morality of a particular practice or when a certain kind of act is deemed to be wrong, regardless of any circumstances, then the ambiguities inherent in the relationship between magisterium and conscience become more pronounced. We do not get any direction from the Council documents about clarifying this relationship. There is no discussion of how to resolve potential conflicts between the views of the magisterium and the conscientious decisions of individuals. This is true both of *Gaudium et Spes* and of *Dignitatis humanae,* the two texts that deal directly with the role of conscience in the moral life.

As we have seen, these ambiguities are part and parcel of the history of conscience. However, they were exacerbated by the fact that in the documents we can see one paradigm, that of law, collapsing and another, that of personalism, beginning to emerge. Since there is a fundamental incoherence in terms of the categories of morality, it is not surprising that such problems arose. Yet, Vatican II simply began a process of renewal that it encouraged the faithful to continue. As a result many of the ambiguities can be resolved by developing the personalist paradigm in moral theology and situating discussions of conscience in that context.

The New Paradigm in Crisis: *Humanae Vitae*

In 1968, before the renewal in moral theology advocated by the Council gained momentum, the encyclical *Humanae Vitae* was issued. It completely changed the character of moral debate within the Catholic Church. Despite the findings of what Pope Paul described as the "broad, varied and extremely skilled international commission,"[37] the traditional ban on artificial contraception and sterilization was confirmed as a basic principle of Christian marriage. The official commentary made it clear that *Humanae Vitae* was not an infallible statement. However, the issue of how it was to inform individual consciences was unambiguous. As a result the commentary concluded that the encyclical "does not leave the questions concerning birth regulation in a condition of vague problematics."[38] In the period before the encyclical, when there was a genuine expectation that the teaching on artificial contraception might change, an element of freedom of conscience operated. However, the commentary on the encyclical made it clear that people could no longer consider the church's attitude to birth control to be unresolved. The position of the church was now absolutely clear. In addition the commentary insisted "there is owed loyal and full assent, interior and not only exterior, to an authentic pronouncement of the magisterium, in proportion to the level of the authority from which it emanates—which in this case is the supreme authority of the Supreme Pontiff."[39] Catholics are thus obliged to give full assent to the teaching, since its authority derives from its status as a pronouncement of the pope.

This draws on the traditional position of the magisterium as the authentic interpreter of the objective moral order. It claims the kind of role for the magisterium that leaves very little room for the individual conscience. The commentary reinforces this further by insisting that the encyclical "prevents the forming of a probable opinion, that is to say an opinion acting on the moral plane in contrast with the pronouncement itself, whatever the number and the hierarchical, scientific and theological authority of those who considered in the past few years that they could form it for themselves."[40] If one were to ask a direct question of the encyclical with regard to the role of conscience in decisions about birth control, how would one fare? For example is the Catholic allowed or even required to decide in his or her conscience what is the morally right thing to do in relation to contraception? The answer, if one was to follow the encyclical and the official commentary, would be "only if the conclusion is the same as *Humanae Vitae.*" This is clearly a problematic position since it subordinates the conscientious judgment of the individual to church teaching.

The reactions to the encyclical are widely known. Within the church there were conflicting views on practically every aspect of its teaching. These views were aired publicly and left the church in no doubt that it faced a significant crisis. Nor, indeed, has this crisis dissipated in the thirty years since the encyclical was published, although the public character of the resistance has changed. The pastoral implications of the encyclical are perhaps the most important of all. Although a resistance to the teaching of the encyclical has evolved in many contexts, it is often characterized by confusion and guilt. The reason for this is evident: Although choosing to use contraception may be in accord with one's informed conscience, it is contrary to church teaching. Lisa Sowle Cahill has claimed that Catholics have, in fact, come to terms with their own conscientious judgments about birth control. She suggests that they "agree on the value of parenthood, the place of sex in expressing intimacy within a committed partnership, and the potential of bearing and nurturing a child together to enhance the quality and depth of marriage."[41] However, the encyclical reduces this complexity of values to one feature, the physical act of sexual intercourse. To focus on this aspect of the marital experience to the exclusion of all other dimensions of married love means that the encyclical operates with a truncated, incomplete understanding of sexuality and marriage. This limited view of marriage is, according to Cahill, counterexperiential. The teaching is increasingly being rejected by Catholics worldwide who seem to be comfortable with making their own decisions with regard to contraception. As an issue of authority and as a measure of the church's position on the dignity and primacy of conscience, however, the encyclical continues to be controversial.

Conformity on the issue of contraception has become a litmus test of one's loyalty as a Catholic. In an increasingly divided church one's view of the role of conscience in decisions about contraception is deemed to be crucial. If one insists that in each and every moral situation, including those that involve the question of birth control, one is obliged to form one's conscience and act accordingly, then one is regarded with suspicion. Yet, this is entirely in accordance with traditional theologies of conscience. Of course the tradition rightly speaks of the duty of each person to inform him- or herself of the church's teaching relevant to the situation. It is certainly the case that no Catholic today could be ignorant of the church's view on artificial contraception. Yet, this does not guarantee that the individual's conscientious judgment about the moral rightness of contraception will coincide with church teaching. Indeed, the overwhelming evidence for three decades now is that a significant portion of the world's Catholic women and men, when they are genuinely free to act on their conscientious decisions (that is, when they are not coerced by restrictive legislation, peer sanction or conditional aid in developing countries), choose to use artificial contraception and consider it to be the morally right course of action.

A Personalist Moral Theology

Vatican II encouraged moral theologians to continue the process of renewal, already begun by theologians like Rahner, Doms and Häring. However, as we saw in chapter 1 this process has been hampered by a reluctance on the part of some to implement any change. Part of the difficulty is that the documents of the Council themselves give out contradictory messages. As a result it is often hard to discern precisely what the Council has mandated. My suggestion is that where ambiguities exist these should be interpreted in light of the spirit and objective of the Council. In relation to moral theology this means a determination to develop a paradigm dominated by the concerns of persons rather than laws. In this final section we will discuss some of the reconceptualizations necessitated by this new paradigm and that are, in some senses, already in process.

1. History and Change in Ethics

In our discussion of the demise of the old paradigm we noted that there was a change in the way the relationship between history and reality was conceptualized. The classical understanding of reality, based on immutable and fixed essences, with the controlling norms being universal and fixed for all time, was challenged. Instead, philosophers argued that change and evolution comprise part of the natural condition of human beings. They suggested that the concept of ethics, too, must be based on such a premise. This involves respecting human experience as a crucial source of moral insight and discernment. It takes account of social, scientific and psychological as well as biological data when assessing the meaning of actions. In addition it recognizes the indeterminacy and complexity of many moral situations. Such a view of morality is founded on "the notion of change through history."[42] It is thus deeply reluctant to make any claims concerning universal or exceptionless moral norms other than in the most abstract and general terms. It does not represent an attack on objectivity since it recognizes the existence of an objective moral order. However, the nature and makeup of that moral order, the kinds of principles it involves and the role given to discernment are each transformed.

2. Actions, Circumstances, Intentions

Some traditional understandings of the relationship among actions, circumstances and intentions are called into question within the personalist paradigm. The revisionists argue that the moral meaning of an act cannot be determined by examining the object alone. They insist that the intention, circumstances and consequences also have a direct bearing on the nature of the act performed. Moral acts are not isolated, single actions that can be separated from the context in which they are performed. They must be recognized as "complex unities involving decisions, historical contexts surrounding the decisions, goals intended by the decisions, and consequences that follow on the decisions."[43] This signals a radical departure for the moral theology of neoscholasticism since it implies that a particular action can have a significantly different meaning in two separate contexts. Melchin gives the example of the act of masturbation to illustrate how circumstances and intention can be included in the moral evaluation of an action to change its meaning. There would be a difference between a person who engaged in this act purely for sexual gratification and a person who engaged in it for the purpose of some medical procedure. Using some traditional analyses, one would not be able to distinguish between these two acts in terms of their nature. It might be possible to argue, from the act of double effect, that masturbation for a medical procedure is permitted, but the moral character of the act itself would remain evil. Some traditional views of the human act disregard context and intentionality in determining the morality of the act. Thus the act is described as either good or evil in itself, the conclusion drawn exclusively from the object of the act.[44]

Within the personalist paradigm theologians sought to include the intention of the person and the circumstances in which they were acting in the moral description of the act. Thus, masturbation for a medical procedure would have a different moral meaning in itself from masturbation for the purpose of sexual gratification. They argued that the concrete situation could alter the meaning of a particular act. They also insisted that it is not possible to describe a particular moral act in itself, that is, independent of the context in which the act is performed. Of course this is not a simple matter. It requires that attention be given to the particular context to ensure that one is describing it honestly and accurately. One must also be able to determine which features of a situation are morally relevant and which are irrelevant. For example, the time of day when an action is performed or the color of the coat a person is wearing has no moral significance in determining the nature of a moral act.[45] However, other particularities, such as one's relationship with one's family, or one's state of mind at the time, may be important.

In reconceptualizing the relationship among actions, circumstances and intentions theologians have argued for the essential unity of the components of morality that aspects of the tradition dealt with separately. The drive to incorporate the intention and the circumstances into the moral meaning of the action has far-reaching consequences, particularly in relation to moral absolutes and the concept of intrinsic evil. It involves a reorientation in the understanding of morality itself. If one has a model of morality in which the intention and context are important for the meaning of the act, then it is impossible to classify particular kinds of acts as good or evil in themselves. Nor is it possible to speak of acts of theft, killing, masturbation or contraception as though each act were morally identical. Including these features in the moral meaning of each act results in a move away from speaking of acts in the abstract. It also means that one cannot judge acts such as contraception, theft or abortion independent of the circumstances in which they are performed.

3. Norms and Principles

This has important ramifications for the way in which moral norms and principles are understood. It raises the question of whether one can have norms and principles that are absolute, exceptionless and universal in their application.[46] Although not all theologians who are committed to a personalist paradigm agree on the approach to the issue of norms, they share a number of important perspectives. The crux of the revisionists' approach is their reluctance to claim that norms can be absolute in anything other than the most general and abstract of terms. Consequently, if the intention and circumstances of a deed enter into the description of what is being done, then it is impossible to evaluate an action or formulate a principle in any but the most general terms. Take again the example of contraception. According to this perspective the nature of the contraceptive act cannot be described exclusively in relation to its physical or biological aspects. To say that the act of contraception is wrong is problematic precisely because it is not possible to speak of the act of contraception in the abstract. One must include an account of the circumstances in which the decision is made, together with the intention of the agent, in the description of the act of contraception. Of course it is possible to conclude that in these particular circumstances, this singular decision to use artificial contraception is wrong. However, this is very different from saying that the act of using artificial contraception is wrong in itself.

Moral norms and principles play a very important role in the moral life of the Christian. They represent the accumulated moral wisdom of the community, wisdom that is a vital source of moral knowledge of each individual. Theologians working within the new paradigm recognize the value of moral norms but caution us to be more precise in our understanding of the different kinds of moral norms and principles that exist within the tradition. They also caution us not to confuse the kinds of applicability that they can have. Within the Christian moral tradition there are three kinds of moral principles—formal, tautological and material. There is no controversy concerning the first two types. The formal principle, for example, human life is to be respected, is a general, abstract principle identifying a particular value. In itself it tells us nothing about the morality of a particular action. It is regarded as universal in its scope. The second type of principle, called tautological, is similarly unproblematic. "Murder is wrong" is an example of a tautology. It simply expresses that which is obvious, that unjustified killing (murder) is wrong. It is also universal in its application because the term *murder* means a killing that is unjustified. Therefore, it is possible to say that it is always and everywhere wrong to engage in unjustified killing. These are points on which both traditionalists and revisionists agree.

However, it is in relation to the third type of moral principle that the most disquiet has been expressed. These are called concrete or material norms or principles. An example of a material principle is "killing is wrong" or "abortion is wrong." But, revisionists ask, is killing always wrong? In other words can this norm be universal in its claim? The answer quite simply is no. It is not possible to say always and without exception that killing is wrong. This is because it is impossible to describe the moral meaning of the act of killing without also including in the description some account of the context. For example, killing can be in self-defense or at the request of the person killed, as in cases of doctor-assisted suicide or voluntary euthanasia. As a result concrete material norms cannot be considered to be absolute, that is, exceptionless. Neither can they be said to be universal in their scope, that is, true always and everywhere. None other than the most vague and general statements of value can be said to be absolute or universal. Any norm or principle that involves concrete action (which, it must be said, encompasses the vast majority of the moral norms associated with Catholicism) must be regarded as provisional and partial. Concrete norms point us in a particular direction and highlight some aspects of morality that are relevant to the situation but should not be thought of as absolute or universal in their purchase.

This revision of thinking on moral norms has an important impact on the way the activity of conscience is understood. This is because it relativizes the claims and scope that characterize the principles and norms of the tradition. If a principle claims that stealing is wrong or killing is wrong, and in the process takes absolutely no account of the circumstances in which these actions are performed, then the role of conscience is redundant. If morality is simply about applying these specific concrete principles to one's actions, then there is no need for conscience. It has no purpose. However if, as the revisionists suggest, these principles are regarded as guides for our behavior, then the role of conscience remains central. A principle such as "killing is wrong" highlights the fact that if a person is to be killed, then this is a very grave matter and worthy of serious thought. Moral norms perform a valuable task in helping us to discern the right thing to do in each situation. But in themselves they are no substitute for the serious, honest and personal judgment of conscience, which must be at the center of any genuine moral decision making.

This approach to morality necessarily brings into focus the thorny issue of intrinsic evil. The concept of intrinsic evil claims that there are particular acts which can never be performed, regardless of the circumstances, the intention or the consequences. This means that the conscience can never entertain the possibility of performing that act. The prohibition is absolutely and universally binding on the conscience. A number of acts have been put into this category at various times. These acts have been described only in terms of their object, with no reference to intentionality or context. In surveying a range of writings on these acts, which are evil in themselves, one finds three distinct areas where they appear. Acts considered to be intrinsically evil were (a) acts "which violated the marriage contract....the prohibition of divorce and remarriage was absolute and exceptionless,"[47] (b) "the direct taking of innocent life" and (c) "the free exercise of the sexual faculty," which "apart from normal sexual intercourse within a marriage relationship, was prohibited, no matter what the intention or the situation."[48] The reasoning behind designating these acts as intrinsically evil differed in each case. What was common to each of these areas was that the tradition, in looking at the object of the act alone, without taking into account anything in the context, insisted that no circumstances could ever justify performing such an act. The prohibition was absolute and universal.

Revisionists are skeptical about claims that these judgments are exceptionless. They insist that it is not possible to judge any action without taking account of the intentionality of the person and the circumstances in which the action is performed. The concept of intrinsic evil ignores these dimensions of morality entirely because it claims that "here exist acts which *per se* and in themselves, independently of circumstances, are always seriously wrong by reason of their object."[49] The core of the revisionist strategy for morality has been to expand the meaning of the moral act and to define it in terms of object, circumstances and intention, not in terms of object alone. One can only speak of particular acts being wrong because of the intention of the person performing them in a specific context. However, such judgments pertain to specific situations, known in all their aspects, and not to "kinds" or "classes" of acts described without reference to circumstances and intention.[50]

Here again the role of conscience is restored. There are no shortcuts for conscience. There are no mechanisms for bypassing the duty to assess every decision in relation to all the morally relevant features. Norms and principles are important sources of moral wisdom and guidance. Traditional principles such as intrinsic evil remind us that we are dealing with very grave situations. They retain a very important role in informing and educating our consciences in moral sensitivity. However, they do not replace the conscience, nor do they provide us with shortcuts to making the right decisions. The conscience remains the center of moral discernment and decision making.

4. Moral Authority

Within the personalist renewal there is a fresh emphasis on the moral authority of the individual. However, the new paradigm is neither individualistic nor isolationist. Moral principles and norms are viewed, not as predetermined solutions to moral problems but as reliable guides in our search for authentic and right moral decisions. Sacred texts and traditions of the church, too, are recognized as excellent sources of moral insight and discernment. The community in which we live and worship is also vital since it educates us in the vision and virtues of our faith. The fund of norms, principles, texts, traditions and witness within the church provides us with a rich source of moral insight. Together with the ongoing dialogue about our behavior in the world, which is properly the task of the church, these resources help us to unravel our moral confusions and uncertainties. They help us to identify the fundamental questions to be answered. They enable us to focus on the important values to be struggled for. They highlight the pitfalls, shortcomings and deceptions present in our own analysis of a situation. But they do not in any sense replace the activity of conscience, which is an essential dimension of the moral life of the individual.

The question of where ultimate moral responsibility and authority reside is extremely fraught. Proponents of the various views argue about the meanings of terms and the roles and responsibilities of the parties involved. Nor is this relevant only when there is disagreement. It is an issue that must be addressed even when there is harmony between the person's behavior and church teaching. The practice of giving donations to charity is a good example of this. If I give regularly to a particular charity *only* because the local priest in his sermon says that I ought, then this cannot be regarded as entering into the realm of morality at all. Since I am doing so only because I am told to, then it cannot be said to be a truly ethical act. It involves the virtue of obedience and nothing more. My action and Christian teaching happen to coincide in this context. However, it does not arise out of a genuine decision to choose to do what is good. This is not to say that it has no value. To the charity receiving the donation the motivation of the person is usually irrelevant. However, when one is interested in the action in relation to the person who is performing it, motivation is a crucial factor. Obedient adherence to norms and principles, although perhaps admirable in itself, is not a substitute for a freely chosen, genuinely motivated decision.

In the Christian tradition, moral responsibility resides with the individual and cannot be circumvented by even the most precise and illuminating advice or teaching, regardless of the source. This is the case whether there is agreement or disagreement between the faithful and the magisterium. It is also the case even when the person is genuinely confused about the right decision in a particular context. Both laity and clergy become nervous when one speaks of this radical responsibility that we all share. We are each ambivalent about the moral authority that we possess. We are unsure about whether we want it or can cope with it. Often, we prefer to relocate the responsibility, to give it to the magisterium or to the pope or to the church. In short we often displace our moral authority and responsibility because it can seem to be too onerous to bear. Yet the Christian tradition of conscience has included an unambiguous assertion that each person has both the responsibility and the right to act according to his or her conscience in each and every situation. Moral norms and principles, together with the ongoing teaching of the church, mean that no individual is without significant help and support in this regard. But such resources, important though they are, can never replace the work of the conscience.

Chapter 5
Toward a Personalist Theology of Conscience

In the previous chapters I have argued for a personalist model of ethics. This model operates on the basis that ethical values derive their authority, not from some static and abstract notion of human nature but from their promotion of the good of the person "integrally and adequately considered."[1] This is the ethical model proposed in both *Gaudium et Spes* and in *Dignitatis humanae*. We have already identified some of the implications of moving to this personalist model. These include (1) a greater recognition of the role of history and change in ethics; (2) a focus on the moral significance of intentions and circumstances in addition to the act itself; (3) a greater degree of sophistication in categorizing the different kinds of moral norms and the kinds of claims they make; and (4) a rethinking of the relationship between the individual and magisterium on the basis of the relocation of moral authority. Each of the changes mentioned above will inevitably have an impact on the way in which the nature and role of conscience is understood. Some of these changes have already been alluded to. However, a coherent account of conscience against the backdrop of this personalist theology still needs to be developed. The purpose of this chapter is to begin that process.

In the first section we will focus on the renewed relationship between the person and her/his actions. This, above all else, is the most significant change in terms of understanding the role of conscience. In the second section we will develop a holistic account of the operations of conscience, which involves the interplay of reason, intuition, emotion and imagination. And in the final section we will explore the limits of human weakness and sinfulness as manifest in the failures of conscience.

Reconceiving the Relationship between Persons and Acts

The traditional understanding of conscience made use of the terms *habitual* and *actual* conscience. The term *habitual* referred to the innate sense of good and evil that all human beings are believed to possess. The term *actual* focused on the judgments of conscience in which such an orientation must be manifested. The habitual conscience corresponded to the term *synderesis* while the actual conscience corresponded to *conscientia.* It is clear from the deployment of such terminology that the traditional account of conscience, as it developed from the theology of St. Paul, had a dual orientation. It involved a focus on the fundamental orientation to the good, which *synderesis* encapsulated, and on the concrete decisions of conscience, which was the work of *conscientia.* However, as the discipline evolved, especially in the centuries when casuistry dominated, attention was ever more focused on the moral act. As a result the Thomistic integration of the habitual and actual dimensions of conscience gave way to a theology preoccupied with the morality of discrete, compartmentalized decisions. So, for example, theologians discussed the morality of contraception, of in vitro fertilization and of warfare, rather than focus on the character and values of the person who chose to use contraception or in vitro fertilization or who engaged in warfare. However, a personalist theology requires that attention be given, not only to actions, not only to the workings of the actual conscience, but also to the character of the person and to her/his orientation vis-à-vis good and evil. In traditional terms the spotlight is once again put on the workings of the habitual conscience. The crucial difference that personalism makes, therefore, is that it places the individual at the center of moral inquiry and understanding. In terms of a theology of conscience, then, the personalist model involves a radical change of emphasis and a reordering of the significance attached to acts and character.

In this new theological framework conscience denotes both the fundamental orientation of the person to seek and do the good, and the actualization of this desire in decisions of conscience. Conscience is thus understood to be more than the sum of particular decisions, although each choice is important. Conscience also refers to the integrated and consistent thrust of the person toward goodness. It is the dimension of one's character that determines the direction of one's moral life, one's self-conscious option for good. This kind of language can give a false impression of our reality as persons. It can suggest that the person is constituted by one singular and unitary narrative. In fact we are not at all like this. We do not possess an innate or essential freedom, as though freedom exists in some abstract or unambiguous way. Nor are our commitments necessarily always harmonious. In reality persons are constituted in a complex unity of fragmentary and varying narratives, commitments and values that change over time and that may pull us in different directions.

These issues of personal identity and subjectivity have been the subject of extensive investigations in recent decades. Feminist and postmodern theorists in particular have problematized the traditional liberal assumptions about personhood. Rosi Braidotti talks about persons as nomadic subjects, ever changing.[2] Judith Butler is reluctant to accept any unifying sense of personal identity at all, save as a performative strategy.[3] Others like Seyla Benhabib recognize that the self is in part socially constituted, fragmented and ultimately always in process. Yet Benhabib also insists that one can talk about a self and about personal identity, albeit in a provisional and partial manner.[4] The essentials of Benhabib's proposal underlie this discussion about conscience. When I speak about the nature of the person or about personal identity it is with a recognition that we are always persons in process and that our identities are multilayered, multiple, ambiguous and necessarily shaped by factors which are beyond either our consciousness or our control. The remit of conscience is thus expanded, to include both the (always incomplete) integrated moral character of the person, and the actions that flow from this and which embody her/his attraction to moral goodness.

This dual emphasis on the direction of the person's life and on the actions that she/he performs has become a cornerstone of the personalist model. The distinction was developed initially in order to rethink the theology of sin, which we will discuss in a later section of this chapter. The central claim is that a theology of sin should focus primarily on the basic direction of a person's life, on his or her fundamental option, rather than on individual acts of failure.[5] This theology of fundamental option, as it has come to be known, is also crucial for rethinking the nature of conscience. The fundamental option is the term given to the basic orientation of a person's life, either toward or against God. At the person's core she/he either responds to the loving invitation of God, or she/he refuses it. A life lived in the context of a "yes" response is a life oriented toward seeking goodness. A fundamental option that says no to such an invitation is directed away from this search. The theory of fundamental option then highlights that persons can be oriented toward good or evil, that they shape their characters in one direction or the other. Each person's fundamental option is actualized in the particular decisions that she/he makes and the virtues or vices that are cultivated. So, in relation to the conscience, it is not that every single decision is decisive, but rather that daily choices and ways of being, repeated over a lifetime, develop a pattern that reveal the person's fundamental option for good or for evil. In effect the theory of fundamental option ascribes significance primarily to the moral character of the person and directs our attention to the general sensitivity and maturity of conscience. The decisions and judgments of the actual conscience are thus regarded as a reflection of the person's fundamental option and are of significance primarily in this regard.

Many moral theologians have adopted and developed the theory of fundamental option. Bernard Häring, Josef Fuchs and Karl Rahner each have based their theological reflections on the idea that human beings, at their core, opt either for a life lived in the direction of goodness or of evil.[6] Although they each have used different reasoning and terminology to analyze the fundamental option, the central tenets of each explanation are the same. We will use Rahner's analysis to discuss workings of the fundamental option in relation to conscience, but we could as easily use that of either Fuchs or Häring. Rahner suggested that one could think of human freedom as having two distinct dimensions. He distinguished between what he called the transcendental level of freedom and the categorical level.[7] According to Rahner human beings possess a basic freedom, a fundamental and deep-rooted freedom, which enables us to determine ourselves as persons. At this level freedom is not about deciding between particular acts or objects; it is concerned with one's entire orientation and direction in life. This is the person's transcendental freedom. In Rahner's theology the choice at this level is either the acceptance of a loving relationship with God or a refusal of it. Fuchs terms this the person's basic freedom. It is on the basis of this transcendental freedom that the person decides her/his fundamental option and determines whether it is for good or bad.

The choice made at the transcendental level shapes completely the moral character of the person and becomes the basis on which the person exercises choice and makes decisions. Rahner calls the daily exercise of choice categorical freedom, in which the person makes decisions on the basis of the options that are before her/him. The free decisions of conscience exercised in everyday situations are vital, because it is in and through each of these distinct choices that the person concretizes her/his fundamental option. Through these free choices, at the categorical level, the person realizes and implements the fundamental option for good or evil. Thus, there is a dialectic in operation here. The person's fundamental option is actualized and reinforced by what Iris Murdoch called the ongoing "acts of attention"[8] to the good. These small, often insignificant acts in which we exercise our freedom are the primary way in which we demonstrate the orientation of our moral lives. They become the incarnation of our fundamental option.

But the choices and decisions a person makes in everyday life not only express the fundamental option, they also reinforce it. This is a point that many proponents of the fundamental option did not emphasize sufficiently. In my view it is unhelpful to conceptualize the fundamental option as radically distinct from and prior to the discrete moments of choosing. Instead, one should think of the person's fundamental option as always in process, as never fully determined once and for all. Rather, it is created in repeated moments of choosing the good over a lifetime. Decisions of conscience, then, are not merely reflections of the person's fundamental option. It is in and through the choices made, both at significant moments in one's life and in the daily routine of minor "acts of attention," that the person determines her/his basic orientation. It is also in the ways we relate to others and our way of being in the world that our fundamental option is cultivated. Earlier theories of fundamental option did not give due attention to the role that categorical freedom plays in constructing the fundamental option. One always got the impression that the person's basic direction or fundamental option was decided at some abstract level, at some time before the person had to make concrete ethical decisions. However, such a view is completely at odds with the experience of the moral life. People do not choose to be oriented to the good in theory at some transcendental level and then go on to make decisions on the basis of that fundamental option. Nor does this happen in a way that disregards the complex psychological makeup of human beings. Rather, imperceptibly over time, in and through the choices they make and the kinds of dispositions and virtues they nurture, people form their moral characters and thereby determine the orientation of their fundamental option. Thus, the person's fundamental option is created in making choices and cultivating virtues and is reaffirmed through the repetition of such behavior.

The precise details of the various theories of fundamental option need not detain us here. The primary purpose in discussing it is to suggest a framework in which to think about the relationship between the character of the person and the choices she/he makes. What is suggested by this is an understanding of conscience as the person's orientation to and desire for goodness. However, this orientation toward goodness can only be actualized in the constant and continuous cultivation of a virtuous character. Of course given the fragile and ambiguous nature of our search for moral goodness,[9] this orientation should not be conceptualized as a single and simple trajectory. In her excellent study *The Fragility of Goodness*[10] Martha Nussbaum reminds us of our limitations as we seek to articulate and live by that which we believe to be good. Our orientation toward "the good" is more appropriately imaged as a stream making its circuitous and uncertain way toward its as yet unknown destination, rather than as an arrow in flight. It needs to take account of the fact that people change and that what seemed to be a good choice in the past may not seem to be so now. Yet, given these limitations, this is an understanding of conscience that sees an intimate connection between the kind of person one is and the actions one performs. It recognizes that the formation of conscience takes place, not by some superficial adherence to rules and laws but rather in working toward goodness rather than evil or indifference in every context, no matter how trivial. It is the way in which these discrete moments of choosing are patterned together that determines the strength and the maturity of conscience. It is through the person's conscience, therefore, that one can see the unity and coherence of the moral character.

We form our consciences over time. We affirm our fundamental convictions through the decisions we have made in the past and the virtues we embody in the present. The mature conscience develops in the attempt to be virtuous and make decisions that further reinforce and continue that pattern.

The good conscience, then, is not merely the sum total of good choices made over time. Rather, it is the disposition or orientation to desire good and is the culmination of a life lived consistently in the pursuit of virtue. The focus on the fundamental option enables one to think of conscience as a continuous process, as an orientation embodied in different contexts and related, not only to past and present, but also to the person's future. This conceptualization of conscience gives most attention to the way in which moments of choosing and ways of relating are patterned into a unity that is the moral self. It allows one to expand discussions of conscience to include considerations of how the emotions, intuitions and imagination of the person shape the moral character. It also focuses attention on the role that the wider community (both secular and religious) has in forming the orientation of the conscience. In short it requires us to abandon the reductionism characteristic of an earlier theology, which was concerned primarily with acts and with specific, unconnected decisions of conscience.

The role of moral communities will be considered at length in chapter 6. However, it is necessary to mention their significance in the formation of conscience at this stage. It is obvious that individuals attempt to orient themselves toward good and form their moral characters within the context of a community or communities. The social context within which a person operates inevitably has a major influence on the conscience. Leonardo Boff, in his book *Liberating Grace,*[11] developed a convincing argument for the strong interrelation between the individual's fundamental project and the society to which she/he belongs. It is not that we are completely socially determined. Of course people can and do resist the expectations and norms of behavior that a society may impose on them. However, the values and virtues that a society embodies do play an important role in the formation of conscience. This is true of the limitations and moral blindness of communities and will be important in our discussion of moral failure. But it is also true of the cultivation of positive dispositions.

The values and virtues that shape a person's conscience arise from beliefs about how the good is constituted and how it can be sought. These convictions—such as, it is good to honor the promises one makes or to deal with people honestly—are present in the society's moral code and are conveyed to the individual in a variety of ways. In the same way as a child learns to belong to a linguistic community, so, too, it learns about moral conduct. This moral development takes place at both the formal and informal levels. Parental guidance, school instruction and moral education in religious communities are very important factors in the formation of conscience. But the stories, narratives and traditions of a community are also vital vehicles of moral codes. These operate at a more informal level but are no less significant for that. Stories of moral exemplars, accounts of moral heroism, articulations of a community's moral vision—each play a part in the development of the individual's conscience. The conscience is formed in community. The individual does not construct her/his basic orientation from a tabula rasa. Rather, the person's conscience is shaped within a received tradition, which conveys its sense of moral goodness in a variety of ways. But no matter how regulatory the community or society may be, the responsibility for educating and nurturing the conscience rests ultimately with the individual.

The Inward Dynamics of Conscience

The formation of conscience involves many aspects of the person. It cannot be reduced to tutoring reason and developing intellectual sophistication. Although reason does indeed have a vital role to play in the activity of conscience, so too have intuition, emotion and imagination. Conscience needs an interplay of each of these elements to operate sensitively and successfully. We make choices by attending to and evaluating our responses at a variety of different levels. Good, integrated and fully personal decisions engage the individual at the intellectual, intuitive, emotional and imaginative levels. Good choices reflect a coherence of these important aspects of the personality so that no one level is ignored or silenced. So, far from being objective, dispassionate judgments of reason, decisions of conscience are embodied and emotional, engaging the whole person and not just the intellect.

A personalist model of conscience should highlight the multidimensional aspects of its decision making. When the focus is directed away from the morality of isolated acts and toward the person who performs these acts, then the person's motivations, dispositions, feelings and intuitions gain tremendous significance. Individuals do not engage in decisions of "pure reason." However, much of Western philosophy and theology operated with the view that "the subject is rational and objective only to the extent that it is disengaged from natural and social worlds and *even* from its own body which then can be seen as an object of study and a source of deception."[12] This clearly is an untenable view of the person. Charles Taylor in his *Sources of the Self* [13] has mapped both the emergence and demise of this punctual self, that is, the self who is "rational, free, but languageless, cultureless, history-less...."[14] In contrast the person at the center of this theology of conscience is not an abstract mind, but a person who is located in culture and history, one who is relational, embodied and ultimately in progress. Of course this self can and must engage in rational inquiry; however, it is a contextual rationality. Indeed, philosophy since Nietzsche has recognized that the idea of pure reason is a myth. Reason is one aspect of our personhood and as such reflects the particularities and limitations of our contexts. In this discussion of the role of reason in the moral life of the person, rationality is understood as embodied and contextual, shaped by the conventions of culture, by religious sensibilities, by desires both conscious and unconscious, by imaginings and fears. Although it is usually difficult to disentangle the complexities of the inward workings of conscience, it is important to discuss, however briefly, the contribution of these elements.

Reason

This is the element in the activity of conscience that has traditionally been given most attention. Indeed, it does play a central role in identifying the nature of problems of conscience and in evaluating possible solutions. I certainly do not want to underestimate the role of reason in decision making, but I do want to emphasize that reason is always contextual. It reflects the presuppositions, values and limitations of our culture, time and place. It is inevitably shaped and tutored by the person's intuitions and emotions. Reason's contribution to the activity of conscience cannot be limited to one particular phase. From the time the person becomes aware of the existence of some kind of dilemma until its resolution, reason may have a contribution to make. Its ultimate role is to help us find a solution internally coherent and consistent with "the bigger picture," notwithstanding the fact that our understanding is always limited and our knowledge always incomplete. The task of providing resolutions both internally coherent and consistent with our general framework of understanding is not an easy one.

One of the most important roles that reason has in moral decision making relates to defining the problem or the issue at stake. This is absolutely crucial since many ethical disagreements arise because people differ about the nature of a problem or indeed whether a particular issue has any ethical significance at all. Take, for example, two businesspeople involved in a company takeover, which results in the loss of two hundred jobs in one small town. One businessman may believe himself to have some responsibility for the employees of the company and may be in a dilemma as to what should be done for them. Should they set up a fund to help the former employees retrain for other jobs? Should they try to enhance the local economy in other ways? Should they compensate the workers beyond the minimal redundancy payments to which they are legally entitled? The other businesswoman may believe that they have no additional responsibilities to the work force over and above those required by law. She may be sorry that economic realities mean that they cannot have as large a work force as the former employers. She may regret that the region is so dependent on that particular company. She may feel genuinely sorry for the people who have lost their jobs. However, all this notwithstanding, she may believe that there is no ethical dilemma to be resolved.

These two businesspeople disagree about whether they have some duty to the former work force and the community affected by their takeover. One does not believe that they have a moral problem; the other does. Identifying and defining the problem is thus the first (often contentious) stage in decision making. Reason has an important role in this process since it accumulates all the evidence, identifies which factors are relevant and scrutinizes the logic of the arguments. This may result in one person changing his mind about the nature of the problem or may lead to the problem being redefined altogether. Of course at various stages the precise nature and scope of the moral problem may again need to be reconceived. We may discover dimensions of the problem that we never envisaged initially. This constant revision of the nature of the problem is itself an integral part of its resolution.

An in-depth discussion of the nature of rationality and its role in the moral life is neither possible nor appropriate at this stage. Suffice it to say that it has been the object of much inquiry through the centuries. Alisdair MacIntyre is one of the many philosophers and theologians concerned with the changing concepts of rationality in ethics.[15] As with the changing understanding of the self, the consensus among many ethicians is that rationality is always historical and contextual. What appears as rational to us is bound in a significant way to our personal histories, community narratives and symbol systems. Terence McCaughey in his groundbreaking *Memory and Redemption* illustrates this point excellently in the context of the Northern Irish conflict.[16] In this work he discusses the profound impact that a community's traditions and symbols can have in shaping what is perceived to be rational. The rational does not exist apart from these contingencies of place, history and culture, but within them. Furthermore, this does not represent the failure of reason, but rather is part of its nature.

For our purposes, however, it is important to note that reason demands that we concern ourselves with issues of "consistency, logic, rules of evidence, appropriateness, coherence, clarity, completeness and congruence with received reality and meaning."[17] Consistency requires that we try to maintain the same standards throughout the whole process of making the decision. Logic points to the need for our thinking to follow a clear and sequential form of argumentation. It helps us to guard against drawing conclusions that are insupportable on the basis of the preceding evidence. The "rules of evidence" remind us to test all our conclusions so that we take care not to include factors that cannot be justified. Reason also necessitates that we search for and include all relevant evidence and that we give to each element the appropriate weight and importance. It also requires that we conduct our arguments with clarity and an internal coherence. We should attempt to ensure that our resolution should not contain any major contradictions. Furthermore, the way in which a particular problem is solved should not contradict what we know to be generally true of our experience of the world and our relationships. For example, if I resolve a problem in a way that leads me to assume that every single person that I have come in contact with over my lifetime has been lying to me, then I need to reexamine my own thinking, since such a conclusion is at odds with what I have experienced heretofore. The solution to my moral problem ought not to be wildly incongruous with the rest of reality.

The significant role that reason performs is evident right through the whole decision-making process. In addition to defining and redefining the nature of the problem, reason plays its part in gathering and evaluating relevant information, judging whether some factors are irrelevant, proposing solutions, assessing their worth in the situation at hand and in relation to the larger context. The work of reason, therefore, involves the person in a constant appraisal of every aspect of the problem and not just a once-for-all judgment. Although such rational decisions are ultimately personal, they must be made with reference to the wider community. When faced with a moral problem we should also investigate how other rational and informed individuals have resolved similar difficulties. We must test the adequacy of our own reasoning and argumentation in the wider domain. It is not sufficient that we are satisfied with the logic and coherence of our analysis. We must be prepared to scrutinize it in public, to seek the advice of friends and to evaluate our own reasoning in the light of the values of moral and religious communities. In short, reason itself requires that we test the adequacy of our rationality by comparing it with that of other thoughtful individuals and communities and by assessing it honestly.

Of course there can be difficulties. Incomplete or inaccurate information can make the reasoning process problematic and can result in unsustainable judgments. We may have assumed that certain individuals will act in a particular way and then find out that they do the opposite. We may depend on particular results that don't materialize or we may ignore the fact that much of the relevant data is missing. But in addition to difficulties that arise in relation to the information needed to make decisions, our rational capacity may also be impaired. Various forms of mental illness, including psychosis and delusions of many sorts, make the kind of thoughtful analysis essential to decision making well nigh impossible. The effects of such limitations can be seen in the many instances of moral failure and self-deception that we encounter daily. These will be discussed in more detail later in the chapter. For the moment, however, it is important to note the central role that reason plays in decisions of conscience and the difficulties that arise from its failures.

Intuition

Making decisions of conscience involves evaluating information of various kinds and not just that which we have acquired through the process of reason. Much of the knowledge we have comes to us from sources that are not strictly intellectual. We tend to class knowledge of this sort as intuitive. By describing something as intuitive we generally mean that we cannot test it by purely intellectual means. It is knowledge that we have instinctively. It is not consciously acquired, but is nonetheless known to us in some indefinable way. I can have an intuition not to trust an individual whom I have recently met. I may not be able to articulate why I am hesitant to trust that person. Yet, I may know instinctively that something is amiss. The essence of an intuition is that it comes to us from a nonconscious place. It is not part of our explicit awareness. We make judgments and decisions on the basis of such tacit knowledge all the time. Our instincts—about the reliability of people, about the eventual outcome of events outside our control, about the way relationships are likely to develop and about many other things—are important sources of information in our moral lives. But although intuitive knowledge by its very nature is unconscious, it is amenable to analysis and evaluation.

The person often experiences intuitions as surprising, as being outside conscious awareness. Yet, even though this may be true superficially, if one investigates it carefully one can usually account for an intuition. Let us take the intuition not to trust a particular person one has recently met. If we scrutinize all our encounters with that individual, we are likely to come up with an explanation for our intuition. It may be that she has been indiscreet about someone she knows or that she has made fun of another person's scruples or that she seems cavalier about people's feelings. Although our encounter with the person may have been perfectly pleasant, one may have picked up something almost imperceptible about the person's behavior that results in the intuition not to trust her. Intuitions usually do have some basis in actual experience. They are rarely completely arbitrary and random. They usually result from being sensitive to the behavior of another person or from conclusions drawn from actions in another context.

Women are generally said to be more intuitive than men. Their intuition is frequently referred to as a sixth sense. If women are more intuitive, it is not because of some biologically rooted, gender-specific faculty. Rather, it may come, as most intuitive insight does, from more careful attention to gestures, reactions, unspoken assumptions and valuations. People reveal a great deal about themselves and their priorities without ever intending to. Intuition is usually based on knowledge and insights gained through sensitivity to all that is implicit and nonconscious in other people's behavior. It may well be that women tend to be more attentive to such things. However, although intuition may be nonconscious knowledge, it cannot remain unexamined. It is never enough simply to act on intuition without evaluating it in the light of our experiences. Intuition can be a very valuable resource for decisions of conscience. It can encourage us to take an unpopular stand on some issue, or it can make one wary of potential but unseen treachery. In short it can operate both as a source of creative insight or as an early-warning signal. However, in order that it does not function simply to reinforce one's prejudices and blind spots, its adequacy must be evaluated.

Our intuition can be affected by a number of complex processes. Memories, dreams, emotions, suppressed experiences and anxieties all contribute to this unconscious knowledge. Sometimes their involvement means that intuition may be mistaken or unreliable. At other times they help explain why someone has come to have such a perception. It is precisely because intuitions are so intimately related to other similarly unreflective elements in the personality that they need to be assessed in many ways, including by the rational, conscious processes of the mind. I may not be able to articulate why I am uneasy in the presence of a particular person or with a course of action, but I can devise ways to identify whether such intuitions are warranted or not. Many of the criteria that have already been mentioned in relation to the operations of reason may also come into play when evaluating the reliability of intuitions. One has to determine if the intuition is well founded, if the conclusions drawn from it are warranted, if this intuition is consistent with the rest of one's beliefs and values, if the normal requirements of evidence are fulfilled. When we are convinced that our intuitions have a reliable basis, then they are a most valuable source of moral knowledge. Intuitive responses to moral dilemmas can cause one to attend to often forgotten or ignored values and can highlight neglected dimensions of the moral life. Many innovative and life-changing insights have occurred because of individuals acting on their intuitive sense of goodness and justice. The key to their reliability, however, rests on the ability of the person to articulate the reasons why such intuitive knowledge ought to be trusted. This clearly points to the integrated activity of conscience.

Emotion

Contemporary psychological theory and practice indicates that the nature of a person's emotional life is highly complex. Psychologists disagree with one another on almost every aspect of this affective dimension of human experience. There are debates about when a person's emotional responses are learned, whether they can be said to be fixed and constant or whether they are subject to continual revision. There are also debates about whether they can be controlled and whether one can ignore or suppress emotions without some serious psychological consequences. Freudians, for example, identify early infant experience and development as the crucial and often definitive stage in forming and tutoring an individual's emotional life. Others disagree with the weight given to this early infant stage and endorse a more progressive and developmental model of the emotions. Important though they are, these debates cannot be the focus of our attention.

If one were to engage in a comprehensive analysis of the nature and role of emotions in the moral life, then one would need to discuss and come to some conclusions on these and related questions. This is certainly work that needs to be done and would greatly enhance our understanding of the detailed workings of conscience. However, our purpose here is to insist that the emotions do have an essential role in the activity of conscience and to suggest that our understanding of conscience will be seriously flawed if their contribution (both positive and negative) is not appreciated.

There is common misconception that emotion hampers rather than facilitates ethical discernment. Such a misconception is based on thinking of the emotions as essentially irrational and involuntary, that is, outside the person's control. However, such a view seriously misunderstands the nature of the emotions and of reason and misconceives the relationship between the two. The multifaceted activity of conscience has often been incorrectly perceived as primarily or even exclusively an intellectual endeavor. However, the emotions, too, play a very prominent role in the work of conscience. In the same way as intuition is not an activity of reason but still must be evaluated, so too with the emotions. They may often be involuntary. I may feel envious at the success of a colleague even though I consciously wish him well. I may have a great desire to be liked and accepted by a particular person although I am not comfortable with his values. But although emotional responses may be generated from a place outside the governance of the intellect, this does not mean that emotions are beyond our voluntary recognition and control. Emotions can be evaluated and accepted in much the same way as intuition is.

We can examine our emotional responses and discover whether particular reactions and feelings should be acted upon or whether they should be rejected as unwarranted or inappropriate. I do not want to suggest that the emotional life ought to be determined by rational concerns. Such an approach would be a denial of the vital role that the emotions play in the apprehension of right and wrong. But neither do I want to suggest a model of the ethical life that views the operations of reason and the emotions as completely separate from or even in opposition to each other. Instead, one should think of the emotions as providing important information and insight for moral deliberation, information that cannot be accessed without reflecting on our emotions. However, the key factor here is that we must reflect on these emotions, we must engage critically with them so that we can be confident that the information they provide is reliable.

One can see how true this is by thinking about all that is involved in making a difficult ethical decision. Important decisions of conscience are usually accompanied by a high degree of emotional intensity. If a young unmarried woman finds herself with an unplanned pregnancy, she has to decide very quickly how she is going to deal with it. The decision she will have to make will have to be contemplated amid a range of unexpected, random and often confused emotions. All sorts of problems will confound and pressurize her. Possibilities will arise in a partial and rather confused manner. She will probably be on an emotional roller coaster, with her feelings changing from one day to the next. She will initially have to choose whether to continue with the pregnancy or not. If she decides to have an abortion, many of her subsequent choices will depend on whether abortion is legally available to her and if so, under which conditions. Will she flout the law and look for a so-called back-street abortionist? Will she go to another jurisdiction? Will she invent some psychological trauma in order to convince doctors to allow an abortion on mental grounds? How will she cope with the aftermath? Will she tell her family? Will she tell the father of the child? In any case is it morally acceptable to be thinking in this way? Is she destroying an innocent life? If she has an abortion, is she murdering a child? On the other hand, if she decides to go ahead with the pregnancy what is in store for her? Should she have the child adopted? If she decides on adoption, what kind of life will her child have? Will the child be raised in an institution? Will he be raised by unsuitable parents? Will he be happy and properly cared for? How will he feel about being adopted? How will he regard his birth mother? Will he come looking for her sometime in the future? Again, should she tell the father that his child will be adopted? What if he objects? But if she decides to raise the child herself, how will she manage? Will she be giving her child the best possible context in which to flourish? Will she be able to support him financially? How will her family react? Will she be putting her job in jeopardy? Will this mean she will be giving up any hope of a future relationship and family? Will her child be discriminated against or ridiculed? Should she involve the baby's father in the child-rearing process, even if she regards him as an inappropriate parent?

Although it is not at all clear what a good resolution of the problem might be for her, it is very obvious that the woman's emotional reactions will play a major part in the process. Emotions—which range from occasional excitement and anticipation, to distress, anger, anxiety about the future, shame and guilt—each has an effect on the decision-making process. In some respects a particular emotion may hamper the resolution of a moral problem. For example, a woman may be so ashamed about being pregnant and unmarried that she may not even consider having the baby, even though deep down that is what she wants to do. She may decide to have an abortion because she could not cope with the shame that she would bring upon herself and her family. On the other hand one's emotional responses may help clarify one's priorities and values. She might decide to acknowledge her mild excitement at the prospect of being a mother and go ahead with the pregnancy, even though conditions are not ideal.

Emotions are spontaneous. We cannot decide how we feel. But we can decide whether and how we are going to act on these emotions. What is most evident, however, is that our emotional reactions are part and parcel of our moral deliberation. The dilemma of what I am to do if I face an unplanned pregnancy has to be confronted in the midst of strong, often conflicting, emotions. The questions I ask myself, the options I am willing to consider and the decision I ultimately come to—all of these are mediated through the filter of my emotions. The fact that I might not consider adoption may be motivated primarily by the fear that someday I may come face-to-face with my child and explain why I gave him away.

But of course one's ethical decisions cannot be completely determined by emotional responses. Part of the process of making a decision of conscience (especially one that is emotionally charged) involves reflecting on such responses. In order for my emotions to be integrated into the decision-making process, I must recognize and acknowledge them. I must try not to deceive myself about the reason for dismissing the option of adoption. I must ask myself if fear of confronting one's child at some time in the future is a good enough reason for dismissing this course of action. In short, I must evaluate my emotional reactions and consider how much importance I should attach to them when making my decision. Evaluation is of a similar kind to that associated with intuition. Are my emotions coherent, proportionate to the situation and consistent with other aspects of my life? Are they reasonable and supportable, or are they illogical and exaggerated?

There is evidence to suggest that, just as a person's rational and intellectual capacities can be impaired, so too, one's emotional life can be limited in significant ways. Such kinds of dysfunction are often responsible for serious moral failure. Inappropriate or disproportionate emotions, lack of control of one's emotions or sometimes the absence of any emotion can lead to unethical behavior. This and other aspects of moral failure will be considered later in the chapter. Clearly, we cannot decide in advance how we are going to feel about a particular event. Indeed, we may be surprised by our feelings, or by their force. But this does not mean that we should slavishly follow our feelings or that we are prisoners to our emotional reactions. The process of making holistic and integrated decisions of conscience involves an interplay of reason and emotion. Reason shapes and evaluates the emotions; emotion contextualizes and gives dynamism to reason. Neither ought to be abandoned, nor should one be considered marginal or peripheral.

Imagination

In some respects this is the most difficult aspect of the integrated activity of conscience to discuss. The operations of the imagination are nebulous and its influence is hard to quantify. We engage our imaginations when we try to come to a decision about what to do in a particular situation. We can imagine different scenarios that would result from various options. We can wonder what a person we admire would do in the same circumstances. We can think about how we will regard the decision in the future. Will we be proud of it, or will we wish we had taken an alternative course of action? Employing one's imagination in this fashion means looking at one's own activity and choices as an outsider would and appraising them on the basis of the decisions made. This involves gaining some critical distance from the problem to be solved. This is often difficult, especially if it is a problem involving great emotional investment. Nonetheless, the imaginative, abstract stage can be very important in allowing one to see possibilities that are not immediately obvious. One's imagination also enables one to view the problem from the perspective of others who may be somehow involved. It helps one to think about how others may be affected, how they might feel, what they might fear or why they might be behaving in a particular manner. By entering their world and experiencing their concerns vicariously we can have a more complete understanding of what may be involved. This is particularly true if a moral problem results in the breakdown of communication between the parties involved. Often, one may not come to appreciate the other person's perspective. Imagination here takes the place of listening.

It can also be vital in situations where one is making a decision that will have far-reaching consequences for people one has never met. Again, engaging imaginatively with their world and their concerns can allow one to empathize with them and to take their interests seriously.

The person's creativity and imagination play a significant role in the moral realm, not only in relation to decisions of conscience made in the present, but also in forming the person's moral character. Here the imagination can cultivate different values, can encourage a person to be more courageous in the pursuit of her/his moral vision and can allow one to confront and then go beyond the boundaries of one's moral heritage. This kind of change and development is vital if any moral tradition or community is to flourish. The process of reevaluating one's commitments and redescribing one's reality is part of the process of being human. As we gain more understanding of ourselves and our world and as we learn from our own and others' moral failures, we need to confront the partiality of our own perspective. Imaginative engagement with other cultures, religious traditions and moral communities can help us to identify the blind spots in our own. So too can creative encounters with literature, drama and art, inspire us to imagine different possibilities for ourselves and our moral communities. Far from being redundant in the moral field, one's imagination helps to articulate one's sense of virtue and enables one to engage in the vital task of constantly renewing one's moral vision.

Conscience and Spiritual Discernment

As is evident from our discussion of the inward dynamics of conscience, the process of decision making is not an exclusively rational one. In addition to reason the person's emotions, intuitions and imagination are involved. So also for Christians is the capacity for spiritual discernment, which has a crucial role to play in the moral life. Christians believe that within the conscience each person has an inner source of moral evaluation. However, it is not entirely reliant on the individual's personal resources. It is also an inner source informed by faith and shaped under the guidance of the spirit.

In *The Making of Moral Theology* Mahoney reminds his readers that the importance of spiritual discernment was part of the traditional Christian understanding of conscience from the earliest centuries. He characterizes it in terms of a Johannine tendency to emphasize "the role of the spirit as internal teacher of all the faithful (and, indeed, of all men)."[18] Over the centuries for various reasons the role of the spirit became associated mainly with the passive reception of magisterial teaching[19] and has only recently been reemphasized, primarily in the texts of Vatican II. However, again as Mahoney argues,[20] it was highly significant in Aquinas's discussions of the role of conscience. Aquinas operated with a theological framework that emphasized the unity of the moral and spiritual realms. He did not regard reason and spiritual discernment to be separate; rather, he thought of them as reflecting aspects of the integrated unity of the person. As a result the rationalism that characterized the later Thomistic tradition is absent in the theology of Aquinas.

As a process of spiritual discernment, the evaluations of conscience involve an element of prayerful reflection and stillness. These are important ways by which the person comes to a deep-seated awareness of the virtues one seeks to cultivate and to embody in one's life. And although there is "a personal uniqueness and a human solitariness about the exercise of conscience,"[21] there is also a sense that this human endeavour is all the while worked at "in the shadow of the spirit." Or, as Mahoney suggests, the conscience is important in discovering where the spirit is leading individuals in response to the call of God in the context of an overall vocation.[22]

Of course we need to engage in a reflective process to help us authenticate the insights arising from this process of discernment, this interior resource, which in the Christian tradition is often spoken of metaphorically as the voice of God. This suggests that the moral insight that comes from genuine and prayerful spiritual reflection forms a significant part of the Christian understanding of conscience. Mahoney describes this interior moral discernment in terms of a taste or a feel for that which is good in a particular context. It is difficult to describe and still more difficult to have confidence in. Indeed, Mahoney recognizes the ambiguities inherent in this process of discernment when he acknowledges that "the moral 'feel' for a situation which Christians are believed to possess by reason of their personal adhesion of faith may be unashamedly of the character of insight in search of arguments or, in terms more generally applicable to theology as a whole, of Christian experience seeking understanding."[23]

Moral Failure

The formation of conscience is a delicate and complex process. It involves the integration of the intellectual and emotional capacities of the individual, together with a commitment to confront one's limitations and weaknesses. The conscience engages the reason, intuition, emotions and imagination of the person. However, distortions can occur at any or all of these levels. Likewise, the process of integrating these dimensions can be problematic. As a result we live with both the history and the prospect of moral failure. Most people experience failure through some kind of dysfunction. Our capacity to make or to carry through good moral decisions can be restricted because some dimension of our ethical discernment may fail. We may be confused or divided over what is in fact good. Our reason may be clouded. Our emotions may be out of control or we may be afraid of the leap of imagination required to resolve a particular problem.

Although the possible reasons for moral failure are innumerable and extremely complex, we must mention at least some of the most common reasons for moral failure and sin. Given that reason plays such an important role in the successful activity of conscience, anything that impairs a person's capacity for rational thinking will obviously have an impact on the working of conscience. Our reason assesses every dimension of the decision-making process. It evaluates not only the evidence before us, but also our own intuitive and emotional responses. It is directed, therefore, not only toward judging external factors, but is also involved in the self-assessment necessary for the mature and honest operations of conscience. There are, of course, many ways in which our capacity to make rational decisions may be stunted. Indeed, many of the failures of reason have to do with our limited or incomplete knowledge and understanding of a situation. Factors that were not considered at the time of the decision may take on great significance with hindsight. We constantly make decisions in situations where we have to act in the face of uncertainty or without all the information we know to be relevant. These gaps in our understanding can, at times, turn out to be so significant that they result in the wrong decision being made. At other times they turn out not to be relevant. At any rate we have to engage in this reasoning process, even though we are aware of lacunae in our knowledge. Other limitations necessarily arise from the incomplete and provisional nature of reason itself. As we have already discussed earlier, our capacity for rationality is inevitably bound up with our histories, communities, symbol systems and narratives. Insofar as these can lead us to ignore important factors or to fail to give attention to an alternative perspective, then these, too, can impair our decision making.

However, apart from these routine difficulties, individuals can experience complications of a far more serious nature. These relate to the functioning of a person's mental capacities and can range from various forms of retardation to neurotic or childish behavior. Although this territory only really came under scrutiny in the late nineteenth and twentieth centuries with the advent of psychology, theologians through the centuries recognized that a person's capacity for rational moral thought can be impaired. Aquinas, for example, spoke of *amentia* and *dementia* (any kind of insanity resulting from the failure of a person's mental powers) as conditions that make it impossible for the person to engage in moral decision making. According to Aquinas and those who followed in the Thomistic tradition, these conditions also limit the moral responsibility of the person. Obviously, modern psychology has taught us a great deal about the failure of a person's rational capacities. Distorted or erratic thinking may be the result of a number of psychological disorders or psychoses. Various forms of brain disease, depression and repressed traumas can seriously damage the person's ability to make good and rational moral decisions.

In the same way, a person's emotional life can also be defective. This, too, can have a serious impact on the ability to make good decisions of conscience. The limitations of a person's emotional engagement can often be more difficult to identify and its effects harder to quantify. Of course to a certain extent we all experience various forms of emotional impairment or dysfunction. If we scrutinize our daily emotional life we can see that it is frequently confused and ambiguous. We experience ambivalent feelings. Our emotional responses can be disproportionate or inappropriate. For example, one can be extremely angry at a friend for what may be a superficial indiscretion, or one might feel full of self-pity over a minor disappointment. One's emotions might also be childish or immature, leading one to perform actions one knows to be wrong. Or, indeed, one might tend to a surfeit or excess of emotion, which distorts one's responses and therefore one's decisions. This can often be the case in instances of high drama or in unanticipated situations. As a result the decision a person makes may, with the luxury of hindsight and once the emotions have become more stable, turn out to be flawed. Excessive or disproportionate emotions may thus distort decision making.

Individuals can also display a lack of emotional response that threatens the successful operation of conscience. This is a complex psychological condition that can manifest itself in a variety of ways. In moral decision making a degree of emotional engagement is essential. It is one of the most important ways in which an individual conveys her/his priorities and values. If I feel no outrage or sorrow at some terrible injustice or violence or if I feel no love or friendship for those who are closest to me, then I am unlikely to be able to respond appropriately in situations of moral choice. Good and genuine emotional responses are essential to leading a successful moral life. Of course a stable emotional life is not something that can be achieved once for all, but rather is a constant process of negotiation and reflection. It is the work of a lifetime. Nonetheless if the emotions are seriously impaired or absent, then all sorts of excesses are possible. Many of the most heinous acts of individuals and of groups have been perpetrated because the emotional responses of those involved were lacking. As a result they felt no guilt or shame, nor did they feel any empathy with, or sympathy for, their victims. Such psychopathic behavior highlights the significant link between the failure of the emotions and moral disorder. It points to the central role of the emotions in the moral life and the severe disruption that impairment at this level can occasion.

In addition to the failure of reason and emotion, there can also be occasions when the person's intuitions may be wrong or when she/he may not be courageous enough to act imaginatively. Sinfulness results from failure on many levels. We can be incorrect in terms of what we decide to do. Dysfunctional reasoning or skewed emotional responses can lead us to do something that we know to be wrong. For example, I can know that it is wrong to deliberately tell an untruth about a particular person, but may do so because I am jealous of her success. But I can also fail in terms of why I decide on a particular course of action. My motivation and intentions may be dishonorable, even though the action itself may be admirable. For example, a colleague may be in trouble and I might go out of my way to help him. However, I might do so in a very public way. My primary motivation may not be to help a friend in distress, but to be seen as kind and caring. The act itself may be good but the reason why it is performed may be dubious.

Much of our moral failure comes from various kinds of inner conflict and weakness. We may be aware of our negative emotions or of our clouded reasoning, and yet we choose to follow what we know to be the wrong course of action. We are, ourselves, fragmented. We experience contradictions within ourselves and we succumb to temptations of various kinds. Our desire for success, wealth or influence can lead us to disregard other things we know to be valuable, such as relationships or family. Our wish for an uncontroversial or quiet life may lead us to ignore the wrongdoings of others or to comply with them. The sinful or wrong behavior of individuals who generally strive to lead good lives can often be the result of conflicting instincts or desires. The struggle to overcome selfishness, cowardice or inertia often fails, and we find ourselves engaged in activities we know to be wrong or avoiding the things we know to be right. Of course these failings can be extremely serious, or they can be less so. The Catholic tradition distinguishes between sinful behavior in terms of mortal and venial sins. This terminology highlights the fact that some kinds of moral failure can be so serious and can involve such a degree of personal investment in wrongdoing as to completely undermine the moral goodness of a person. Known as mortal sin, this involves three distinct elements. First, the act itself must be very serious; second, the person must choose to do it with the full knowledge of what she/he is doing; and finally the person must be doing it freely, without coercion, that is, with full consent. Venial sin involves wrongdoing of a far less serious kind.

Of course individuals can also engage in wrongdoing, not because of inner conflict and weakness, but because of deliberately choosing evil. This is very difficult to comprehend and, I think, quite rare in human experience. Nonetheless, it often accounts for some of the worst excesses of human behavior. There have been, and are, individuals who avow a disdain for all morality, who delight in disregarding even the most basic requirements of ethics and who set themselves up as the absolute arbiters of their own (and, if possible, others') behavior. The actions of Adolf Hitler are often understood in this way, but of course there have been many others through history who have also perpetrated acts of terrible savagery, genocide and indiscriminate torture. It is difficult to determine why and indeed how individuals can embody such absolute degradation. It is as if not only their specific decisions but also their entire moral sense has been fatally flawed.

This kind of immoral behavior has raised some difficult questions about human nature. The Christian tradition has always operated with an assumption of the essential goodness of all human beings. In terms of the traditional language of conscience it has held that even if individuals make many bad or wrong decisions, they still have a desire (if only a faint one) to do good. But the question that must be confronted here is whether it is possible for a person to turn away completely from the habitual conscience, that is, from the orientation toward good, which people are believed to possess. Of course genetic inheritance, social background, parenting and education each may play its part in the disintegration of a person's moral sense. But the issue here is more fundamental than that. It relates to whether an individual can so reject even the most minimal conditions of morality as to freely and deliberately, continually over a lifetime, choose evil. St. Jerome and subsequent medieval thinkers were adamant that the human being's fundamental moral inclination is indestructible. They held that even after unspeakable evil, the "spark" of conscience still resides in the person. Jerome, in his *Commentary on Ezekiel*, reinforces the point that "this light of conscience was not extinguished in the heart of Cain even after he was expelled from paradise. It is by it that we are conscious of sinning even when we are overcome by pleasure, anger or false reasoning."[24] This image highlights the claim of Jerome that the habitual conscience refers to such a basic orientation that, even though it may be dulled or dormant as a result of deliberately choosing evil, it is never completely extinguished.

It is clear however, that individuals and groups can radically turn away from good. This is a highly complex issue and is impossible to consider without representing the discussions in extremely superficial terms. Indeed, psychologists and others are amassing a great deal of evidence from conducting in-depth interviews with people who have been convicted of serious and often heinous crimes. It is only when we as a society take the time to consider the lives and experiences of people who, either individually or collectively, participated in acts of great violence that we can hope to understand such events and people. Very often the traditional definitions and boundaries are of little help in such extreme circumstances. In the chapter, "Moral Failure and Self-Deception," Sidney Callahan discusses the inconsistency and irrationality that deliberately choosing evil occasions. She discusses the psychological states that individuals who avow immorality exhibit and documents the inevitability of paranoia and self-destruction that follow. Although such cases are on the margins of our study, they do confront us with some uncomfortable questions about the reliability or sturdiness of the person's innate moral sense. Do humans have a desire for the pursuit of goodness, as many Christian theologians would claim? If so, how does it happen that the behavior of some individuals appears to contradict this? Did they lose the appetite for goodness? If so, how? What of other individuals who appear to be seduced by the immoral behavior of these charismatic figures? Is the human desire for good so fragile that large numbers of individuals can be deflected from its path? Those who abandon any commitment to moral worth challenge, in a fundamental way, the Christian optimism about the goodness of human nature. Of course the doctrine of original sin points to the limited and fallible nature of human beings. It goes some way to explain the weakness of the human condition, which leads us to do evil deeds. However, it does not really help us understand why certain individuals dedicate their lives to the pursuit of evil.

Self-Deception

Deceiving oneself about one's actions and motives often plays an important part in the person's participation in wrongdoing. We may know at some level that what we are doing is wrong but may engage in all sorts of evasions and lies so that we don't have to confront the truth about our behavior. Experts disagree with one another about whether we can, in fact, lie to ourselves, whether we can be so divided in ourselves to allow a complete fragmentation. There are, undoubtedly, degrees of self-deception. Most well-meaning and honest individuals, at some stages in their lives, refuse to acknowledge the realities of their moral failure. In fact there is likely to be a degree of self-deception or flattery at work most of the time in our lives. We may describe our motives and intentions in positive terms. We may rationalize and explain our actions. We may silence any internal criticism, all in an effort to avoid the reality of our unethical behavior. This sort of evasion helps to explain moral failure in a person who is essentially committed to living a morally good life.

When we come face-to-face with moral conflict we can often be divided about desires and motivations. For example, I may believe that a friend is being abusive to his wife, although I might be unsure about the extent of that abuse. I might "choose" not to know anything about it because if I did, I would feel obliged to do something about it. I might close my eyes to obvious evidence, such as violent rows and bruises. I might demonize his wife in order to justify my friend's actions. I might refuse to believe other people who try to tell me about the situation. I might choose to believe my friend's denials when I confront him, even though I know deep down that these denials are untrue. There are numerous strategies that people use in order to avoid what they ultimately know to be true. Avoiding finding things out, ignoring vital information, looking the other way, burying inconvenient information—each of these strategies helps us to give an alternative, more acceptable account of our behavior. This avoidance of self-knowledge allows us to create false descriptions of reality and of our own moral characters. It allows us to participate in what we regard to be wrong, while pretending to ourselves that we are acting with integrity. Minor acts of self-deception are an inevitable part of the confused and unresolved nature of human behavior. These distortions of situations and contradictory reasoning suggest that the moral identity of the person is always incomplete and immature.

But self-deception can also be of a more serious order. It can be so "successful" as to allow a person to participate in or collude in acts of great evil and destruction without ever confronting the reality of such an engagement. Albert Speer is an extremely interesting historical figure in this regard. It may be unfair to single him out from among the many high-ranking individuals in Hitler's regime. However, his case is very illuminating because he reflected on and tried to explain his own participation in this evil. Albert Speer was an architect who joined Hitler's National Socialist Party in 1931. He rose through the ranks quickly and eventually occupied the position of minister of armaments in Hitler's government. As such he had responsibility for providing the military hardware for the war and was directly implicated in the use of Jews and other "enemies of the Reich" as slave laborers in his factories.

Speer's involvement provides important insights into individual collusion with evil. He gave many different accounts of his activities in these years. He spoke during his trial at Nuremberg and was the only one among Hitler's senior officers to accept responsibility for his actions. Many saw this as a cynical move that saved his life. He produced a number of different versions of his years in the Nazi party. He wrote an early account during his first years in Spandau prison. He then published a subsequent version, *Inside the Third Reich,*[25] and yet another, in conversation with Gita Sereny for the biography *Albert Speer: His Battle with Truth.*[26] Each of these accounts shows an individual who at one level is struggling to confront the enormity of his involvement with evil. And yet, all the while that he was "accepting responsibility," he was still trying to deceive himself and others about the extent and nature of his involvement.

The crucial question for him was whether he actually knew about the fate of the Jews. He evaded the question many times and gave explanations as to why he would not have known anything beyond his own particular sphere. He always denied that he actually knew about the policy of extermination. But in *Inside the Third Reich* he admits that he saw burnt-out Jewish homes and synagogues and saw evidence of mass deportation. He also tells of being warned by his friend Gaultier Karl Hanke never to go to a camp that he later concluded must have been Auschwitz. In an extraordinarily revealing passage in conversation with Sereny he tells how at one level he knew that terrible things went on there but deliberately chose not to know. Then Speer says,

> He [Hanke] had seen something there which he was not permitted to describe and moreover could not describe. I did not query him. I did not query Himmler, I did not query Hitler, I did not speak with personal friends, I did not investigate—for I did not want to know what was happening there. Hanke must have been speaking of Auschwitz and then *during those few seconds, while Hanke was warning me, the whole responsibility had become a reality again.* Those seconds were uppermost in my mind when I stated to the International Court at the Nuremberg trial that as an important member of the leadership of the Reich, I had to share the total responsibility for all that had happened. From that moment on, I was inescapably contaminated morally; from fear of discovering something which might have made me turn from my course, I had closed my eyes....I still feel, to this day, responsible for Auschwitz in a wholly personal sense.[27]

This moment of choice indicated a policy of self-deception on small matters which, when confronted with the reality of evil, allowed him to evade knowledge and thereby responsibility. This condition is often described as "middle knowledge." It operates on the basis of selecting and filtering the knowledge and experience that we allow ourselves to know. It is a choice of ignorance that isn't really ignorance at all. It is a self-imposed ignorance, a false naiveté. In many respects it is a feature of all of our lives. In an affidavit in 1977, in order to prevent a neo-Nazi pamphlet being published, Speer in fact confronted the reality of his life of self-deception. He said, "...to this day I still consider my main guilt to be my tacit acceptance of the persecution and the murder of millions of Jews."[28] When asked by Gita Sereny why, after denying this for so long, he admitted it directly, he gave a radically honest answer. He said simply, "For this purpose and with these people [neo-Nazis who were insisting that the Holocaust never happened] I didn't wish to—I couldn't—hedge." It captures in one sentence an important truth about all self-deception, that is, at some level and in some essential way the truth is known. A person cannot close her/his consciousness completely. The self-deception can never be absolute.

Nonetheless, we often try to hide from the reality of our moral failure. The great Dutch theologian Wilhelm Visser't Hooft partly explained the human tendency to self-deception when he spoke about the Holocaust. He suggested that "people could find no place in their consciousness for such...unimaginable horror....they did not have the imagination, together with the courage, to face it. It is possible to live in a twilight between knowing and not knowing."[29] This refusal or inability to accept the reality of one's moral failures is what drives us to try to ignore what we already know and to weave a narrative that is more pleasing to us. The complex psychological patterns accompanying all self-deceptions make it difficult to explain fully. One of the most pressing questions is whether it is possible to avoid self-deception or whether we are always engaged in constructing a more favorable account of reality. There is no doubt that we often flee from the distress that confronting our wrongdoing causes. Furthermore, we are inclined to remember our behavior in flattering terms and have a tendency to forget events that show us in an unfavorable light. But although such tendencies exist in most people, there is also an alternative drive—to be true to the things we know, to confront and thereby overcome our moral failures.

The process of shaping and educating the conscience has to take this ambivalence about moral failure on board. On the one hand it is only if we recognize and learn from our past sinfulness that we can develop our ethical sense. Yet, we do this fully aware of our impulse to hide from or reinterpret the reality of such failures. But the authentic development of conscience needs a significant degree of honesty with regard to our behavior, past and present. Self-consciousness is a crucial element in making decisions of integrity. The evaluation of one's past actions forms a central part of this self-consciousness. It is obvious that such evaluation must be vigilant about the all-too-human tendency to deceive oneself about the worthiness of one's history. Yet, this vigilance is not something that we can accomplish unproblematically but, rather, needs to be learned over time. It is a central component of the formation of conscience. It is learned through attempting to confront the reality of one's actions, through scrutinizing one's motivations, through checking one's own memory of the events. There are many strategies that we can develop in order to limit our own self-deception. However, the key factor in every strategy is the recognition that a well-formed conscience is prepared to confront its own failures and learn from them.

Sin: Original and Social

The tradition has many mechanisms for considering such limitations. The metaphors of original sin and social sin have relevance in this regard. Each highlights a dimension of the human condition that makes moral failure inevitable. They enable us to understand in some respect why decisions of conscience are always immature and imperfect. Our decisions are limited by factors constitutive of both the human condition (original sin) and by our social embeddedness (social sin).

Original sin is currently out of favor. It is associated in people's minds with the church's traditional fear and mistrust of human sexuality and with its antifemale bias (communicated, for example, through its treatment of Eve in the tradition). However, if we disregard these elements, which unfairly dominated traditional understanding of original sin, we can see a far more profound truth in the concept. Of course the doctrine of original sin involves complex theological claims about creation, judgment and redemption. These cannot be of concern to us here. Instead, we use the concept of original sin in a looser and more metaphorical fashion, to point to the manner in which the nature of the person is understood in the Christian tradition.

The account of the Fall in Genesis, in fact, speaks of the frailty and vulnerability of people's moral sense. It does so metaphorically, through a story about a man and a woman in their struggle to confront their conflicting desires and avoid temptation. It is a narrative in which they fail and subsequently have to come to terms with the consequences of that fact. Although the actual doctrine of original sin involves other theological claims, one thing we can draw from the concept is that as human beings we are born into a situation characterized by moral failure. It is part of our heritage and will inevitably form part of our future. But this condition of sinfulness is not the result of or specifically associated with any one of our faculties—for example, our sexuality. This tendency in the tradition was really the result of an unresolved ambivalence about sex that somehow mistakenly became attached to the concept of original sin. Instead, one aspect of the notion of original sin points to the reality that our knowledge and understanding are always partial and incomplete, that our desires are often conflicting, and that our emotions often immature. In part it articulates a fundamental truth about our condition, that is, that limitations of many sorts are embedded in our origins and that our desire to do the good is lived out in this context of frailty and finitude.

But in addition to this inheritance of original sin we live in a social environment that also bears the marks of social and institutional failure. This is usually referred to as social sin. It points to the fact that the social, cultural and religious context often functions to obscure value and to hinder our moral development. We have already discussed the many ways in which one's sense of value is tied up with the community to which one belongs and the social context in which one lives. However, this context can also function in a negative manner, hiding values, giving priority to inessentials or desensitizing us to particular injustices. There is no doubt that the biases and blindness of the prevailing cultural ethos limits the extent to which a person can come to a truly free and responsible decision of conscience. Systemic racism and sexism, for example, perpetuate injustices against particular groups. The fact that these were hidden in ideologies and reinforced in many different cultural assumptions and patterns of behavior meant that people were often unaware of their participation in this social sin.

The pervasiveness of social sin profoundly influences the ability to see and resist these destructive attitudes and actions. The person's apprehension of good may thereby be seriously flawed by the prevailing cultural values. Individual choice and behavior are closely bound to and shaped by social context. It is difficult to maintain a sense of self-direction in the context of all the external factors that ground and influence one's morality. Yet, the Christian tradition is built on the assumption that although social and cultural practices play an important role in shaping our sense of morality, they do not determine it. We do have a sort of freedom that enables us to evaluate, and then either reject or endorse the dominant culture. Social embodiment is important but not decisive in the individual's pursuit of good.

This talk of freedom brings us back to our earlier discussion of the fundamental option. There is no doubt that an individual's ability to orient her/his fundamental option toward seeking the good is influenced by her/his sensitivity to the limitations of the social context. The conscience is the part of the person that attempts to negotiate the many frailties of the human condition and yet act in accordance with one's understanding of moral goodness. As such there can never be an absolute certainty about the rightness of one's decisions. There are many flaws, both conscious and unconscious, that distort the operation of conscience. Yet, even though this be the case, we have to act on the truth as we know it. This is because although our best and most truthful effort to understand what is good and right in a particular situation may be incorrect, it is still the best that we can do. And in the final instance all that is asked of us is that we act with integrity and pursue what we believe to be good.

Chapter 6
Living with Contradictions: Disagreement and Dialogue in the Church

The divisions that exist within the church today can partly be explained by the presence of competing theologies of conscience. Throughout this book I have suggested that it is entirely understandable that such differences have emerged, given the confused and contentious history of conscience in the Catholic tradition. Not only have there been disagreements among theologians about the precise nature and role of conscience in the life of the Christian, but there have also been inconsistencies and contradictions with regard to the practical application of the various theological principles. However, it is not only that conscience itself has been the subject of theological debate, but also that such discussions inevitably involve other equally contentious issues, such as the importance of circumstances and intentionality in morality or the nature of moral authority within the institutional church. Each theology of conscience reflects and embodies a particular understanding of the nature of the person, of morality and of ecclesiology. And since each of these categories is and has long since been the subject of intense theological debate, the possibilities for continued disagreements are innumerable.

The nature of conscience itself involves such difficult questions that disagreement is somewhat inevitable. We can never be absolutely certain that our theologies are complete. Neither can we be sure that we have understood different theologies or perspectives accurately and properly. As such, within the church we will need to begin to live with the contradictions that flow from the ambiguous nature of conscience itself. So too will we need to live respectfully with the reality of differing and conflicting responses to important moral and ecclesial concerns. In this chapter we will deal with such issues, with the firm conviction that not only is difference and diversity in the moral realm inevitable, it is also immeasurably valuable.

The language of conscience refers to the personal discernment of moral truths and as such attempts to integrate the subjective and objective aspects of Christian morality. However, since these are somewhat vague and abstract, theologians through the ages have struggled to delineate precisely what each involves. They have had difficulty expressing the parameters of each and the relationship between them. Inevitably, throughout history theologians have tended to emphasize either the objective or the subjective aspect, and neglect the other equally important one. As a result theologies of conscience tended to be either theologies of obedience or of freedom. However, neither adequately encapsulates the complexity of conscience and its contextualization within the church.

In earlier chapters I discussed the necessary components for a theology of conscience that would deal with the ambiguities in the category itself and in the myriad contexts within which it operates. At the most basic level conscience is understood as a personal discernment of good and evil, in the context of relationship with a loving God. As such it is not purely subjective, arbitrary nor private. It is an understanding of conscience that draws heavily on the personalist theology of Vatican II. Although it is concerned with individual, discrete moments of choosing, it also reflects the manner in which particular choices are patterned into a unity that is the moral character. As a result conscience embodies the culmination of reflection, which can be rational, intuitive, emotional or imaginative, or which may draw on a combination of these faculties.

Conscience also reflects the fact that Christians do not profess a purely private faith but, rather, belong to a worshiping community. Although it is thoroughly personal, conscience is formed in the faith community, past and present. It is rooted in the narratives and traditions of the church and necessitates a personal engagement with the cumulative wisdom of the community. This view of conscience reflects the Aristotelian and Thomistic conviction that ethics is not an exact science and that we should not expect the same degree of precision and certitude from morality that one might expect from some other disciplines.[1] This is so because "circumstances alter cases" and intentions and consequences do have a bearing on the morality of a particular practice or decision. Conscience must take account of this reality in the way it attends to the particularities of each situation. As a result it must reject moralities that evaluate acts in isolation from the context in which they are performed. In short this is an understanding of conscience that confronts the complexities of persons and of contexts.

An inevitable result of these complexities is the presence of serious disagreement among Catholics regarding the morality of particular issues. The nature of the moral enterprise makes this inescapable, as do the limitations and failures that are part of the human condition. Thus, in my opinion, it is not only the presence of conflicting views on morality that is problematic within the church today; difficulty also resides in the church's inability to live fruitfully amidst the reality of difference and disagreement.

A Church in Crisis or Transition?

The church today faces a significant challenge in attempting to find a way of acknowledging and valuing the diversity that exists within as well as outside its borders. We have already discussed this diversity in the context of decisions of conscience as they are expressed at an individual level. However, the more obviously institutional and community-related aspects also need to be attended to. Of course this involves many complex issues relating to ecclesiology and doctrine, most of which cannot be the focus of this discussion. These have been considered extensively by theologians and by those associated with pastoral ministry over the past thirty years. Among those who have made significant contributions to the church's developing sense of its own nature and mission are reformers like Karl Rahner and Bernard Häring, feminist theologians such as Rosemary Radford Ruether, Ursula King and Mary Grey and liberation theologians like Juan Luis Segundo and Gustavo Gutierrez. Although it is impossible to summarize or indeed quantify the significance that these and numerous others have had, it is not an exaggeration to suggest that they have contributed to a worldwide renaissance within the Catholic Church.

It may seem rather optimistic to speak of a renaissance. Yet, it is my estimation that we are witnessing a slow and somewhat unsteady rejuvenation within the Catholic Church. There are many signs of hope. The emergence and continuance of the *communidades de base* in many Latin and South American countries, despite serious political repression, is one such sign of hope. Another is the global movement of women-church and of feminist worshiping communities. Still another is the growth of church-based development agencies and justice-oriented groups that embody the now firm conviction that action for justice forms an integral part of the church's ministry. The growth of lay involvement (both formal and informal) in parishes worldwide is yet another sign of hope. The vibrancy and commitment that exists among these still marginal and marginalized communities is a testimony to the renewal promoted and fostered by Vatican II. Mary Grey speaks of the many instances of renewal as "an attempt to take with absolute seriousness the intuition of the Second Vatican Council that the pilgrim people of God, the baptized community of faithful, do constitute the pulsating heart of the community of discipleship."[2] The faithful are now beginning to articulate their vision for the future church with increasing confidence. There is a sense in which the mandate for change and renewal given by the Second Vatican Council has been internalized and adopted by significant numbers of Catholics worldwide. Mary Grey's inspiring and challenging *Beyond the Dark Night: A Way Forward for the Church?*[3] expresses well the ambiguity that is borne of living in these twilight decades. She speaks of the collapse of the edifice of an overly centralized church and of being left in a place wherein we only have fragments and hints of other ways of being church. In this place of hope and uncertainty it is entirely understandable that many seek to reestablish the old patterns of thought and practice and to reaffirm the certainties of an earlier time.

The Nature and Authority of Church Teaching

At the heart of the contemporary struggle within the church to articulate a renewed way of being church in the world is a complex discussion regarding the role of church teaching on moral matters. The context of this discussion is the recognition of the need for clear and authoritative teaching on a variety of difficult and intricate moral issues. The magisterium has a vital role to play in articulating the values that ought to shape our moral sense and in providing clear guidance in the ever more complicated situations of contemporary life. However, within the church there exists a number of different and often contrary perspectives regarding the rightful nature and authority of church guidance and teaching, especially on moral matters. One recent instance of this debate was occasioned by the 1998 apostolic letter *Ad Tuendam Fidem*. In this text Pope John Paul II announced the insertion of new canons into the Code of Canon Law and also expanded the already controversial 1989 Profession of Faith.[4] The reason given for the inclusion of the new canons was that there is no rule in the existing code to deal with the "acceptance of doctrine definitively proposed by the church."[5] In response to this Ladislas Örsy suggested that this new phrase, "definitive teaching," used by the magisterium, is problematic. The reason, he claimed, is that a definitive teaching "is not an infallible pronouncement, it does not require surrender in faith, yet it must be 'embraced and held' as irreformable"; moreover, he wrote that here "is the crux of the problem; how can a point of teaching not guaranteed by the assistance of the Holy Spirit (as infallible definitions are) be irreformable?"[6] Örsy's point addresses what has popularly been termed as a creeping infallibility within the church today. He argues that teachings representing the church's current but not conclusive thinking on a range of issues are being presented with excessive weight and authority. As a result, in many cases the faithful seem to be presented with a choice: Either obey or risk excommunication.

The commentary accompanying the papal letter discusses the issue of definitive teaching more fully. Signed by the prefect and secretary of the Congregation for the Doctrine of the Faith, it states, with regard to this type of teaching, which includes the doctrine that priestly ordination is reserved only to men and the teaching on the invalidity of Anglican orders, that "whoever denies these truths would be in a position of rejecting a truth of Catholic doctrine and would therefore no longer be in full communion with the Catholic Church."[7] Many theologians and pastors have expressed their concern that the logic of this position seems to be that the faithful cannot continue a respectful and loyal dialogue within the church on a number of unresolved issues. Others have suggested that a worrying aspect of this new initiative is that a person may be declared out of communion with the church because of the desire to continue to discuss certain issues.

One of the most problematic aspects of these debates is that they tend to facilitate the creation of false distinctions between respect for church teaching and the necessity for personal moral responsibility. These conflicts can perpetuate the mistaken assumption that the teaching church corresponds to the magisterium and that the learning church is the clergy and laity. Furthermore, they can promote a false sense of the nature of obedience in the context of a community of faith and morals.

Of course we must give careful consideration to the teachings that come from the magisterium. However, as is clear from the many texts we have examined throughout this book, the Christian tradition has continuously insisted that moral responsibility and choice reside ultimately with each individual. We cannot export our moral choices or hand over our decision making to any other person or body. As such we must be obedient to our own discernment of the Spirit; we must adhere to our own consciences. Obedience, therefore, can never be construed as the blind submission of one's will and intellect, even to the magisterium of the church, particularly if one's considered judgment pulls one in the opposite direction.

Through its history the church's own understanding of the nature and authority of its teaching has been extremely nuanced and sensitive. However, another cause of difficulty according to some is that some recent pronouncements ignore the subtle gradations of authority inherent in different forms of church teaching and that they claim a status that is at odds with their nature. Francis Sullivan has discussed this issue at length, both in regard to this recent tendency in the church and in relation to specific cases.[8] He makes the point that the church's sophisticated and nuanced account of the nature and scope of its teaching is, in some cases, being ignored. Moreover, he argues that this sophisticated form of teaching is being replaced by statements containing excessive claims regarding the degree of obedience that is due to them.

In a contribution to this debate Richard Gaillardetz makes the point that

> ...all Catholics have a right to know that ecclesiastical pronouncements differ significantly, not only in their content but in their authoritative character. They must also know that their response to church teaching can and should be correlated to the particular character of the teaching itself. What is at stake here is nothing less than a proper understanding of what constitutes church membership and the fact that, in Catholic teaching, not all disagreement with

ecclesiastical pronouncements necessarily separates one from the Roman Catholic communion.[9]

Gaillardetz's text is concerned with identifying and discussing the nature of the doctrinal and moral teaching authority of the church. While a detailed consideration of the issue is beyond the scope of this book, it is important to consider the way in which the nature and scope of church teaching on moral matters relate to the authority of conscience.

In addition to advocating a renewal in moral theology, Vatican II also initiated a change in the church's understanding of the nature and scope of its doctrinal authority. One of the most significant transformations that the Council prompted was a move away from an autocratic notion of authority and toward a collegial and consultative one. Gaillardetz suggests that one of the greatest achievements of the Council is that it offered the "beginnings of an account of ecclesial authority grounded in an ecclesiology of communion."[10] This grows out of the conviction that the whole people of God are addressed by the word of God, thereby rejecting the view that divine revelation is communicated primarily to the hierarchy.[11] It also emphasizes a vision of church that is oriented toward participation and modeled in terms of mutual and reciprocal relationships.[12] The account of ecclesial authority that it presents reflects this ecclesiology of communion, thereby recontextualising and ultimately transforming traditional models.

There was a corresponding development in the theology of divine revelation that also had a significant impact on the church's understanding of the content of its teaching. In *Dei verbum,* the church's constitution on divine revelation, the Council suggested a subtle shift in emphasis. It moved away from what has been described as a propositional and positivistic model of revelation, that is, one which viewed revelation in terms of a collection of discrete propositional truths, concerned primarily with the transmission of conceptual truths and having the authority of divine utterances.[13] Within this model the hierarchical magisterium was regarded as the primary mediator of these truths. In its place, albeit tentatively, the Council offered an understanding of revelation as God's personal self-disclosure in Jesus Christ as a living word addressed to all humanity and alive in the Christian community. Of course the Council did not ignore the essential role of church teaching in the articulation and communication of this living word; however, it did shift the focus away from an immediate preoccupation with formal pronouncements. Furthermore, it reinforced the already existing but much ignored recognition that not every doctrinal teaching of the church is related to divine revelation in the same way.[14] In doing so it reminded us to be aware that there are many forms of church teaching, each with its own centrality and authority and each making a different claim on our intellect and will.

It takes a significant degree of knowledge and reflection to discern the authority of the various forms of church teaching. Indeed, one of the most frequent criticisms of the teaching offices of the church is that they have failed to help the faithful identify the appropriate weight that should be given to any pronouncement. The important distinctions present in the tradition regarding these gradations of authority can frequently be blurred. Örsy develops this point by suggesting that as a result of this the authority of certain pronouncements can sometimes be upgraded, "affecting (and falsifying) the binding force of its message."[15] Indeed, André Naud makes the point that "along with the infallible magisterium properly exercised in the Church, there is another 'uncertain' magisterium that teaches with less authority and must honestly acknowledge the possibility of error."[16] Yet the faithful are rarely appraised of the nature and authority of this important and voluminous form of teaching.

In the field of morality most conflict tends to arise over the nondefinitive authoritative teachings of the church. This is the category containing much of the church's moral pronouncements over the centuries.[17] The distinctive aspect of this type of teaching is that there is a recognition that we are dealing with issues on which the church cannot make a definitive statement. It may not be able to do so for a variety of reasons. It may realize a possibility that its view may be in error, or there may be a degree of uncertainty regarding how the church should respond to a particular issue. In addition, particularly in the moral field, there are many issues that cannot be properly considered or answered in unambiguous statements about right and wrong. Many ethical issues require a degree of nuance and attention to detail that the general statements of formal teaching cannot provide. As a result they are more properly discussed and considered by other means.

These teachings, which actually form the bulk of the church's moral instruction, are highly significant and need to be given due consideration by the believer. The kind of response that any individual is required to give to such teaching has, unsurprisingly, been the subject of much discussion over the years. *Lumen gentium* teaches that all authoritative teaching is to be given a religious *obsequium* of intellect and will.[18]

However, the precise meaning of this term *obsequium* has been the subject of serious academic debate within the church.[19] It is variously translated as "submission" or "due respect." Örsy, in fact, suggests that the meaning of the term *obsequium* changes depending on the nature of the teaching to which the *obsequium* is due. Certain teachings are due a faithful submission of the intellect and will of the believer, while others may be due serious attention or respectful listening. The overriding concern, according to Örsy, is that a particular attitude of loyalty and respect is due toward the church and its teaching.[20] The believer ought to be informed of and take serious cognizance of the church's view on each moral issue and should only dissent from that position for serious conscientious reasons.

Assent and Dissent

Much ink has been spilled during the last twenty years, particularly among theologians, over the issue of assent and dissent. Although it impacts directly on theologians, it also affects all the faithful to a greater or lesser extent. As a result it would be wrong to construe the discussion too narrowly and to consider issues of assent and dissent only as they impinge on the lives and work of theologians.[21] The issue of assent to or dissent from church teaching, especially moral teaching, has profound importance in the life of the church. However, we should remember that the church teaches in many different ways and with different gradations of authority and that not all instances of church teaching are equally contentious. It is in the field of morality that the nature and degree of the assent due to each instance of church teaching are especially problematic. This is unsurprising given the complex and ambiguous nature of morality and given the depth of disagreement among thoughtful and good individuals on the ethics of many issues.

As Richard Gaillardetz suggests, it is important for the faithful to be informed about the nature and degree of authority claimed for each instance of church teaching.[22] Indeed, if this was made clear to people, much of the anxiety relating to the degree of assent that a person is expected to give to a particular teaching would disappear. This is because, especially although not exclusively in the moral field, when one examines closely the nature of much contentious teaching, one can see that the degree of assent it is due is a good deal less extreme than is generally supposed. In fact since most of the contentious moral teaching is not classed as definitive, dissent from such teachings is not only to be expected but should also be foreseen. The inevitable tension relating to moral teaching often arises because its nondefinitive nature is obscured.

However, instead of focusing on questions like What is the status of the church's moral teaching? What kind of authority does it have? and What degree of obedience is it due? I wish to propose a different approach. This approach reflects the reality that ultimately the issue is not about legalistic requirements but about seeking to do the good. Our attention should be directed toward working out how a person should act on her/his conscientious decisions and what one's response should be when church teaching does not coincide with one's best estimation of the right thing to do in a particular situation. If we begin at this point, then our attention is focused on the essential and crucial aspect of each instance of moral deliberation, that is, the process by which one comes to a sense of the good. The heart of

Christian ethics is the individual's discernment of value and its embodiment in each context. When this becomes our central concern, then conflicts of authority assume far less importance. The issue no longer revolves around whether and to what extent one has the right to dissent from a particular kind of church teaching, but how one can understand oneself as a loyal and committed member of the church while at the same time disagreeing with a particular teaching.

This approach is greatly influenced by one of Kevin Kelly's excellent reflections on the Charles Curran case. In a short piece entitled "Serving the Truth," which appeared initially in *The Tablet*, Kelly suggests that by making the issue of dissent the central one, Charles Curran and Cardinal Ratzinger have not done full justice to themselves.[23] In a remark that has far wider application than the Curran case, Kelly explains that

> *dissent* is a negative word. It belongs to the same stable as terms like *deny, oppose,* and *contradict.* There is nothing positive or affirmative about it. Focusing on the issue of dissent, therefore, has two unfortunate consequences. It creates a climate of confrontation and it makes true dialogue impossible. Moreover, it deflects attention from the fundamental question that underlies the whole dispute: the respective roles of the teaching authority, theologians and all believers in the Church's mission of serving and proclaiming the truth.[24]

Indeed, Kelly's words were to prove prophetic, for in the intervening years the church has become preoccupied with the question of dissent, including who can dissent, under what circumstances, for what reasons and from what kind of teaching. It is not only the theologians who have made this a central concern; the Vatican, mainly through the Sacred Congregation for the Doctrine of the Faith, has also devoted what one might regard as a disproportionate amount of time and attention to the problem. Of course it is a matter of concern, and there are disagreements that need to be resolved. However, one does wonder whether, almost fifteen years after the Curran affair, which in many ways was just a catalyst for the controversy, we

have come any nearer to an agreement on or greater understanding of the role of individual moral discernment within the
institutional church. The intervening years have prompted serious reflection and some great moral insight; however, what
they have not produced is any likelihood of consensus. To apply
a phrase taken from the acrimonious debates surrounding the
abortion controversy, it has regrettably been a dialogue of the
deaf.[25] The past fifteen years truly have been ones of confrontation, in which true dialogue has proved impossible.

However, Kelly's criticism of the terms in which the Curran
case was debated is more substantial than the effects of the
dispute. His objection to the preoccupation with dissent lies in
his sense that the debate was too narrowly construed to deal
with the heart of the matter. His comments are more generally
pertinent when he suggests that "the term *dissent* has no feel
for all that is positive in such a position—respect for tradition,
concern for the truth, love of the Church, shared responsibility for the Church's mission in the world. It does not express
the respect for teaching authority in the Church which moti-
vates someone adopting this kind of stance."[26] He is pointing
the way to a different approach that would seek to avoid constructing two distinct moral authorities, one individual, one
institutional, each vying with the other for prominence. And
although it is true that it was not the intention of those who
engaged in the debate on dissent to create such a climate, it
was undoubtedly one of the side effects.

If one continues to conduct the discussion exclusively in
terms of dissent, one inevitably perpetuates a legalistic model
of morality. With such a model the complexities of the moral
enterprise are discussed primarily in the language of obedience. In addition relationships in an already fragmented
church are fractured further, and entrenched positions
become even more solid. Instead, following Kelly, I suggest
that we focus first on what is, after all, of central concern in all
moral debates, that is on the issue of how best to understand
and articulate the good and loving thing to do in each given
situation. When disagreements occur, as inevitably they will
given the nature of the moral enterprise, then a further issue

of how to harmonize the insights of each perspective would need to be considered. With such a model, however, we would be more inclined to keep our attention focused on creating a dialogue to achieve agreement and to find ways of living fruitfully in the midst of difference.

Kelly alludes to the differences between the two approaches when he compares two possible ways of expressing one's disagreement with certain church teachings. One way is simply to say, "I dissent from the church's teaching"; however, according to Kelly this does not capture the essence of the person's stance. The other, which Kelly recommends, embodies the model proposed earlier and could be verbalized by a statement such as:

> ...drawing on the richness of the Church's tradition and in the light of the Church's deeper knowledge of this aspect of human life gained through its dialogue with the human sciences today, I believe that what I and many Christians are saying is a more adequate expression of the richness of our present Christian understanding than is found in the current statement of the Church's teaching.[27]

Such an approach acknowledges the important role that the church has in the formation of conscience. It also reflects the reality that the church operates within the constraints of culture and time and that its own understanding is inevitably limited by such factors. In addition it conveys a sense of the church's tradition as developmental and dynamic rather than unchanging. But most of all it reminds us that one's ultimate concern must be with what is good and true in a given context. The duty of conscience is not to assent to magisterial teaching but to work earnestly and courageously for the articulation of the good in each context. One hopes and expects that normally these two will coincide. However, when they do not, one's duty continues to be to strive to embody, in one's decisions, that which one has come to understand to be good and true. It is not that situations of disagreement will be avoided with this approach; such a claim would be fanciful. However, when the unambiguous intention is to seek the good, albeit often in complicated and indeterminate circumstances, then the issue of assent or dissent remains of secondary importance.

The paradigm of law as conceived within a hierarchical church cannot accommodate the many possible reasons for dissent among the faithful, and as such is wholly inappropriate as a way of understanding and resolving the complexities of the moral life. Differences of opinion tend to be put down to error on the part of the faithful. The possibility that the position of the magisterium may be in error is rarely even considered. Nor is the possibility that a final resolution of particular issues may not yet be achieved because of our continued lack of understanding. However, within a personalist paradigm differences of opinion between individuals and the magisterium can be regarded as an inevitable aspect of the dynamic nature of human growth and understanding. Furthermore, they are recognized as arising necessarily from the unity-in-difference that is the essence of vibrant communities. Rather than being ruled out, loyal opposition is essential if a community is to flourish. Loyal opposition signals a primary commitment to seek the truth, even if it leads one to depart from one's community's understanding of that truth. But it also signals a degree of confidence in the community, so that even when there are differences of opinion, one remains faithful to it.

Development and Change in the Moral Tradition

In his poem "The Settle Bed," Seamus Heaney evokes the seemingly unchangeable nature of tradition. He speaks of an inheritance

> upright, rudimentary, unshiftably planked
> In the long long ago, yet willable forward
> Again and again and again, cargoed with
> Its own dumb, tongue-and-groove worthiness
> An un-get-roundable weight....[28]

This is precisely how many people experience the heritage of the church's moral teaching. Respectful of its upright and worthy purpose, we feel trapped by its un-get-roundable weight. Its weight can paralyze one's sense of purpose and confidence in one's own discernment. Yet, this is not at all what is intended for a community with a rich moral inheritance. Once we can see that the tradition of moral guidance and teaching is nothing more than the accumulated wisdom and insight of our forebears, then it becomes something supple we can work with, planked in the long ago, yet willable forward.

One of the reasons why the tradition of moral teaching seems to be weighty and unyielding stems from our failure to give due attention to the developments and changes that are themselves part of the tradition. We tend to operate with an overly simplistic and unified view of the moral teaching of the church. We assume that the position now being taught on, for example, slavery, marriage or human rights is essentially the same as, or at least consistent, with what the church taught in the past. Yet, with the example of human rights this is clearly not the case. When, in 1789 the National Constituent Assembly of France declared that "men are born and remain free and equal in rights" and that "the aim of every political association is the preservation of the natural and inviolable rights of man,"[29] the Vatican reacted immediately to condemn it. In 1791 Pius VI in his *Quod Aliquantum* claimed that it was anathema for Catholics to accept the Declaration of the Rights of Man and of the Citizen. He insisted that "this equality, this liberty, so highly exalted by the National Assembly, have then as their only result the overthrow of the Catholic religion."[30] Yet by 1963, a mere two centuries later, John XXIII insisted that

> any human society if it is to be well ordered and productive, must lay down as a foundation this principle, namely that every human being is a person, that is, his nature is endowed with intelligence and free-will. Indeed precisely because he is a person he has rights and obligations flowing directly and simultaneously from his very nature. And as these rights are universal and inviolable so they cannot in any way be surrendered.[31]

This is not simply a conflict between two texts pulling in alternative directions. The tradition has changed, and changed radically. Once the concept of inviolable and natural rights was anathema; today it forms a central plank of the church's understanding of how the dignity of the person is to be protected and promoted.

In his article "Development in Moral Doctrine"[32] John Noonan discusses other examples of change in the church's moral teaching. In the cases of usury, marriage, slavery and religious freedom Noonan documents the real and substantial changes that have taken place in the church's teaching over the centuries. In respect to usury, Noonan explains, "from at least 1150 to 1550, seeking, receiving, or hoping for anything beyond one's principal—in other words looking for profit—on a loan constituted the mortal sin of usury."[33] Furthermore, it was a doctrine "enunciated by popes, expressed by three ecumenical councils, proclaimed by bishops, and taught unanimously by theologians."[34] It cannot be regarded as an obscure or minor teaching; it formed a substantial part of Christianity's approach to the market. Although there were many debates through the centuries about what precisely constituted usury, "the great central moral fact was that usury, understood as profit on a loan, was forbidden as contrary to the natural law, as contrary to the law of the church, and as contrary to the law of the gospel."[35]

But of course we know that this fundamental moral doctrine has changed. Furthermore, the change, like that in relation to human rights, cannot be described as a minor emendation but one of substance. It is also a change that has been thoroughly absorbed into the tradition; thus "the idea that it is against nature for money to breed money, or that it is contrary to church law to deposit in a savings institution with the hope of a profit, or that hoping for profit at all from a loan breaks a command of Christ—all these ideas, once unanimously inculcated with the utmost seriousness by the teaching authority of the Church, are now so obsolete that one invites incredulity by reciting them."[36] The nature of the church's moral doctrine is such that it seems to be able to absorb this kind of radical change and yet retain its authority. And yet we do not immediately or easily think of this kind of flexibility when we speak of the church's moral doctrine or teaching.

There were similarly dramatic changes in the church's moral teaching in relation to marriage. Noonan points out that even within the New Testament itself a perceptible change occurs, one that was subsequently developed and exaggerated through the centuries. As a result the idea of monogamy without divorce, which many regard as the "law of the gospel," was modified to allow converts to Christianity to remarry if their spouses had not converted. This exception, known as the Pauline privilege, was radically extended in the sixteenth century so that slaves taken from Africa could remarry, even though there was no way of knowing whether absent spouses would abandon them or not.[37] In the case of slavery until the teaching of Leo XIII prevailed there was no institutional outrage at the practice of owning slaves. Indeed, the church itself was a slave owner; it approved of and perpetuated the trade in human beings for many centuries. There were dissident voices within the Catholic tradition, voices that condemned slavery as a great evil. However, in both its practice and its teachings the institutional church was supportive of slavery. Yet, today one could not imagine the church condoning any kind of slavery, whether it be the chattel slavery which persisted in the United States into the nineteenth century, or the modern equivalent of the indentured slavery of men, women and children in the sweatshops of Burma, Malaysia, the Philippines and other developing countries.

The changes in church teaching with regard to torture, religious freedom and the execution of heretics are similarly dramatic. When we examine the substance of what is often presented to us as an unchanging tradition, we can see that the notion of a singular tradition of moral teaching is a myth. Of course there has long since been an acceptance of the idea of development in the church's moral teaching in the abstract. Even in *Veritatis Splendor* there is recognition that "within Tradition, the authentic interpretation of the Lord's law develops, with the help of the Holy Spirit."[38] Yet, while the principle of development and change in the church's moral doctrine is widely accepted, individual moral doctrines are presented as if they were universal in their scope, exceptionless in their application and timeless in character. In short, when it comes to particular moral teachings, the possibility of change and development, which is conceded in the abstract, is rarely acknowledged. As a result certain moral teachings, such as those relating to contraception, homosexuality, or divorce and remarriage, are invested with an unwarranted degree of certainty and inflexibility.

This raises the issue of how the church understands the nature of its moral tradition. When one examines the relevant literature, however, one realizes that although there is a vague sense of the nature of the "moral tradition," there has, as yet, been little sustained analysis of what the church's moral tradition is, how it functions and how we can explain the ambiguity of continuity and change that is at its core.[39] The question of how the tradition can be both bound to the past and yet open to the possibility of the new is perhaps the most central. Many theologians have discussed this problem specifically in relation to the church's theological doctrines. For example, John Henry Newman, in his 1843 *Essay on the Development of Christian Doctrine*,[40] attempted to explain the extent to which doctrinal change is possible and the limits of that change. In the twentieth century Yves Congar,[41] Karl Rahner,[42] Jaroslav Pelikan[43] and others have attempted to analyze and articulate the complicated nature of the church's tradition, but primarily with doctrinal rather than moral matters in mind. Yet Noonan suggests,[44] wisely I think, that we can draw on the insights gained from these investigations of changes in propositions of faith and we can apply them to the field of moral doctrine.

In a synthesis of insights drawn from recent discussions of continuity and change in theological propositions, together with a consideration of the ways in which tradition has functioned in moral theology, Johnstone tentatively proposes "a synthetic idea of tradition as moral tradition."[45] He suggests that we should think of tradition as denoting a comprehensive range of factors "from the unconscious, through shared symbols, to official written documents, to faithful action."[46] Tradition is the "life of the historical community of the Church" in its fullest sense and has a fundamental community structure; "it shapes community and is shaped by community."[47] It must be understood as a living tradition, one that does inevitably change and develop. However, Johnstone is also keen to suggest that change within the tradition "is not brought about by a series of breaks with the past. It is the permanent continuous elements which provide the basis of possibility of change."[48] Here, in particular, one is confronted with the ambiguity of the concept of tradition as employed by the church. It is out of continuity that change is made possible, and yet it is in the context of change that the church most vociferously articulates its moral tradition or doctrine.

This expanded notion of tradition, which encompasses symbol systems, official documents and faithful action provides a valuable framework for the alternative approach to instances of disagreement between individuals and the magisterium that I proposed earlier in the chapter. It allows for the recognition that the church's moral tradition is composed of more than magisterial teachings. Indeed, it enables one to claim that, for example in the case of slavery, the church's tradition is composed not only of the institutional pronouncements supporting slavery, but also of the prophetic voices and practices of those Catholics who opposed it. This account of tradition also designates the whole church, rather than just the magisterium, as its authors. When discussing cases of disagreement, then, it enables one to move away from the conventional model of the individual conscience up against the weight of tradition, since the conscientious judgment of the individual, too, is part of the tradition. Indeed, the individual's insight may have an important function in prompting a particular development or change in the church's apprehension of value.

Of course Catholics believe in the teaching authority of the church which, although it is present through the Spirit in the whole church, is thought to be enjoyed in a special way by its pastors.[49] The intricacies of the nature and authority of the various teaching roles within the church are subtle and complex. Furthermore, they too are the subject of ongoing development. Pastors, bishops, pope, theologians and laity each have distinctive responsibilities and duties as both learners and teachers. The individual's moral judgment must be exercised in a manner that is mindful of this rich and diverse model of learning and teaching.

Traditionally, the concern to give due recognition to the beliefs and moral sensibilities of the faithful was expressed in terms of the *sensus fidelium*. Commenting on the recent use of this concept Gaillardetz reminds us that although this term "would not always be employed explicitly, the fundamental concept, namely the inerrancy of the faith of the whole community of believers, can be traced back to the very origins of Christianity."[50] And although it went through periods of neglect, through the centuries important theologians, and especially Newman, continued to give prominence to the idea of the "significance of the witness of the faithful," to use Gaillardetz's phrase. However, this witness was conceptualized in a corporate sense. Drawing on Newman's comprehensive and ecclesially sensitive understanding, Gaillardetz imagines the *senus fidelium* as a "process of articulation, which leads to pedagogy, which leads to reception, which in turn engenders a new articulation."[51] He speaks of it as a spiral-like movement in the church's traditioning process, one which "can be helpful in dispelling the tendency toward a linear conception of church teaching, which...starts with the deposit of faith, which first resides in the hierarchy and then is being dispensed to the faithful...."[52]

In the theological developments of the documents of Vatican II the *sensus fidelium* refers to the believers' instinctive sense of the faith. It is regarded as infallible, not in terms of the individual exercise of this *sensus fidei*, but in terms of the corporate belief of the whole people of God. In the context of this approach an understanding of the *sensus fidelium* is important for two reasons. First, it reinforces the dialectical nature of tradition, especially moral tradition, which is a model we have already proposed. But more than this, it points to the central role of the faithful in engendering such change. Second, it gives due recognition to the important function that the community has in the discovery and articulation of value. Individual moral judgment is not exercised in a vacuum. It is shaped by and shapes the believing community's witness to the faith. However, neither is individual moral judgment the prisoner of past understandings. One need not be paralyzed by a misconceived notion of the moral tradition as monolithic and unchanging. For, as Seamus Heaney reminds us, we can "conquer that weight" because

> whatever is given
> Can always be reimagined, however four-square
> Plank-thick, hull-stupid and out of its time
> It happens to be....[53]

The Church and Moral Failure

In the same way that individual moral discernment is a complex and delicate phenomenon, so too is the institutional process. It may seem inappropriate to speak of the institutional church in such terms, but being in part a human institution, it is subject to some of the same difficulties that complicate individual moral deliberation. Indeed, not only is the church limited by its human frailties, but it is further hampered by the inevitable conflicts that arise as a result of the variety of views and roles that legitimately comprise the institution. This makes moral failure inevitable. In chapter 5 we spoke of the failures of reason, emotion, intuition and imagination that account for many of the instances of individual moral failure. Although one cannot speak of the institutional church as possessing rationality or an emotional life, the limitations that comprise the church's moral failures can be seen in similar terms.

When the institutional church, through the magisterium, comes to a judgment regarding whether or not a particular practice or process is acceptable, it does so using the same resources that are available to the faithful. Moral judgments are made with the guidance of the Spirit, in dialogue with the inherited wisdom of the tradition and in the context of the community's religious narratives and symbols. But they are also made by people who are subject to the limitations of the human condition. We trust that each judgment and teaching is well reasoned. However, in the same way that an individual's assessment may be flawed through limited or incomplete knowledge or through a misunderstanding of the situation, so too can an institution's. Just as individuals occasionally have to make decisions in the face of uncertainty or without all the information we know to be relevant, so too does the church. The emotional responses of the individuals who make up the magisterium also come into play when it teaches. These can take the form of excessive emotions, lack of an appropriate emotional response because of the inability to empathize with a particular kind of abuse or a deep-seated fear of change. The intuitions at play within the community may also lead it to disregard important new insights or to ignore voices long marginalized. Nor is it difficult to envisage how a failure of imagination might be possible. When an institution, through its members as well as through those entrusted with its governance, becomes locked into a mindset and way of being, then it is difficult for it to make necessary leaps of imagination. It is often when such failure occurs that the prophetic voices of our age are most urgently heard. All institutions are susceptible to the failure of imagination; it is a hazard of institutional life. Yet, many of the most significant and enduring moral insights of the institutional church have come when, against the tide of history, and with great imaginative courage, the magisterium has articulated a truly radical position.

One could see the change in the church's teaching on religious freedom as an example of this imaginative leap. The belief that error has no rights totally determined the church's approach to religious liberty for centuries. Many theologians and bishops believed in using imperial force to compel heretics to return to the church. In fact Noonan claims that "it was universally taught that the duty of a good ruler was to extirpate not only heresy but heretics" and that "the vast institutional apparatus of the church was put at the service of detecting heretics, who, if they persevered in their heresy or relapsed into it, would be executed at the stake."[54] And as Curran reminds us, Leo XIII, who in many other respects was truly prophetic, condemned liberty of worship, which "goes against the chiefest and holiest human duty demanding the worship of the one true God in the one true religion which can easily be recognized by its external signs."[55] Yet, in response to the growing recognition of the values of different religious traditions, during Vatican II the church took a truly bold and imaginative step and reversed the teaching of centuries. In *Dignitatis humanae* the church insisted that "the human person has a right to religious freedom, that it is based on the very dignity of the human person and that this right must be given recognition in the constitutional order of society."[56]

Institutional moral failure can be compounded by self-deception. In order to preserve the reputation and standing of the institution, there can be a refusal to acknowledge or accept the reality of past moral failures. Bad decisions can be rationalized, mixed motives can be explained in a positive light, the memories and narratives of the past can be constructed in order to flatter and internal critics can be silenced. As with individual self-deception much of this can be unconscious or at least not deliberately intended. Institutional self-deception can also be accomplished in a more indirect manner. The institution can avoid finding things out, it can ignore uncomfortable or troubling signs, it can bury inconvenient information and it can look the other way. Indeed, much of the sexual abuse of children that took place in religious contexts was able to continue because of this kind of self-deception on the part of the institution. It could be said to fall into the "twilight of knowing and not knowing,"[57] which we spoke of in an earlier chapter.

The avoidance of self-knowledge or the construction of false and flattering accounts of one's past and present is a temptation as real for institutions as it is for individuals. And, indeed, just as in our own lives, where we can learn honesty through confronting our past failures, so too can the church. The church, too, needs to take account of its own moral failures and must learn from its past sinfulness. In instances of suspected moral failure it can draw significant insight from scrutinizing its own motivations and checking official versions of events. This will allow the church to reconstruct a more truthful account of the past and will thereby enable it to create a more promising future. The recent papal announcement that one of the church's bleakest stories, the Inquisition, will be subject to such scrutiny is a welcome example of this kind of self-examination.[58]

In recent years the Catholic church worldwide has gone through a series of crises that have rightly caused it to reflect not only on its past, but also on its future. Financial and sex-abuse scandals, internal divisions on a range of ethical issues, expressed dissatisfaction with the leadership of the church and the lack of substantial progress in ecumenism all suggest that the church is in the midst of what Mary Grey calls its dark night.[59] Yet the only way out of this dark night is a process of remembering and repentance of past sinfulness, together with a determination to learn from such failures. The church, too, is confined by the limitations of the human condition. However, in the same way that all persons are believed to be both imperfect yet redeemed, the church too is believed to share this ambiguous nature. Recalling Karl Rahner's call for "faith in a wintry time," Enda McDonagh insists that "the winter name of church can only be *metanoia*, repentance, a radical change of human minds and hearts, of human structures and practices."[60]

Beyond the Impasse

A key component of the *metanoia* of which McDonagh speaks must be a renewed theology of conscience. The model of conscience that I have been proposing throughout this text has its roots already within the tradition. Indeed, from the earliest centuries the conscience was respected as the individual's personal discernment of the Spirit in moral matters and as such is worthy of deep respect and authority. The renewal of Vatican II returned this understanding of conscience to center stage, although it must be said that it was never abandoned within the tradition, just occasionally ignored or minimized. Despite the unease that the promotion of this model of conscience has caused in some quarters, the paradigm of moral responsibility it has generated is being enthusiastically embraced by the faithful.

This personalist model of conscience holds tremendous promise together with great challenges for individuals and for the institutional church. It proposes a model of moral responsibility that recognizes its irreducibly personal character. Yet, the nature of that personal responsibility is dialogical and communitarian. The moral self is a self-in-relation: It is formed through the narratives and symbols of the tradition and seeks to exercise ethical responsibility in this context. The church forms the moral community within which the individual strives to live an ethical life. As such it must provide the resources to enable individuals to develop their own moral sensibilities and must nurture them in that task. Teaching through word and example will form an important part of that nurturing role. However, when the church teaches, it must do so with respect for the seriousness with which most people engage in ethical reflection and with a supportive attitude toward their conscientiously held beliefs and values. It is only when such a model is accepted that the church will be able to recreate itself as a truly visionary moral community.

Notes

Introduction

1. Fagan, Sean, *Has Morality Changed?* (Dublin: Gill & Macmillan, 1997), p. 92.

2. D'Arcy, Eric, *Conscience and Its Right to Freedom* (New York: Sheed & Ward, 1961).

Chapter 1

1. Callahan, Sidney, *In Good Conscience: Reason and Emotion in Decision Making* (New York: HarperCollins, 1991), p. 5.

2. Ibid., p. 15.

3. Bolt, Robert, *A Man for All Seasons* (New York: Random House, 1962), p. 77.

4. Statement from a briefing by Bishop Harries, Anglican bishop of Oxford, October, 1993, p. 9.

5. The encyclical *Veritatis Splendor* figures prominently in this chapter. I have used it here as representative of the official church's analysis of the current moral climate. It is an important encyclical in many respects; however, the main purpose of its employment in this chapter is to illustrate the magisterium's view of the moral sense of ordinary people, including Catholics.

6. *Veritatis Splendor*, # 32.

7. Ibid.

8. Murdoch, Iris, *The Sovereignty of Good* (London: Routledge & Kegan Paul, 1970), p. 97.

9. *Gaudium et Spes*, # 16.

10. Noonan, John, "Development in Moral Doctrine," *Theological Studies*, 54 (1993): 662–77.

11. Delhaye, Philippe, *The Christian Conscience* (New York: Desclee, 1968), p. 20.

12. *Gaudium et Spes*, # 16.

13. *Veritatis Splendor*, # 57.

14. Ibid., # 60.

15. Ibid., # 63.

16. Ibid., # 61.

17. Finnis, John, *The Tablet*, January 1994, p. 9.

18. Ibid., p. 10.

19. Ibid.

20. *The Tablet*, December 1993, p. 1619.

21. Ibid.

22. Cosgrove, William, "Structures of Authority," in *Authority in the Church*, ed. Sean Mac Reamoinn (Dublin: Columba Press, 1995), p. 30.

23. "The Manual System of Moral Theology Since the Death of Alphonsus," *Irish Theological Quarterly* 51, no. 1 (1985): 1–17.

Chapter 2

1. Diels, Hermann, *Die Fragmente der Vorsokratiker* (Berlin: Wiedmannsche, 1951), 68, B, 297.

2. Davies, W. D., "Conscience," in Buttrick et al., *Interpreter's Dictionary of the Bible* (Nashville: Abingdon Press, 1981), vol. 1, pp. 671–76.

3. Euripides, *Orestes*, 396.

4. Plutarch, *On Tranquility of Mind*, 11, 479 ff., Loeb edition.

5. Plato, *Republic*, 1, 330d–331a.

6. Aristotle, *Nicomachean Ethics*, VI, 5.

7. Plato, *Apology*, 31d, Penguin edition, p. 64.

8. D'Arcy, op. cit., p. 5.

9. Maurer, Christian, "Conscience," in Kittel, Gerhard, *Theological Dictionary of the New Testament*, translated by Bromiley, Geoffrey (Grand Rapids Mich.: Eerdmans, 1964), p. 905.

10. Epictetus, *Diss.*, 111, 22, 94, discussed in Maurer, op. cit.

11. This text is usually attributed to Epictetus, although there is some dispute regarding who the author is. It may be another Stoic philosopher (Davies, op. cit., p. 671).

12. Seneca, *de ira*, III, 6, quoted in Maurer, op. cit., p. 906.

13. Davies, op. cit., p. 672.

14. Cicero, *De Senectute*, 3, 9.

15. Cicero, *De Finibus,* I, 51.

16. Cicero, *De Natura Deorum*, III, 85.

17. Seneca, *Epist.* 41, 1.

18. Seneca, *Epist.*, 43, 5.

19. Maurer, op. cit., p. 907.

20. Jonsen, Albert, and Toulmin, Stephen, *The Abuse of Casuistry: A History of Moral Reasoning* (Berkeley: University of California Press, 1988), p. 47.

21. Cicero, *De Officiis*, 1, 32.

22. Ibid., 1, 59, quoted in Jonsen and Toulmin, op. cit., p. 79.

23. Ibid., p. 75.

24. Wisdom 17:11.

25. Psalm 139: 1, 23, 24.

26. Maurer, op. cit., p. 908.

27. Job 27:6.

28. Ecclesiastes 7:22.

29. Exodus 7:13.

30. Zecheriah 7:12.

31. Jeremiah 23:9.

32. Psalm 51:10.

33. Maurer, "Conscience," op. cit., p. 910.

34. Ibid., p. 913.

35. Jonsen and Toulmin, op. cit., p. 57.

36. Many translations do not include this phrase. See, for example, the RSV and the NRSV translations.

37. Romans 2:14.

38. Romans 9:1.

39. Delhaye, op. cit., p. 35.

40. 2 Timothy 1:3.

41. 2 Corinthians 1:12.

42. Eight of the fourteen mentions of conscience occur in relation to eating meat sacrificed to idols. Most of these appear in 1 Corinthians, 8, 9 and 10.

43. 1 Corinthians 8:7.

44. 1 Corinthians 8:13.

45. 1 Corinthians 10:25.

46. Romans 13:5.

47. Maurer, op. cit., p. 916.

48. D'Arcy, op. cit., p. 11.

49. Delhaye, op. cit., p. 48.

50. Mahoney, John, *The Making of Moral Theology: A Study of the Roman Catholic Tradition* (Oxford: Clarendon, 1987), p. 186.

51. Quoted in Delhaye, op. cit., p. 73.

52. There is a useful and detailed discussion of conscience in patristic thought in Delhaye, op. cit.

53. Ibid., p. 74.

54. Ibid.

55. D'Arcy, op. cit., p. 15, quoting Patrologia graeca 14, 893.

56. Jerome, *Ep.*, 100, I, Patrologia latina 22, 814 A in Delhaye, op. cit. p. 75.

57. See chapter 3.

58. Apology I, 28, Patrologia graeca 5, 372, B, C, quoted in Delhaye op. cit., p. 77.

59. Ibid., p. 80.

60. Ibid.

61. D'Arcy, op. cit., p. 15.

62. Jerome, *Commentarium in Ezechielem*, 1,1, PL 25, 22 in D'Arcy op. cit., p. 16.

63. *Penitential of Bede*, quoted in Jonsen and Toulmin, op. cit., p. 97.

Chapter 3

1. Leff, Gordon, *Medieval Thought* (Chicago: Quadrangle Books, 1958).

2. D'Arcy, op. cit., p. 20.

3. Potts, Timothy, "Conscience," in *Cambridge History of Later Medieval Philosophy*: *From the Recovery of Aristotle to the Disintegration of Scholasticism 1100–1600,* ed. Norman Kretzmann, Anthony Kenny & Jan Pinborg (New York: Cambridge University Press, 1982), p. 687.

4. D'Arcy, op. cit., p. 22.

5. Potts, Timothy, *Conscience in Medieval Philosophy* (New York: Cambridge University Press, 1980), p. 95.

6. Potts, "Conscience," in *Cambridge History*, op. cit., p. 694.

7. Ibid., p. 695.

8. D'Arcy, op. cit., p. 29.

9. D'Arcy, op. cit., p. 27.

10. Potts, "Conscience," in *Cambridge History*, op. cit., p. 691.

11. Ibid., p. 30.

12. Luscombe, David, *Peter Abelard's Ethics* (Oxford: Clarendon, 1971), p. xv.

13. Ibid., p. xxxii.

14. Ibid., p. xxxiv.

15. *Summa Theologiae* (*S.T.* in later references) 1a, q. 79, a. 12.

16. Delhaye, op. cit., p. 114.

17. Ibid.

18. Aquinas would refer to these elsewhere as the primary precepts of the natural law.

19. Mahoney, op. cit., p. 188.

20. *S.T.*, 1a2ae q. 94, a. 1.

21. *S.T.*, 1a, q. 79, a. 13.

22. Ibid.

23. Ibid.

24. Ibid.

25. Ibid.

26. This dilemma comes from the Moral Dilemmas Forum, which is run by Bernard Treacy, editor of *Doctrine and Life*. It appeared in *Doctrine and Life* in November 1998.

27. D'Arcy, op. cit., p. 77. Augustine defended this view by insisting that we judge the will by its own proper object. Now

the proper object of the will is the good, not as it is in itself, but as it is presented by the reason; and this is just what we mean by the judgment of conscience. Hence, that which conscience judges (whether correctly or not) to be obligatory, by that very judgment binds the will.

28. *Sermo vi De Verbis Domini*, cap. 8, in D'Arcy, op. cit., p. 77.

29. D'Arcy, op. cit., p. 87.

30. Ibid., p. 95.

31. Ibid., p. 98.

32. Aquinas describes this view thus: "...reason or conscience obliges on neutral matters, so that an act of will against it is bad and a sin. But that when reason or conscience is mistaken in commanding what is bad in itself, or forbidding what is good in itself and necessary for salvation, then it is not binding; and in that case an act of will that goes against it is not bad." *S.T.*, 1a2ae, q. 19, a. 5.

33. Ibid.

34. Ibid., "...when the reason is mistaken its judgment, though not issuing from God, is nevertheless put forward as true, and therefore as issuing from God, from whom is all truth."

35. Ibid., a. 6.

36. Ibid.

37. A central plank of Aquinas's theology is that only actions that are voluntary, or freely chosen and intended, can be judged to be good or evil.

38. Ibid.

39. Ibid.

40. Ibid.

41. Mahoney, op. cit., p. 183.

42. Ibid.

43. Zedeen, Ernst, *The Legacy of Luther* (London: Hollis and Carter, 1954), p. 79.

44. *Martin Luthers Werke, Kritische Gesammtuasgabe* (Weimar, 1883), 7, 838, 4–9. The translation is Michael Baylor's in *Action and Person, Conscience in Late Scholasticism and the Young Luther* (Leiden: E. J. Brill, 1977), p. 1.

45. The nature of the relationship between Luther's theology and that of late Scholasticism has been and continues to be seriously contested by theologians down through the centuries. Many of these discussions have proceeded on narrowly denominational lines. For a sample of these diverse views see Karl Adam, *The Roots of the Reformation* (Garden City, N.Y.: Doubleday, 1957); Ronald Bainton, *The Reformation of the Sixteenth Century* (London: Hodder & Stoughton, 1953); and Elmore Harbison, *The Age of the Reformation* (Ithaca, N.Y.: Cornell University Press, 1955).

46. See, for example, many of the essays in *Transition and Revolution*, edited by Robert Kingdon (Minneapolis, 1974) and the essays of Steven Ozment, *The Reformation in Medieval Perspective* (Chicago: Quadrangle Books, 1971).

47. Baylor, op. cit., p. 114.

48. Ibid., p. 158.

49. See H. Oberman, *Luther and the Dawn of the Modern Era* (Leiden: Brill, 1974) and B. Gerrish, *Grace and Reason* (Oxford: Oxford University Press, 1962) for some initial soundings on this subject.

50. Baylor, op. cit., p. 202.

51. Ibid., p. 247.

52. Ibid.

53. For an excellent analysis of the Christian tradition of casuistry see Jonsen and Toulmin, op. cit.

54. Ibid., p. 164.

55. Ibid., p. 165.

56. Ibid., p. 166.

57. As discussed in Gallagher, John, *Time Past, Time Future*: *Historical Study of Catholic Moral Theology* (Mahwah, N.J.: Paulist Press, 1990), pp. 44 ff.

58. Ibid., p. 81.

59. Ibid., p. 82.

Chapter 4

1. This phrase has been appropriated by theologians from the philosophy of science. Famously, Thomas Kuhn used the term to describe the very fundamental ways in which our

understanding of the universe has changed since the renaissance as a result of the great advances in science. Cf. *The Structure of Scientific Revolutions* (Chicago: University of Chicago Press, 1970).

2. O'Murchu, Diarmuid, "New Paradigms in Theology," *Priests and People* 4 (1990): 388.

3. Johnstone, Brian, "The Revisionist Project in Roman Catholic Moral Theology," in *Studies in Christian Ethics* 5, no. 2 (1992): 19.

4. Modernism was condemned as "the synthesis of all heresies" by Pius X in his 1907 encyclical *Pascendi dominici gregis*. This phrase refers to the work of a number of theologians who argued that the church needed to respond to the challenges of modernity. They were united in their opposition to the rigidities of neo-Thomism and sought to introduce the ideas of historical change and development into the church's understanding of its tradition.

5. Rahner, Karl, "Der Einzelne in der Kirche," in *Stimmen der Zeit* 39 (1946–47): 260–76, quoted in Gallagher op. cit., p. 241.

6. See McCormick, Richard, *Corrective Vision: Explorations in Moral Theology* (Kansas City: Sheed & Ward, 1994), op cit., p. 19.

7. See Gallagher op. cit., p. 171 ff.

8. Sheed & Ward, New York; originally *Vom Sinn und Zwek der Ehe*, 1935.

9. Cahill, Lisa, "Catholic Sexual Ethics and the Dignity of the Person," *Theological Studies* 50 (1989): 121.

10. Mahoney, op. cit., p. 203.

11. Jacques Neuner and Jacques Dupuis, *The Christian Faith in the Doctrinal Documents of the Catholic Church* (London: Collins, 1983), p. 595

12. Mahoney, op. cit., p. 206.

13. Neuner and Dupuis, op. cit., p. 596.

14. Mahoney, op. cit., p. 207 ff.

15. Fuchs, Josef, "On Christian Moral Theology" in Latourelle, Rene, *Vatican II: Assessment and Perspectives* (Mahwah, N.J.: Paulist Press), 1989.

16. Fuchs, Josef, *Christian Morality: The Word Made Flesh* (Dublin: Gill & McMillan, 1981), p. 21.

17. Ibid

18. Ibid.

19. Kelly, Kevin, *New Directions in Moral Theology* (London: Chapman, 1992), p. 30.

20. *Gaudium et Spes*, # 51.

21. McCormick, *Corrective Vision*, op. cit., p. 14.

22. Gaffney, J., *Matters of Faith and Morals* (London: Sheed & Ward, 1987), pp. 115–33.

23. *Dignitatis humanae*, #3.

24. Ibid.

25. Ibid.

26. Fuchs, "On Christian Moral Theology," op. cit., p. 490.

27. *Gaudium et Spes*, # 50.

28. Ibid., # 16.

29. Fuchs, "On Christian Moral Theology," op. cit., p. 439.

30. Ibid., p. 493.

31. Ratzinger, quoted in Michael Allsopp, "Conscience, the Church and Moral Truth: John Henry Newman, Vatican II, Today," *Irish Theological Quarterly* 58 (1992): 197.

32. Keenan, James, *Goodness and Rightness in Thomas Aquinas' Summa Theologiae* (Washington, D.C.: Georgetown University Press, 1992), p. 143.

33. Ibid., p. 137.

34. Gleeson, Gerald, "When a Good Conscience Errs," *Pacifica* 8 (1995): 67.

35. Allsopp, op. cit., p. 197.

36. *Gaudium et Spes*, # 50.

37. Mahoney, op. cit., p. 265.

38. Ibid., p. 271.

39. Ibid.

40. Ibid.

41. Cahill, Lisa, "Sex and Gender: Catholic Teaching and the Signs of Our Times," *Milltown Studies* 34 (Autumn 1994): 43.

42. Johnstone, op. cit., p. 24.

43. Melchin, Kenneth, "Revisionists, Deontologists and the Structure of Moral Understanding," *Theological Studies* 51 (1990): 369.

44. It is important to note that although some neoscholastics separated the object from the intention, many did not. As a result it would be wrong to read this criticism as pertaining to all neoscholastic theologies since many did recognize that the object was in the intention.

45. Theologians hold different opinions regarding how one determines the moral significance of the various features of the context.

46. See, for example, Charles Curran and Richard McCormick, *Readings in Moral Theology No.1: Moral Norms and Catholic Tradition* (Mahwah, N.J.: Paulist Press, 1979).

47. However, we will see in chapter 6 that the church itself introduced an exception to this exceptionless norm in the guise of the Pauline privilege.

48. O'Connell, Timothy, *Principles for a Catholic Morality* (New York: Seabury, 1976), p. 166.

49. *Veritatis Splendor,* # 80.

50. Confusion has also arisen because the phrase *intrinsic evil* has been misused throughout history to refer to very serious actions needing great justification to be performed. The encyclical *Veritatis Splendor* is a case in point. It includes a list of actions, some of which have been traditionally considered to be intrinsically evil and some that are considered to be serious issues but not themselves intrinsically evil. This adds to the confusion of the issue and also leads to the term being used in popular discourse to convey moral censure in relation to particular actions.

Chapter 5

1. This phrase is characteristic of personalist theologies and is used by both Louis Janssens and Kevin Kelly.

2. Braidotti, Rosi, *Nomadic Subjects* (New York: Columbia University Press, 1994).

3. Butler, Judith, *Gender Trouble* (New York: Routledge, 1991) and, particularly, *Bodies That Matter: On the Discursive Limits of Sex* (London: Routledge, 1993).

4. Benhabib, Seyla, *Situating the Self: Gender, Community and Postmodernism in Contemporary Ethics* (Cambridge, England: Polity Press, 1992).

5. This is developed by Häring in many texts including *The Law of Christ*, vol. 1 (Cork: Mercier Press, 1960).

6. See, for example, Häring, Bernard, *Free and Faithful in Christ*, vol. 1 (New York: Seabury, 1978), pp. 164 ff., Fuchs, Josef, *Human Values and Christian Morality* (Dublin: Gill and Macmillan, 1970), pp. 92 ff. and Rahner, Karl, *Theological Investigations*, vol. 6 (New York: Crossroad, 1982).

7. Rahner, op. cit.

8. Murdoch, Iris, op. cit., p. 37.

9. The issue of how we understand the nature of moral goodness is much debated. As is evident throughout this text, I am operating with a view that regards moral goodness not as an abstract ideal or form, but rather something contextual and embodied, something ultimately uncertain and provisional, something our understanding and apprehension can change.

10. Nussbaum, Martha, *The Fragility of Goodness* (Oxford: Oxford University Press, 1986).

11. Boff, Leonardo, *Liberating Grace* (Maryknoll, N.Y.: Orbis, 1979).

12. Soskice, Janet Martin, "The God of Hope" in *Doctrine and Life* 44 (April 1994): 203.

13. Taylor, Charles, *Sources of the Self: The Making of Modern Identity* (New York: Cambridge University Press, 1989).

14. Soskice, op. cit., p. 204.

15. See Alasdair MacIntyre, *Whose Justice: Which Rationality?* (Notre Dame, Ind.: University of Notre Dame Press, 1988), for a comprehensive discussion of this point.

16. McCaughey, Terence, *Memory and Redemption, Church, Politics and Prophetic Theology in Ireland* (Dublin: Gill and Macmillan, 1993).

17. Callahan, op. cit., p. 126.

18. Mahoney, *The Making of Moral Theology*, p. 222.

19. Ibid.

20. Ibid., p. 207.

21. Mahoney, John, "Conscience, Discernment and Prophecy in Moral Decision Making," in William O'Brien, ed., *Riding Time Like a River: The Catholic Moral Tradition Since Vatican II* (Washington, D.C.: Georgetown University Press, 1993), pp. 81–97.

22. Ibid.

23. Mahoney, *The Making of Moral Theology*, p. 209.

24. Delhaye, op.cit., p. 26, quoting Jerome, *Commentary on Ezekiel*, 1 Patrologia latina 25, 22.

25. Speer, Albert, *Inside the Third Reich*: *Memoirs* (London: Weidenfield & Nicholson, 1970).

26. Sereny, Gita, *Albert Speer: His Battle with Truth* (London: Macmillan, 1995).

27. Ibid., p. 463.

28. Ibid., p. 707.

29. Ibid., opening inscription.

Chapter 6

1. Aristotle, *Nicomachean Ethics*, 1.3. 1–4, 1094b.

2. *Beyond the Dark Night*: *A Way Forward for the Church* (London: Cassels, 1997), p. vii.

3. Op. cit.

4. For a discussion of the controversy surrounding this 1989 Profession of Faith, see Ladislas Örsy, *The Profession of Faith and the Oath of Fidelity*: *A Case Study* (Wilmington, Del.: Michael Glazier, 1990).

5. Örsy, Ladislas, "Intelligent Fidelity" *Ceide* 2, no. 2 (1998): 29.

6. Ibid., p. 30.

7. Cardinal Ratzinger, "For the Defense of the Faith," *The Tablet*, July 11, 1998, p. 921.

8. Sullivan, Francis, *Creative Fidelity*: *Weighing and Interpreting Documents of the Magisterium* (Mahwah, N.J.: Paulist Press, 1996) and "Recent Theological Observations on Magisterial Documents and Public Dissent," *Theological Studies* 58, no. 3 (1997): 509–15.

9. Gaillardetz, Richard, *Teaching with Authority: A Theology of the Magisterium in the Church* (Collegeville, Minn.: Liturgical Press, 1997), p. 271.

10. Ibid., p. 63.

11. Ibid., p. xi.

12. Ibid.

13. Ibid., p. 70.

14. Ibid., p. 99.

15. Örsy, "Intelligent Fidelity," p. 30.

16. Quoted in Gaillardetz, op. cit., p. 290.

17. However, as already noted earlier, in very recent years there has also been a tendency to expand and upgrade the authority of the category of definitive teaching. As a result many moral pronouncements previously believed to be in the category of nondefinitive teaching are now given the status of teachings definitively held. There are many detailed discussions of this problem, including Richard Gaillardetz, *Teaching with Authority: A Theology of the Magisterium in the Church;* Francis Sullivan, "Recent Theological Observations on Magisterial Documents and Public Dissent," in *Theological Studies;* and Richard McCormick, *Corrective Vision: Explorations in Moral Theology.*

18. *Lumen gentium,* # 25.

19. Rahner, Karl, "Dogmatic Constitution on the Church," chapter 3 in Vorgrimler's *Commentary on the Documents of Vatican II* (New York: Crossroad, 1989), pp. 208–10; also Butler, B. C., "Infallible: *Authenticum: Assensus: Obsequium.* Christian Teaching Authority and the Christian's Response," *Doctrine and Life,* 31 (1981): 77–89.

20. Örsy, Ladislas, *The Church: Learning and Teaching* (Wilmington, Del.: Michael Glazier, 1987), p. 85.

21. There are many excellent discussions of how issues of dissent and assent affect the nature of theological inquiry. Those of Sullivan and Örsy mentioned above are important. There are also some interesting articles on the topic in Charles Curran and Richard McCormick's *Readings in Moral Theology No. 6: Dissent in the Church* (Mahwah, N.J.: Paulist Press, 1988). In his article "Compelling Assent: Magisterium, Conscience

and Oaths," *Irish Theological Quarterly* no. 57 (1991): 209–27, James Keenan also makes some very insightful comments on the issue.

22. Op. cit., p. 271.

23. *The Tablet,* June 21, 1986, pp. 647–49; reprinted in Curran and McCormick, *Readings in Moral Theology No. 6: Dissent in the Church*, pp. 478–83.

24. Ibid., p. 478 (quotation taken from the Curran and McCormick text).

25. This is a phrase used by Richard McCormick.

26. Curran and McCormick, *Readings in Moral Theology No. 6,* p. 480.

27. Ibid., p. 479.

28. "The Settle Bed," from *Seeing Things,* 1991, reprinted in Seamus Heaney, *Open Ground: Poems 1966–1996* (London: Faber and Faber, 1998).

29. "Declaration of the Rights of Man and of the Citizen," in Hans Küng and Jürgen Moltmann, *The Ethics of World Religions and Human Rights,* Concilium, 2, pp. 3–5 (New York: Seabury, 1990).

30. Quoted in Bernard Plongeron, "Anathema or Dialogue? Christian Reactions to the Declarations of the Rights of Man in the United States and Europe in the Eighteenth Century," in Alois Muller and Norbert Greinacher, eds., *The Church and the Rights of Man,* Concilium, 12, pp. 1–16 (New York: Seabury, 1979).

31. *Pacem in Terris,* # 9

32. Noonan, John, "Development in Moral Doctrine," *Theological Studies* 54 (1993): 662–77.

33. Ibid., p. 662.

34. Ibid.

35. Ibid.

36. Ibid., p. 663.

37. Ibid.

38. *Veritatis Splendor,* # 27.

39. See Brian Johnstone's "Faithful Action: The Catholic Moral Tradition and *Veritatis Splendor,*" *Studia Moralia* 31 (1993): 283–305 for an interesting comment on this subject.

However, this is a subject that still warrants further serious historical and theological analysis.

40. Newman, John Henry, *Essay on the Development of Christian Doctrine*, ed. Charles Frederick Harrold (New York: Longmans, Green, 1949).

41. Congar, Yves, *La Tradition et les traditions*: *Essai historique* (Paris: Fayard, 1960); *La Tradition et les traditions*: *II Essai theologique* (Paris: Fayard, 1963).

42. Rahner, Karl, "The Development of Dogma," in *Theological Investigations* 1 (London: Darton, Longman & Todd, 1961), pp. 39–77.

43. Pelikan, Jaroslav, *The Christian Tradition*: *A History of the Development of Doctrine* (Chicago: University of Chicago Press, 1971–89).

44. Noonan, op. cit., p. 670.

45. Johnstone, op. cit., p. 302.

46. Ibid.

47. Ibid., p. 303.

48. Ibid.

49. McCormick, Richard, "The Search for Truth in a Catholic Context," reprinted in Curran and McCormick, *Readings in Moral Theology No. 6*, p. 425.

50. Gaillardetz, op. cit., p. 230.

51. Ibid., p. 232.

52. Ibid.

53. Heaney, "The Settle Bed," op. cit.

54. Noonan, op. cit., p. 667.

55. Curran, Charles, "Changing Anthropological Bases of Catholic Social Ethics," in *Readings in Moral Theology No. 5*: *Official Catholic Social Teaching*, eds., Charles Curran and Richard McCormick (Mahwah, N.J.: Paulist 1986), p. 189.

56. *Dignitatis humanae*, #2

57. Visser't Hooft, quoted in Sereny, op. cit.

58. Reported in *The Observer*, November 1, 1998.

59. Grey, Mary, *Beyond the Dark Night: A Way Forward for the Church* (London: Cassels, 1997).

60. McDonagh, Enda, *Faith in Fragments* (Dublin: Columba Press, 1996), p. 32.

Bibliography

Adam, Karl. *The Roots of the Reformation*. Garden City, N.Y.: Doubleday, 1957.

Allsopp, Michael. "Conscience, the Church and Moral Truth: John Henry Newman, Vatican II, Today." *Irish Theological Quarterly* 58 (1992): pp. 192–208.

Aquinas, Thomas. *Summa Theologiae*. Blackfriars edition. London: Blackfriars, 1963.

Aristotle. *Nicomachean Ethics*. Translated by J. Thomson. Harmondsworth, U.K.: Penguin, 1976.

Bainton, Ronald. *The Reformation of the Sixteenth Century*. London: Hodder and Stoughton, 1953.

Baylor, Michael. *Action and Person: Conscience in Late Scholasticism and the Young Luther*. Leiden: Brill, 1977.

Benhabib, Seyla. *Situating the Self, Gender, Community and Postmodernism in Contemporary Ethics*. Cambridge: Polity Press, 1992.

Bernardin, Cardinal J. *Consistent Ethic of Life*. Kansas City: Sheed & Ward, 1988.

Bernardin, J., and Oscar Lipscomb. *Catholic Common Ground Initiative, Foundational Documents*. New York: Crossroad, 1997.

Boff, Leonardo. *Liberating Grace*. Maryknoll, N.Y.: Orbis, 1979.

Bolt, Robert. *A Man for All Seasons*. New York: Random House, 1962,

Boyle, Joseph. "Theologians and Bishops: Freedom and Assent." *Catholic Theological Society of America Proceedings* 44 (1989): pp. 91–102.

Braidotti, Rosi. *Nomadic Subjects*. New York: Columbia University Press, 1994.

Butler, B. C. "Infallible: *Authenticum: Assensus: Obsequium*. Christian Teaching Authority and the Christian's Response." *Doctrine and Life* 31 (1981): pp. 77–89.

Butler, Judith. *Gender Trouble*. New York: Routledge, 1991.

———. *Bodies That Matter: On the Discursive Limits of Sex*. London: Routledge, 1993.

Cahill, Lisa. "Catholic Sexual Ethics and the Dignity of the Person: A Double Message?" *Theological Studies* 50 (1989): pp. 120–50.

———. "Sex and Gender: Catholic Teaching and the Signs of Our Times." *Milltown Studies* 34 (Autumn 1994): pp. 31–47.

Callahan, Sidney. *In Good Conscience: Reason and Emotion in Decision Making*. New York: HarperCollins, 1991.

———. "Conscience," In William O'Brien, ed., *Riding Time Like a River: The Catholic Moral Tradition Since Vatican II*. Washington, D.C.: Georgetown University Press, 1993, pp. 99–112.

Cicero. *De Officiis*. Translated by W. Miller. London: Heinemann, 1913.

———. *De Finibus*. Translated by H. Rackham. Cambridge, Mass.: Harvard University Press, 1914.

———. *De Senectute*. Translated by W. Falconer. Cambridge, Mass.: Harvard University Press, 1946.

———. *De Natura Deorum*. Translated by H. McGregor. Harmondsworth, U.K.: Penguin, 1972.

Congar, Yves. *La Tradition et les traditions: Essai historique*. Paris: Fayard 1960.

———. *La Tradition et les traditions: II Essai theologique*. Paris: Fayard 1963.

Conn, Walter. *Christian Conversion, A Developmental Interpretation of Autonomy and Surrender*. Mahwah, N.J.: Paulist Press, 1986.

Cosgrove, William. "Structures of Authority." In *Authority in the Church*, edited by Sean MacReamoinn. Dublin: Columba Press, 1995, pp. 26–47.

Crotty, Nicholas. "Conscience and Conflict." *Theological Studies* 32 (1971): pp. 208–32.

Curran, Charles, and Richard McCormick, eds. *Readings in Moral Theology No.1: Moral Norms and Catholic Tradition.* Mahwah, N.J.: Paulist Press, 1979.

———. *Readings in Moral Theology No. 5: Official Catholic Social Teaching.* Mahwah, N.J.: Paulist Press 1986.

———. *Readings in Moral Theology No. 6: Dissent in the Church.* Mahwah, N.J.: Paulist Press, 1988.

D'Arcy, Eric. *Thomas Aquinas.* London: Ernest Benn Ltd., 1930.

———. *Conscience and Its Right to Freedom.* London: Sheed & Ward, 1961.

Davies, W. D. "Conscience." In George Arthur Buttrick et al., *Interpreter's Dictionary of the Bible.* Nashville: Abingdon Press, vol. 1, pp. 671–76.

Davis, Charles. *A Question of Conscience.* London: Hodder & Stoughton, 1967.

Delhaye, Philippe. *Christian Philosophy in the Middle Ages.* London: Burns & Oates, 1960.

———. *The Christian Conscience.* New York: Desclee Company, 1968.

Diels, Hermann. *Die Fragmente der Vorsokratiker.* Berlin: Wiedmannsche, 1951.

Euripides. *Orestes.* Translated by Vellacott. Harmondsworth, U.K.: Penguin, 1972.

Fagan, Sean. *Has Morality Changed?* Dublin: Gill & Macmillan, 1997.

Fuchs, Josef. *Human Values and Christian Morality.* Dublin: Gill & Macmillan, 1970.

———. *Christian Morality: The Word Made Flesh.* Dublin: Gill & Macmillan, 1981.

———. "A Harmonization of the Conciliar Statements on Christian Moral Theology." In Latourelle, Rene, *Vatican II: Assessment and Perspectives.* Mahwah, N.J.: Paulist Press, 1989, pp. 479–500.

————. *Moral Demands and Personal Obligations*. Washington, D.C.: Georgetown University Press, 1993.

Gaffney, James. *Matters of Faith and Morals*. London: Sheed & Ward, 1987.

Gaillardetz, Richard. *Teaching with Authority: A Theology of the Magisterium in the Church*. Collegeville, Minn.: Liturgical Press, 1997.

Gallagher, John. *Time Past, Time Future: Historical Study of Catholic Moral Theology*. Mahwah, N.J.: Paulist Press, 1990.

Gallagher, Raphael. "The Manual System of Moral Theology Since the Death of Alphonsus." *Irish Theological Quarterly* 51, no. 1 (1985): pp. 1–17.

Gerrish, Brian. *Grace and Reason*. Oxford: Oxford University Press, 1962.

Gilson, Etienne. *The Philosophy of St. Thomas*. Cambridge, U.K.: Heffer & Sons Ltd., 1924.

Gleeson, Gerald. "When a Good Conscience Errs." *Pacifica* 8 (1995): pp. 53–73.

Grave, Selwyn. *Conscience in Newman's Thought*. Oxford: Clarendon Press, 1989.

Gres-Gayer, Jacques. "The Magisterium of the Faculty of Theology of Paris in the Seventeenth Century." *Theological Studies* 53 (1992): pp. 424–50.

Grey, Mary. *Beyond the Dark Night: A Way Forward for the Church*. London: Cassels, 1997.

Grisez, Germain. "Infallibility and Contraception: A Reply to Garth Hallet." *Theological Studies* 47 (1986): pp. 134–45.

Hallet, Garth. "Infallibility and Contraception: The Debate Continues." *Theological Studies* 49 (1982): pp. 629–50.

————. "Contraception and Prescriptive Infallibility." *Theological Studies* 43 (1988): pp. 517–28.

Harbison, Elmore. *The Age of the Reformation*. Ithaca, N.Y.: Doubleday, 1955.

Häring, Bernard. *The Law of Christ*. Vol. 1. Cork: Mercier Press, 1960.

————. *Free and Faithful in Christ*. Vol. 1. New York: Seabury, 1978.

———. "More than Law and Precept Commandments # 2052-2195." In Michael Walsh, ed., *Commentary on the Catechism of the Catholic Church*. London: Chapman, 1994, pp. 357–66.

Hauerwas, Stanley. *Truthfulness and Tragedy: Further Investigations into Christian Ethics*. Notre Dame, Ind.: University of Notre Dame Press, 1977.

Heaney, Seamus. *Open Ground, Poems 1966–1996*. London: Faber and Faber, 1998.

Hughes, Gerard. "Our Human Vocation #1691–2051." In Michael Walsh, ed., *Commentary on the Catechism of the Catholic Church*. London: Chapman, 1994, pp. 336–56.

Janssens, Louis. "The Non-Infallible Magisterium and Theologians." *Louvain Studies* 14 (1989): pp. 195–259.

Johnson, Mark. "Proportionalism and a Text of the Young Aquinas: Quodlibetum IX, Q.7, A.2." *Theological Studies* 53 (1992): pp. 683–99.

Johnstone, Brian. "The Revisionist Project in Roman Catholic Moral Theology." *Studies in Christian Ethics* 5, no. 2 (1992): pp. 18–31.

———. "Faithful Action: The Catholic Moral Tradition and *Veritatis Splendor*." *Studia Moralia* 31 (1993): pp. 283–305.

Jonsen, Albert, and Stephen Toulmin. *The Abuse of Casuistry: A History of Moral Reasoning*. Berkeley: University of California Press, 1988.

Keenan, James. "Compelling Assent: Magisterium, Conscience and Oaths." *Irish Theological Quarterly* 57 (1991): pp. 209–27.

———. *Goodness and Rightness in Thomas Aquinas' Summa Theologiae*. Washington, D.C.: Georgetown University Press, 1992.

Kelly, Kevin. *Conscience: Dictator or Guide?* London: Chapman, 1967.

———. "Serving the Truth." *The Tablet*, June 21, 1986, pp. 647–49, reprinted in Curran and McCormick, *Readings in Moral Theology No. 6: Dissent in the Church*. Mahwah, N.J.: Paulist Press, 1988, pp. 478–83.

———. *New Directions in Moral Theology*. London: Chapman, 1992.

Kingdon, Robert. *Transition and Revolution*. Minneapolis: 1974.

Knowles, David. *The Evolution of Medieval Thought*. London: Longman, 1962.

Kuhn, Thomas. *The Structure of Scientific Revolutions*. Chicago: University of Chicago Press, 1970.

Küng, Hans, and Jurgen Moltmann. *The Ethics of World Religions and Human Rights*. Concilium, 1990/2.

Leff, Gordon. *Medieval Thought*. Chicago: Quadrangle Books, 1958.

Luscombe, David. *Peter Abelard's Ethics*. Oxford: Clarendon Press, 1971.

———. "Natural Morality and Natural Law." In *Cambridge History of Later Medieval Philosophy: From the Recovery of Aristotle to the Disintegration of Scholasticism 1100–1600*, edited by Norman Kretzmann, Anthony Kenny and Jan Pinborg. New York: Cambridge University Press, 1982, pp. 705–19.

Luther, Martin. *Martin Luthers Werke, Kritische Gesammtuasgabe* (Weimar, 1883).

MacIntyre, Alasdair. *Whose Justice: Which Rationality?* Notre Dame, Ind.: University of Notre Dame Press, 1988.

Magill, Gerard. "Moral Imagination in Theological Method and Church Tradition: John Henry Newman." *Theological Studies* 53 (1992): pp. 451–75.

———. "Interpreting Moral Doctrine: Newman on Conscience and Law." *Horizons* 20 (1993): pp. 7–22.

Mahoney, John. *The Making of Moral Theology: A Study of the Roman Catholic Tradition*. Oxford: Clarendon, 1987.

———. "Conscience, Discernment and Prophecy in Moral Decision Making." In William O'Brien, ed., *Riding Time Like a River: The Catholic Moral Tradition Since Vatican II*. Washington, D.C.: Georgetown University Press, 1993, pp. 81–97.

Maurer, Christian. "Conscience." In Gerhard Kittel, *Theological Dictionary of the New Testament*, translated by Bromiley, Geoffrey. Grand Rapids: Eerdmans, 1964, pp. 898–919.

McBrien, Richard. "A Response to Francis Sullivan." *Catholic Theological Society of America Proceedings* 43 (1988): pp. 76–79.

McCaughey, Terence. *Memory and Redemption, Church, Politics and Prophetic Theology in Ireland*. Dublin: Gill & Macmillan, 1993.

McCormick, Richard. "Notes on Moral Theology, 1984, Moral Norms: An Update." *Theological Studies* 46 (1985): pp. 50–64.

————. "The Search for Truth in a Catholic Context." Reprinted in Curran and McCormick, eds, *Readings in Moral Theology No. 6: Dissent in the Church*. Mahwah, N.J.: Paulist Press, 1988, pp. 421–34.

————. "Tradition in Transition." In William O'Brien, ed., *Riding Time Like a River: The Catholic Moral Tradition Since Vatican II*. Washington, D.C.: Georgetown University Press, 1993, pp. 17–33.

————. *Corrective Vision Explorations in Moral Theology*. Kansas City: Sheed & Ward, 1994.

McDonagh, Enda. *Faith in Fragments*. Dublin: Columba Press, 1996.

Melchin, Kenneth. "Revisionists, Deontologists and the Structure of Moral Understanding." *Theological Studies* 51 (1990): pp. 389–416.

Mitchell, Basil. *Morality: Religious and Secular*. Oxford: Oxford University Press, 1980.

Murdoch, Iris. *The Sovereignty of Good*. London: Routledge & Kegan Paul, 1970.

Nelson, Carl Ellis. *Conscience, Theological and Psychological Perspectives*. New York: Newman Press, 1973.

Neuner, Jacques, and Jacques Dupuis. *The Christian Faith in the Doctrinal Documents of the Catholic Church*. London: Collins, 1983.

Newman, John Henry. *Essay on the Development of Christian Doctrine,* ed. Charles Frederick Harrold. New York: Longmans, Green, 1949.

————. *Grammar of Assent*. New York: Doubleday, 1955.

————. *Letters and Diaries*, edited by C. S. Dessian et al. Oxford: Clarendon Press, 1961.

Noonan, John. "Development in Moral Doctrine." *Theological Studies* 54 (1993): pp. 662–77.

Nussbaum, Martha. *The Fragility of Goodness*. Oxford: Oxford University Press, 1986.

Oberman, Heiko. *Luther and the Dawn of the Modern Era*. Leiden: Brill, 1974.

O'Connell, Timothy. *Principles for a Catholic Morality*. New York: Seabury, 1976.

O'Keeffe, Mark. "Social Sin and Fundamental Option." *Irish Theological Quarterly* 58 (1992): pp. 85–95.

O'Murchu, Diarmuid. "New Paradigms in Theology." *Priests and People* 4 (1990): pp. 388–96.

Örsy, Ladislas. *The Church: Learning and Teaching*. Wilmington, Del.: Glazier, 1987.

————. *The Profession of Faith and the Oath of Fidelity: A Case Study*. Wilmington, Del.: Glazier, 1990.

————. *Theology and Canon Law, New Horizons for Legislation and Interpretation*. Collegeville, Minn.: Liturgical Press, 1992.

————. "Intelligent Fidelity." *Ceide* 2, no. 2 (1998): pp. 29–31.

Ozment, Steven. *The Reformation in Medieval Perspective*. Chicago: Quadrangle Books, 1971.

Pelikan, Jaroslav. *The Christian Tradition: A History of the Development of Doctrine*. Chicago: University of Chicago Press, 1971–1989.

Pierce, Claude Anthony. *Conscience in the New Testament*. London: SCM Press, 1955.

Plato. *Apology*. Translated by Tredennick and Tarrant, Harmondsworth, U.K.: Penguin, 1954.

Plato. *Republic*.

Plongeron, Bernard. "Anathema or Dialogue? Christian Reactions to the Declarations of the Rights of Man in the United States and Europe in the Eighteenth Century." In Alois Muller and Norbert Greinacher, eds., *The Church and the Rights of Man*. Concilium 12 (1979): pp. 1–16.

Plutarch. "On Tranquility of Mind." In *Moralia*. Vol. VI, translated by W. Helmbold. London: Heinemann, 1939.

Potts, Timothy. *Conscience in Medieval Philosophy*. New York: Cambridge University Press, 1980.

————. "Conscience." In *Cambridge History of Later Medieval Philosophy: From the Recovery of Aristotle to the Disintegration of Scholasticism 1100–1600*, edited by Norman Kretzmann, Anthony Kenny and Jan Pinborg. New York: Cambridge University Press, 1982, pp. 687–704.

Rahner, Karl. "The Development of Dogma." *Theological Investigations*. Vol. 1. London: Darton, Longman & Todd, 1961, pp. 39–77.

————. *Theological Investigations*. Vol. 6. New York: Crossroad, 1982.

————. "Dogmatic Constitution on the Church." (Chapter 3). In Herbert Vorgrimler, *Commentary on the Documents of Vatican II*. New York: Crossroad, 1989, pp. 208–10.

Sacred Congregation for the Doctrine of the Faith. *Instructions on Certain Aspects of the Theology of Liberation*. London: Catholic Truth Society, 1984.

Selling, J., and Jan Jans. *The Splendor of Accuracy: An Examination of the Assertions Made by* Veritatis Splendor. Kampen: Kok Pharos, 1994.

Selling, Joseph. "*Veritatis Splendor* and the Sources of Morality." *Louvain Studies* 19 (1994): pp. 3–17.

Seneca. *Ad Lucilium Epistulae Morales*. Translated by R. Gummer. London: Heinemann, 1917.

Sereny, Gita. *Albert Speer: His Battle With Truth*. London: Macmillan, 1995.

Soskice, Janet Martin. "The God of Hope." *Doctrine and Life* 44 (April 1994): pp. 195–207.

Speer, Albert. *Inside the Third Reich: Memoirs*. London: Weidenfield & Nicholson, 1970.

Sullivan, Francis. *Magisterium: Teaching Authority in the Catholic Church*. Dublin: Gill & Macmillan, 1983.

————. "Magisterium and Theology." *Catholic Theological Society of America Proceedings* 43 (1988): pp. 65–75.

————. *Creative Fidelity: Weighing and Interpreting Documents of the Magisterium*. Mahwah, N.J.: Paulist Press, 1996.

————. "Recent Theological Observations on Magisterial Documents and Public Dissent." *Theological Studies* 58, no. 3 (1997): pp. 509–15.

Taylor, Charles. *Sources of the Self: The Making of Modern Identity*. Cambridge: Cambridge University Press, 1989.

Zedeen, Ernst. *The Legacy of Luther*. London: Hollis and Carter, 1954.

Index

65 Propositions (Innocent XI), 95

Abelard, Peter, 65, 73–74, 75
Action and Person (Baylor), 88–89
Ad Tuendam Fidem (Pope John Paul II), 169–70
Africa, 182
Agamemnon, 39–40
Albert the Great, 70–71, 80
Albert Speer: His Battle with the Truth (Sereny), 159
Albigensians, 4
Ambrose, 56–57, 58
Amnesty International, 13
Anglican bishop, 16–17
Apology (Justin), 58
apostle, 57
Aquinas, Thomas, Saint, 4, 66, 72, 98, 111, 113, 115, 152, 195n. 18
  on conscience, 75–76, 87, 149–50, 196n. 32
  authority of, 80–81
  erroneous, 81–85

nature of, 76–79
  on moral authority, 65, 85–86, 97, 196n. 37
Aristotle, 40–41, 64
  view of reality, 86, 90
Augustine, Saint, 55–56, 73–74, 80–82, 99, 195–96n. 27
  on conscience, 57
  theology, 92–93
Auschwitz, 159
Azor, 93

Benhabib, Seyla, 129–30
Bernard of Clairvaux, Saint, 4
Beyond the Dark Night (Grey), 169
birth control, 115–18, 120–21
Boff, Leonardo, 134
Bolt, Robert, 12–13
Bonaventure, Saint, 64–65, 70
Book of Ecclesiastes, 47
Book of Job, 47
Book of Wisdom, 46
Briadotti, Rosi, 129–30

Burma, 182
Burmese, 13
Butler, Judith, 129–30

Cahill, Lisa Sowle, 32, 117
Cain, 60, 156
Callahan, Sidney, 10–11,
    156–57
Can a Rich Man Be Saved?
    (Clement of
    Alexandria), 58–59
Caramuel-Lebkowitz, Jean,
    93
Cassian, 55–56
casuistry, 44, 61, 92–94,
    98–99
  Jewish, 49–50
  Roman, 44–46
Catholic moral theology, 1, 2,
    22–23, 27–28, 33–34,
    65, 92–93. *See also*
    casuistry; conscience;
    ethics; *Gaudium et
    Spes;* moral norms
    and principles
  and historical
    consciousness, 103–4,
    118–19
  and paradigm shifts,
    101–2, 107–9
  resistance to neo-
    Thomism, 104–5
  and situation ethics, 105–7
  in transition, 102–3
Celtic monasteries, 61
Chenu, 103
Christ. *See* Jesus Christ

Christianity, 14–15, 21, 23,
    38, 82, 181, 182, 185
  and belief, 82
  and faith, 82, 96–97
  and life, 85, 99, 104, 106,
    110
  and marriage, 115–16
  and morality, 22–23, 27,
    31, 33–34, 46, 55,
    62–63, 107–8, 166
  and theology, 23–24, 49,
    53, 156–57
  and tradition, 2, 5, 15,
    34–35, 50, 99, 126,
    155–56, 162, 163, 171
  and values, 112
Christians, 14–15, 18, 36–37,
    51, 53, 54, 62, 89–90,
    111, 149, 150, 167,
    178
  and ethics, 31, 176
Chrysostom, John, 56–57, 58
Cicero, 42–43, 44–46
Clement of Alexandria, 57,
    58–59
Code of Canon Law, 169–70
Commentary on Ezekiel
    (Jerome), 59–60, 66,
    156
Commentary on the Sentences
    (Aquinas), 75–76, 81
communidades de base, 168
Congar, Yves, 103, 183
Congregation for the
    Doctrine of the Faith,
    170, 176
Congregation of the Holy
    Office, 105

conscience, 9–14, 33–35, 62–63, 98–99, 124, 129, 189–90. *See also* casuistry; ethics, personalist; moral climate; moral failure; nominalism; probabilism; Second Vatican Council
actual, 128
Catholic context, 13–16, 165–67
dynamics, 135–36
and emotion, 143–47
and goodness, 132–35
habitual, 128
history, 2–5, 36–38
and imagination, 147–49
and individual moral values, 17–20
and intuition, 140–43
medieval views, 64–65
   early, 65–73
and the "moral law," 25–28
and reason, 137–40
and spiritual discernment, 149–50
and subjectivism, 21–25, 52, 73–75
theology of, 2, 25, 28–33
traditions, 5–6, 15–16, 183–84
   Greek, 38–42
   Jewish, 46–50
   Latin, 42–43, 44. *See also* casuistry
   manual, 96–98
   New Testament, 50–55
   patristic, 55–61
   penitential, 61–62
conscientia, 37, 42, 55, 66, 69, 71–72, 76–80, 88, 128
contraception. *See* birth control
Corinthians, letters to, 36–37, 50, 51, 52–53, 194n. 42
Council of Trent, 93
Curran, Charles, 1, 176–77, 187–88
Cyprian, 58
Cyril of Alexandria, 58

daimon, 41
Danielou, 103
D'Arcy, Eric, 41, 54, 59, 70
Davies, W. D., 42–43
De Finibus (Cicero), 43
De Lazaro (Chrysostom), 56
De Officiis (Cicero), 44–46
De Senectute (Davies), 42–43
De Veritate (Aquinas), 75–76, 81
Declaration of the Rights of Man and of the Citizen, 180
Dei verbum, 172–73
Delhaye, Phillippe, 40, 57, 58, 76–77
Democritus of Abdera, 38–39
"Development in Moral Doctrine," 181
Diet of Worms, 88
Dignitatis humanae, 110–11, 115, 127, 188
Dionysius, 84–85

Dominicans, 70–71, 94
Doms, Herbert, 104–5, 118

Ecclesiastes, 47, 77–78
Egypt, 13
Enlightenment, 88
Epictetus, 41–42
Epistle (Seneca), 43, 89–90
*Essay on the Development of
    Christian Doctrine*
    (Newman), 183
ethics, 118–19, 127–28, 167,
    174. *See also*
    Christians, and ethics;
    Roman Catholicism,
    ethics; situation ethics
    personalist, 118–26, 136
    relationship between
        persons and acts,
        128–35
Ethics (Abelard), 74
Euripides, 38–39
Europe, 61
evil, intrinsic, 120, 200n. 50
Exodus, 48
Ezekiel, 59–60

Finnis, John, 1, 30–32
Fragility of Goodness
    (Nussbaum), 133
Freudians, 143
Fuchs, Josef, 1, 108, 110–11,
    131

Gaffney, James, 109–10
Gaillardetz, Richard, 171–72,
    175, 185
Gallagher, Raphael, 34, 97

Gaudium et Spes, 27–28,
    107–8, 109, 110–11,
    115, 127
Genesis, 162
Gentiles, 54–55, 57
God, 5–7, 12–13, 27–28,
    33–34, 41–42, 54–56,
    73–74, 80–81, 97,
    103–4, 110–11,
    112–14, 130–31,
    166–67, 168–69,
    185–86
    and commands, 87
    and law, 46–47, 62
    and love, 108
    and word, 46, 52, 92,
        172
Greece, 36–37, 38–39, 66
    culture, 46
    philosophy, 42, 48, 49
    and text, 37–38, 39, 55
    thought, 41–42, 46, 49
    and translation, 47
Greeks, 59–60
Gregory of Nyssa, 57
Grey, Mary, 168–69, 189
Grisez, Germain, 1
Gutierrez, Gustavo, 168

Halakhah, 50
Hanke, Gaultier Karl, 159
Häring, Bernard, 67, 104,
    118, 131, 168
Harries, Bishop, 16–17
Heaney, Seamus, 179, 186
Hebrew Bible, 46–49
heretics, and torture, 26–27,
    182–83

Himmler, 159
His Battle with the Truth
    (Sereny), 159
Hitler, Adolf, 155, 158–59
Holocaust, the, 160–61
Holy Spirit, 24–27, 31–32,
    51–52, 105–6,
    170–71, 182–85,
    186–87, 189–90
Hooft, Wilhelm Visser't,
    160–61
Humanae Vitae, 101–2
  and new paradigm
    crisis, 115–18

Indo European, 37–38
Innocent XI, 95
Inside the Third Reich (Speer),
    158–59
Institutiones Morales, 93
*Instruction of the Holy Office on
    "Situation Ethics"*
    (Pope Pius XII), 106
International Court at
    Nuremberg, 159
Ireland, 61

Jansenism, 96
Jeremiah, 48
Jerome, Saint, 57, 58, 59–61,
    64–65, 66, 70, 79
  on conscience, 155–56
Jesuits, 44
Jesus Christ, 14–15, 50, 51,
    53, 82, 91, 173,
    181–82
Jewish text, 36–37, 47
  and homes, 159

and Jews, 51, 54–55, 83,
    158, 159, 160
and law, 49–50
and philosophers, 48–49
and theology, 50
and thought, 46, 49–50
and tradition, 55–56
Job, 47
Johnstone, Brian, 100–101,
    183–84
Josephus, 48–49
Judaism, 46–47, 49–50
Justin, 57, 58

Keenan, James, 113
Kelly, Kevin, 176, 177–78
King, Ursula, 168
Kuhn, Thomas, 197–98n. 1

Langdon, Stephen, 66–67,
    69–70, 76–77
Law of Christ (Häring), 104
Laxists, 95
Liberating Grace (Boff), 134
Liguori, Alphonsus de, 96
Lombard, Peter, 64–65,
    75–76
Lumen gentium, 33, 174
Luther, Martin, 26–27, 197n.
    45
  on conscience, 87–92

MacIntyre, Alisdair, 138
Mahoney, 55–56, 77, 106–7,
    149–50
Making of Moral Theology
    (Mahoney), 149–50
Malaysia, 182

Man for All Seasons, A (Bolt), 12–13
marriage, 104–5, 123–24. *See also* Second Vatican Council, on marriage
Master Udo, 66–67
Maurer, Christian, 41, 46, 48
McCaughey, Terence, 138
McCormick, Richard, 1, 103–4, 109
McDonagh, Edna, 189–90
McHugh/Callan, 97–98
Meaning of Marriage, The (Doms), 104–5
Medina, Bartolomeo, 94, 96
meditation, 42
Melchin, Kenneth, 119
Memory and Redemption (McCaughey), 138
metanoia, 189
Middle Ages, 70, 72
Mishnah, 49–50
modernism, 198n. 4
moral authority, 125–26
moral climate, 16–17
moral failure, 150–57, 186–89
"Moral Failure and Self-deception," 156
moral norms and principles, 121–24, 125
moral teaching, 180–83
moral theology. *See* Catholic moral theology
More, Sir Thomas, 12–13
Murdoch, Iris, 18, 132

Nasreen, Taslima, 13
National Assembly, 180
National Constituent Assembly of France, 18
National Socialist Party, 158–59, 160
natural law, 26, 195n. 18
Naud, André, 173
Navarrus, 93
Nazi Party. *See* National Socialist Party
neoscholasticism, 119, 200n. 44
New Law, 91
New Testament, 36–37, 104, 182
Newman, John Henry, 183, 185
Nietzsche, Friedreich, 136
Nigeria, 13
Noldin/Schmitt, 97–98
nominalism, 85–87
Noonan, John, 181, 183, 187–88
Norfolk, Duke of, 12–13
Northern Irish conflict, 138
nouvelle theologie, 103
Nuremberg, 82–83, 158–59
Nussbaum, Martha, 133

obsequium, 174
Occam, William of, 86, 92–93, 99
Occamism, 86–87, 88
Old Testament, 55–56
On Duties (Cicero), 44–46

On the Freedom of a Christian (Luther), 91
On the Proper Wisdom and Will (Luther), 90
On the Treatment of Lapsed Christians (Cyprian), 58–59
Orestes, 39–40
Origen, 55–56, 57
Orsy, Ladislas, 169–70, 173, 174
Oxford, 16–17
Oxford English Dictionary, 44

"paradigm shift," 100, 197–98n. 1
Paradise, 12–13
Paris, University of, 75–76
Pars Prima (Aquinas), 75–77
Pascal, Blaise, 44, 95
Paul, Saint, 36–37, 43, 57, 58. *See also* Corinthians, letters to; Romans, letter to
on conscience, 50–55, 128
Pelagian, 90
Pelikan, Jaroslav, 183
Penitential of Bede, 61
Pentateuch, 49–50
Peter of Poitiers, 66–67
Pharaoh, 48
Philip the Chancellor, 64–65, 67–69, 70, 72, 76–77
Philippines, 182
Philo, 48–49
phronesis, 40–41
Plato, 40–41, 59–60
Plutarch, 39–40

Pope Alexander VIII, 96
Pope John XXIII, 180
Pope John Paul II, 169–70
Pope Leo X, 26–27
Pope Leo XIII, 182, 187–88
Pope Paul, 115–16
Pope Pius VI, 180
Pope Pius XII, 26–27, 106–7
Prima Secundae (Aquinas), 75–76, 81–82
probabilism, 94–96
Profession of Faith (1989), 169–70
Provincial Letters (Pascal), 44, 45, 95
Psalm 51, 48
Psalm 139, 46–47
Psalms, 89–90

Questiones Disputatae de Veritate (Aquinas), 75–76
Quod Aliquantum (Pius VI), 180

Radford Ruether, Rosemary, 16
Rahner, Karl, 103–4, 131–32, 168, 183, 189
Ratzinger, Cardinal, 112–13, 114, 176
Regulus, 45
Republic (Plato), 40
Roman Catholicism, 2, 13, 16, 102, 122–23, 172. *See also* Catholic moral theology; Roman Catholics;

Second Vatican
        Council
and the Church, 22, 28,
        34–35, 93, 95,
        115–16. *See also* moral
        failure
    assent/dissent issues,
        174–79
    authority of Church
        teaching, 169–74,
        184–85
    in crisis, 167–69
    divisions within, 165–67
    moral tradition, 179–86,
        183–84
    doctrine, 170
    ethics, 101
    teaching, 2, 5, 171–72,
        178
    and theologians, 103–4
    thought, 2–3, 87–88
    and tradition, 2, 5, 15,
        34–35, 44, 87–88,
        105–6, 107, 154–55,
        165–66
Roman Catholics, 16, 21–22,
        30, 72, 116, 117–18,
        167, 171–72, 180,
        184–85
Romans, letter to, 14, 15,
        36–37, 51–52, 54, 57,
        89–90, 91
Rome, 4, 36–37, 44

Sacred Congregation for the
        Doctrine of the Faith,
        176–77
San Sui Kyi, Aung, 13

scholasticism, 65, 89–90,
        92–93, 197n. 45
Scito to ipsum (Abelard), 73
Second Vatican Council
        (Vatican II), 5–7, 22,
        33, 65, 98, 106,
        166–67, 168–69,
        172–73, 188, 189–90.
        See also Catholic
        moral theology, and
        paradigm shift; ethics
    on conscience, 109–10
    and discernment,
        111–12
    erroneous, 112–14
    and the law, 110–11
    and the role of the
        magisterium, 114–15
    on marriage, 105, 109
    on morality, 106–8, 118
Segundo, Juan Luis, 168
self-deception, 157–61
Seneca, 42, 43
sensus fidei, 185
sensus fidelium, 185–86
Sentences (Aquinas), 75–76
Sereny, Gita, 159, 160
"Serving the Truth," 176
"Settle Bed, The," 179
sexual morality, 20, 83–84,
        104–5, 116–18,
        119–20, 123–24
sin
    original, 161–64
    social, 161–64
    theology of, 130

situation ethics. *See* Catholic moral theology, and situation ethics
slavery, 182
Socrates, 41
Sources of the Self (Taylor), 136
South America, 168–69
Speer, Albert, 158–59, 160
Stoic philosophers, 41–42, 44
subjectivism. *See* conscience, and subjectivism
Sullivan, Francis, 171
Summa Theologiae (Aquinas), 66, 75–77, 79, 81
synderesis, 37, 38–40, 42, 46, 48, 55, 59–60, 66, 76–80, 88, 90, 110, 128
synoida, 47

Tablet, The, 176
Talmud, 49
Taylor, Charles, 136
theology of divine revelation, 172–73
Third Reich, 158, 159
Thomism, 65, 79, 94, 96–97, 103–4, 105–6, 150, 167

Tillman, 104
Timothy, second letter to, 52
tutiorism, 95–96

United States, 182

Vatican, the, 176–77, 180
Vatican II. *See* Second Vatican Council
Veritatis Splendor, 16–19, 20, 21–23, 29–30, 102, 182–83
via moderna, 88
voluntas, 70
Vulgate, 47

Wales, 61
war crimes, 13–14
Western philosophy, 136
William of Auxerra, 66–67
Wiwa, Ken Saro, 13
World War II, 83

Yahweh, 48

Zechariah, 48